Writing for Museums

Writing for Museums

Communicating and Connecting with All Your Audiences

Second Edition

Margot Wallace

ROWMAN & LITTLEFIELD
Lanham • Boulder • New York • London

Published by Rowman & Littlefield
An imprint of The Rowman & Littlefield Publishing Group, Inc.
4501 Forbes Boulevard, Suite 200, Lanham, Maryland 20706
www.rowman.com

86-90 Paul Street, London EC2A 4NE

British Library Cataloguing in Publication Information Available

Library of Congress Cataloging-in-Publication Data

Names: Wallace, Margot A., 1941– author.
Title: Writing for museums : communicating and connecting with all your
   audiences / Margot Wallace.
Other titles: Communicating and connecting with all your audiences
Description: Second edition. | Lanham : Rowman & Littlefield, [2022] |
   Includes bibliographical references and index. | Summary: "Whether
   written by administrators, staffers, freelancers, or interns, words are
   delivered by people in your museums with the knowledge to be interpreted
   by strangers. This new edition features seven new chapters and a focus
   on inclusivity and accessibility"— Provided by publisher.
Identifiers: LCCN 2022019518 (print) | LCCN 2022019519 (ebook) |
   ISBN 9781538166246 (cloth : alk. paper) | ISBN 9781538166253
   (paper : alk. paper) | ISBN 9781538166260 (electronic)
Subjects: LCSH: Communication in museums. | Museums—Public relations. |
   Museums—Social aspects. | Museums—Educational aspects. | Museum
   visitors. | Authorship. | Rhetoric.
Classification: LCC AM125 .W35 2022 (print) | LCC AM125 (ebook) | DDC
   069/.1—dc23/eng/20220519
LC record available at https://lccn.loc.gov/2022019518
LC ebook record available at https://lccn.loc.gov/2022019519

Contents

Preface

Museums are intermediaries. Long before media entered our usage, museums have been the medium where creators met the public. Museums collect the work of creators and communicate them to the public. Fragments of an anchor can't talk about their history; the four walls of a house don't have ears or tell stories. Weavings make us wonder about the weavers, paintings get framed, and the night sky needs a script writer.

Enter the writers, the people to whom this writer is speaking.

Writers, you are a diverse group of talented and long-hours heroes. Many of you have been handed to you a task that's unexpected. All of you wonder where the next words will come from.

Words turn up most reliably to those who read a lot. Hence, the pattern of this book, the interweaving throughout of examples you can read from other museums' writing. How do other museums write e-newsletters, videos, announcements, or tour scripts? You can read selections of the best, here.

When you read what museums of all sizes and genres say, it's a thesaurus of good ideas: ways to write about a speaker or a venue, words that speak to diverse audiences, synonyms for dull subject lines of an e-mail.

Writers, here's a tip: get on the mailing list of other museums and snoop around.

Museums amaze and astound with their deep understanding of equity. To these community institutions, inclusion is a goal reached daily with common sense initiatives like evening hours—because some audiences work shifts; closed captioning of videos—because some audiences have hearing problems; smaller tours for families with a need for quieter surroundings; volunteer openings for people with professional skills and interests; awareness in every department that, for many, English is a second language; programming and exhibitions that acknowledge our kaleidoscopic culture. Writers fulfill the intent of inclusiveness by writing about the details already enacted.

Museums need words, and that's also a foundational belief of this book. Despite galleries and classrooms and spaces immersed in visuals, museums rely on writing. Writing covers the landscape of websites and dives deep. Writing makes possible these activities: e-mail, newsletters, blogs, tour scripts, education outlines, fundraising, volunteerism, research archives, videos, store merchandising, volunteer recruitment, community partnerships—twenty chapters' worth of communications.

Writers, use the index as well as the contents listing to search for your own writing needs.

As a museum researcher, I've amassed a treasury of contacts; I get a lot of e-mail from museums keeping me informed of their activities. My research antennae pick up mentions of museums in dozens of publications and uncounted conversations. I have the advantage of dropping in on any room in any museum I want, with just a few clicks and Search. When I notice something exceptional, it's in the book.

Images reveal more than you think, and many museums excel at teaming words and pictures. Photos demonstrate diversity better than mere words. Photos imply the wondrous depth of collections, where full lists would be tedious. Good charts are easier to read than paragraphs. Creative use of the camera is to be applauded.

Writers, work with the designers and graphics professionals, because words and pictures work together. When you talk about inclusion, diversity, and equity, show it. When you write a blog about research, find a photo, or take your own, to illustrate your breadth of knowledge. This concept, visual literacy, is promoted throughout the following pages.

Strategy underpins every chapter. You can't write anything unless you've first asked "why?" and ascertained "so what." Readers are impatient and won't stick around while you fumble to explain yourself. Strategies keep museums from wasting money and time. They are businesses, and writers will do well to notice hints of marketing on many pages.

Writers, when you first get an assignment, ask for the strategy. Keep everyone thinking straight.

Writing encompasses eight competencies: strategic thinking; knowledge of the audiences who will be reading the words; editing; hatred of platitudes; appreciation of visuals; thorough research; business sense; organization. Writers will be reminded of these in every chapter.

This book is a second edition, and these are the justifications for the redo. First and foremost is the realization that change happens. External situations require a changed book, of course. And human nature also demands change. Stasis is unnatural and doesn't succeed.

A big change for museums are videos. They enliven and enrich every written communication. External changes catapulted online media into every audience's life. Video would have gotten there, anyway. It appears in several chapters because scriptwriters are the experts who tell the ear what the cameraperson sees.

E-mail now gifts everyone with e-newsletters, announcing the wonders that lie just beyond the entrance.

Collection display and interpretation has flourished into new perspectives and pathways.

Museums are expanding, and that's another reason for a second edition. They have built larger exhibition areas, better classrooms, sophisticated theaters, more office space, more storage, richer archives, more nature environments, more social spaces, and, in recognition of new museum audiences, expanded facilities rental. Writers will write about all these improvements.

Inclusiveness is expansive. Writing will expand to communicate to the wide range of audiences you reach out to. Writers will describe existing programs in diverse ways, and help educators communicate their new, more widely targeted initiatives.

Research management allows researchers to communicate their excellent work to a broader public and open their archives to storytelling.

Historical societies, places of remembrance, and visitor centers are adopting the precepts of museums, and they need to get their messages out to the public.

Museum Studies programs at undergraduate, graduate, and certificate levels answer many of the questions asked by museum professionals; those questions change daily.

Demographics change. Behavior changes. Technology changes. What made sense a few years ago seems dated now. Hi Writers, you need to adapt to the current manner of speaking.

Another truth about writing never changes: organized thinking. This bane and triumph of all writers requires that books, this book, be divided into neat chapters. Each one deals with a specific topic, because that's how writing assignments are made. Chaptered thinking helps writers stay on topic. However, there are no walls around chapters, and sometimes similar material appears in several chapters. The index is helpful in locating information that crosses borders.

The index also recognizes the many museums mentioned in the book. Their professionalism, creativity, hard work, ingenuity, and decency deserve attention and will enlighten every professional who reads their words. I'll vouch for that.

CHAPTER 1

Audiences

Can you characterize your museum's target audience? If not, be reassured. The people in your "audience" are so varied and ever-changing, you can never definitively categorize them. What once was called targeting audiences is now referred to as "letting audiences find you," a process by which their interests and your offerings search for each other. It's the digital world everyone lives in. Audiences are fluid, following different paths to your door, the traditional appeals as well as hashtags. Don't talk to or at them; use the right words and they will come.

This chapter is about communicating with sensitivity to the multiple personalities that make up the museum universe. Listen to them and watch them. Read their comments. When you write a newsletter, blog, website, didactic panel, or tour script, keep several of those persons in mind.

Here are some first steps:

- Review your traditional audience.
- Know your current audiences.
- Look at your museum's parts and departments to assess the different audiences that they serve.
- Visit other museums and cultural institutions to discover.
- Be open to anybody different—notice them.

The taxonomy of audiences, always in flux, follows.

- Visitors, local
- Individuals who like your collection—partisans
- Members—a more predictable and approachable partisan
- Companions of the person who made the plan, not the initiator
- Parents of children—virtual programming has expanded this group

- Caregivers of children—may have age, interest, or ESL challenges
- Businesspeople on a lunch break
- People who've attended a meeting in one of your meeting spaces
- Newcomers to community
- Young people on a date
- Retired people—more time, wide interests, estate planning prospects
- Walkers—this for museums such as botanic gardens and zoos that have large campuses
- Lifetime learners—repeat purchasers of tickets for virtual and in-person lectures, performances, and tours
- The hearing and visually challenged
- Suppliers

WHAT WRITERS SHOULD KNOW ABOUT YOUR AUDIENCES

Good writing starts with looking and listening. Spend even one hour in the galleries, the lobby, and on the comments in social media. Get to know who's talking about museums. Several audiences are sketched below.

Local Visitors, in General

Local visitors are the people who live in the area and return to the museum once a year or more for exhibitions and programs. These repeat visitors are loyal and possibly members. They are prospects for donors. Repeat visits to local museums, and the income they represent, are an American phenomenon; few of the world's museums rely for support on nongovernmental funds, or money from citizens. As museums welcome global residents, this might be another of the diversity and empathy issues to consider. Writers: speak to local visitors using local references and appeals.

Individuals Who Like Your Collection

Call them partisans; these visitors are knowledgeable about your objects and return for exploration. They come from near and, possibly, far. Writers: when writing about objects, programs, or books in the store dealing with the collection, be comfortable with more academic terms.

Members are a more predictable and approachable partisan.

When a local person invests in a membership, the investment is emotional, logical, and financial. Members believe in the institution's goals and value to the community. Writers: use words like goals, mission, believe, trust, pride, sensible, worthwhile.

Companions of the Person Who Made the Plan

The second person is a nightmare and must be confronted head on. These visitors haven't planned the outing or bought the tickets, but they paid for tickets and came through your door, actual or virtual, to see the museum for themselves. Get their names and add them to mailing lists. They comprise a sizable fraction of fans who never hear from you. Writers: when writing a reminder message or after-performance follow-up message, include "the people who attended with you" in the note. Add a link for the name of those people who came along.

Parents of Children

Figure out who your audience is: five-year-olds or parents. Virtual programming has expanded the group of people who attend Story Hour. Writers: avoid risk and address messaging to both parents and children.

Caregivers of Children

The adults in the room may not be parents. They could be grandparents, nannies, caregivers, or friends. Their demographics may differ from those of the parents. Age, education, culture, and language all figure in the learning that happens when a museum, facilitator, child, and caregiver join forces.

Businesspeople on a Lunch Break

Urban museums attract people who work. These visitors take a museum break physically or virtually. Perhaps they've attended a meeting in a conference room. Writers: add a sentence to suggest these daytime visitors return on the weekend with their families.

Newcomers to Community

In a version of the welcome wagon, new residents may singled out on websites or social media, and be sent discounted tickets or parking along with letters of welcome from the museum. Writers: look for place to add a welcome to newcomers. Talk about the museum's place in the community when describing programs.

Retired People

The instant people retire, they have more time and wider interests. Discover their interests and plan daytime programs accordingly. Writers: talk about the time to explore long-standing interests. Use energetic words. Don't stress lots of benches. Retired people don't surge through the door because of age but because of excess energy.

Walkers

Many people love to walk, and for them botanic gardens, zoos, and multi-building campuses hold great allure. Hail them with words of action, nature, fresh air, and natural beauty. Be assured this group will include many cultures and backgrounds for whom walking is a given, not an impediment.

Lifetime Learners

Some audiences breathe learning like air; they love virtual lectures, the more the better. They'll come to series of classes. Writers: for these repeat purchasers of tickets for lectures and classes, talk to them as if they were students, which they are.

Hearing and Visually Challenged People

Accessibility comes in many forms, including people who aren't blind or deaf, but, rather, challenged with sight and hearing. Writers: recommend and learn to script audio guides for the visually impaired. Write basic information on signage in galleries and at the front desk. For people who don't hear well, asking even the simplest instructions is painful. For slide presentations, in-person or virtual, if slides are used, keep the text short and enlarge the type.

SUPPLIERS

Furnace repair people. Taxi drivers. Printer salesman. Cleaning crew. Don't forget your suppliers, who may work evenings or live outside your zip code. They are part of that valuable audience of people who have already set foot inside the museum's front door. They see your exhibits, know some of your staff, and importantly, know your location and how to get there. They all have colleagues, friends, families, and communities. They come in all ages and backgrounds. Let them get to know you better. For writers, this could amount to a handout given at the time of sign-in, delivery, or billing.

"Come back and bring your family. Touch here for your ticket." Include your museum's name, address, website next to the QR code.

Underrepresented minorities and out-of-sight members of your community comprise the biggest group of all because they are your "unknown unknowns." You don't know who you don't know. "Unknown unknowns" was a phrase famously coined by the late Donald Rumsfeld, secretary of defense under George W. Bush. He never knew that twenty years later an author of a museum book would find his quote invaluable in the new world of audiences.

Writers who read to the bottom of this list have a head start. They understand the vastness of the territory and will be sensitive to their innumerable readers and viewers. Whether you're writing a blog, tour script, or counter card for the store, the following opening lines may start the words flowing:

Good morning, Indiana history buffs.

Say this in your head, not on the page. Local references are a technique speakers use to connect to an audience. It helps writers find a way into the lead paragraph of a blog, newsletter item, or a tour.

The annual barbecue gives our donors a chance to meet other rich people.

Say this, too, in your head. Start to think about the real reason for the paragraph you're writing for an event. Be straightforward about its purpose.

Ask questions about a specific topic or object. Then, answer them yourself.

What's an artist's favorite time to work?
What do paleontologists dislike?
Would my grandmother like this exhibition?
Why would I go to a museum on a date?
What would my visiting brother-in-law like about this gallery?

Look at this newel post.

Start small. Think about the size of an object, one plant in the botanic garden, one animal's breakfast, one figure in a painting, the opening word of a play.

Think big. In writing panels or newsletter announcements or signs on a campus path, think about the person who wore the sixteenth-century breastplate. Write about the town surrounding the historic house in 1843.

What are you going to do with that? Ask a shopper how they'll use the purchase they're talking home, or whom they're giving it to. Surprisingly, buying stuff reveals more good things about people than you'd imagine. And as we've discovered in this chapter, people are more surprising than we ever dreamed.

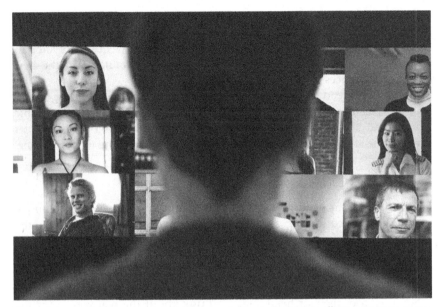

Figure 1.1.   Audiences come in all shapes and sizes, including small squares on a screen, originating in 24 time zones.
LeoPatrizi/ E+ via Getty Images

ACADEMIC MUSEUMS

Of course, not all museum audiences are visitors, and not all museums are like the ones a writer is currently working for. Audiences of academic museums are the students and professors of the parent college or university. Visitors to the campus are often overlooked audiences. Don't underestimate the scope of your marketing area. The Museum of Contemporary Photography at Columbia College Chicago attracts visitors from all over the world. At six o'clock one evening, two very well-dressed women were seen at the just-closed doors. It will be open tomorrow morning, they were told. Ah! But the visitors were from Paris, they'd heard for years about the fine collection at this Chicago museum and, *malheureusement*, they were returning to France the next day. Add global aficionados to the roster of academic museum visitors.

For writers who want to reach out to these audiences, assume they are enlightened amateurs, visitors with an interest they will go to the ends of the earth—or at least the quad—to explore.

Add curators to the list of audiences. They enable creators of all genres to be collected and cataloged. And they collaborate with a variety of institutions.

If the academic museum is an art museum, faculty from many other departments will find educational tools for their science and history students.

Part of the writer's job is to point out the connection between paintings and the medical school, or sculpture and AR and AI people.

Include people who come to campus for other reasons: parents, conferees, guest lecturers, researchers.

Remember that academic museums are accountable in ways large and small to the college or university they adjoin, part of its brand and a contributor to its standing. Write with the appropriate gravitas.

MUSEUMS WITH LARGE PHYSICAL CAMPUSES

Botanic gardens, zoos, many historic houses, and museum villages have grounds—lawns and plantings, walks and trails. Some are extensive enough to offer autumn hayrides and farm visits. Writers must include these walkable spaces when talking to prospective visitors. Inform them of distances, inclines, and weather. Encourage the walkers to explore history and art and science physically.

If your museum is called a center, you're probably a complex of museums or cultural institutions. That's complicated, all right, considering all the different audiences you'll be writing for. The Buffalo Bill Center of the West calls itself "five museums under one roof," and they can't be corralled easily. These are audiences who like William Cody, rodeos, firearms, Western history, Native American history, Yellowstone geology and ecology, art, a good library, and experiences. For cultural institutions also housing playhouses, concert halls, and full-time schools, the possibilities go exponential. This chapter will stick with museum writing, but writers should be alert to the cross-cultural collaborations that may sometimes need your attention.

INTERNAL AUDIENCE

Remember that your internal audience is big and important because it's comprised of people who know you well and have a stake in your success. They have a voice in your challenges and solutions that writers must be attuned to. Here are typical internal audiences:

- Curators, yours and other institutions'
- Your professional staff
- Your support staff
- Board of Trustees
- Finance
- Volunteers
- Suppliers

Museums pay special attention to audiences that can be relied on for return visits. These are people who support the institution by bringing friends, attending programs and fundraising events, spreading word-of-mouth news, posting and tweeting, broadcasting their loyalty, and providing financial support at many levels.

- Members at all levels
- Donors
- Supporters
- Patrons
- Corporate sponsors
- Partners
- Collaborators

All these friends are quasi staff in their familiarity with your institution and stake in it. They speak the language of museums, and writers have to talk differently to them than they would to the general public. Use words like thank you, members, museum community, friends, volunteers.

Audiences that share in your cultural and educational goals deserve special comment. Their thoughtful yet intangible support is invaluable. You rise higher because of them.

- Educators in local schools
- Government, all levels
- Scholars from other museums and cultural institutions
- Artists in all fields (e.g., SFMOMA auxiliary gallery of California artists' works, available for purchase by individuals and businesses, proceeds going to artists, exhibitions, and the museum).

This taxonomy of audiences is not complete. Consider it instructive.

AUDIENCES AND SENSITIVITY

There are many audiences your museum may not target directly, but need to be sensitive about when writing labels, panels, timelines, newsletters, podcasts, or print. Here are some of them and brief advice about writing for them:

- Gay parents
- Mixed-race parents
- Gender identity
- Older parents

- Caregivers who aren't a child's parents
- People speaking English as a second language
- Veterans
- Families entering with more than four children
- Visitors younger than the reader of this chapter
- Foreign visitors—seesaw parable
- Out-of-town visitors
- People who don't know history
- People who know history better than you do
- Wealthy
- Americans
- Canadians

Gay Parents

Writers: don't write "Mom and Dad" when "Your Parents" might describe them better.

Mixed-Race Parents

This might be a photo issue. Pattern your photo shoots after television commercials where you often see parents of different races. Writers: identify them as parents.

Gender Identity

Gender pronouns are commonly used by individuals in e-mail signatures and Zoom photo name tags. They're an option of the individual, not the organization. Writers: when interviewing people, ask their pronouns. Whether they, or your institution, uses them, it shows respect for their gender identity.

Older Parents, Grandparents, Aunties

Writer: watch out for ageism. For picture captions, get the relationship right.

Babysitters, Nannies, Caregivers

It may be surprising how many household employees are charged with taking children to the museum. Those people who button the jackets, fold and unfold the strollers, and seek out the story-telling room do not read labels and think like parents. Loving and conscientious they might be, but they haven't designed the child's cultural activities. They may not understand your museum's signage. Writers: labels and maps should be short and simple. Signs at the front desk can be headed "Children's Activities," and then followed with a QR code that includes graphics that aid directions. Consider getting a translator.

Veterans

Writers: don't include them only when offering free entry or discounted tickets. Inclusiveness is needed here. Include military men and women in designing lectures and projects. Include veterans in advisory councils and fundraising. Include the military in your education department. According to Pew Research Center, veterans represent about 10 percent of the U.S. adult population.

Younger Visitors

Don't be shocked by the youth of some adults. If they were born after 1990, but you weren't, beware. Writers: when using examples, check for relevance to a younger audience. A reality-checking professor always asked her students if they knew the name of the round object on the wall with two sticks and numbers from 12–11 around the edges. The students laughed, but the professor retired five years ago.

Visitors Speaking English as a Second Language

When English is a second language, there are several implications. Speakers are new immigrants and speak and read very little English. Or, they're professionals who speak English beautifully. Maybe they're foreigners who understand only tourist English. Writers: since you don't know who your ESL viewers and listeners are, make a few assumptions. Large urban museums will welcome a lot of these visitors. Small-town museums will meet many people who use American culture as a learning tool. Art museums can rely, to a certain extent, on their visuals. Write tour scripts, signs, and lecture introductions with no more than three-syllable words. Remember that children learn English quickly, possibly faster than their parents. Realize that the most fluent and confident speakers don't understand all the nuances of American language. Writers: for online and teleconference programs, closed captioning is advised. If your museum offers workshops and demonstrations, write your script to track exactly with the visuals. Wherever bullet points are used—website, slide presentations, handouts, newsletter—the rule of thumb is brevity and a large typeface. You can use colloquialisms with children but they might confuse adults. In fundraising communications, add a short paragraph that paraphrases this concept: "The Smith Jones is grateful for the support of individuals like you. Government support supplies only a small percentage of our budget." Explain the meaning of a 501(c)3 organization. In holiday or seasonal messages that mention events from different cultures, triple-check spelling and usage. Don't offend in enduring print.

Foreign Visitors

In tour groups, foreigners may not understand the references Americans use. A tour group at a contemporary art museum was shown a sculpture of a teeter-totter, aka a seesaw. The visitors, when asked their nationality, turned out to be 50 percent from foreign countries. What did they call that playground thing: teeter-totter or seesaw? Writers: fact check.

American Visitors

Americans are defined, in any dictionary, as people living in, or citizens of, North America or Latin America. When "American" is used to describe a citizen or resident of the United States, that leaves out Argentineans, Costa Ricans, and Canadians. Sometimes it doesn't matter in the context of your message, but sometimes it does. Be alert. There's further danger in recklessly using "American" or "America" to mean "me and you." The writer and speaker at a museum located in the United States may well be an American, but not everyone else will be. In any schoolroom, office, town meeting, factory, concert venue, or Little League bleachers, there's likely to be non-Americans. Watch what you reminisce about. If the person reading this is not an American citizen, or doesn't reside in the U.S., share some of your observations with your American colleagues.

Canadian Visitors

Canadians prefer to be called North Americans. Americans are people who need a passport to enter Canada. Names become really problematical when identifying native people. In Canada, they're called First Peoples.

Writing Faux Pas to Avoid

Some writing needs more subtlety: Mom and Dad versus Dad and Dad, or my moms. When conducting a family workshop, for instance, it's easy to mention Moms and Dads, when that might not apply to some parents in the group. When speaking in a military museum, sensitivity to gender rules is essential. In talks about jobs or industries that once were gender oriented—nursing, trucking, space exploration—gender awareness is honored more in the breach than in reality.

COMPETITION WITHIN THE COMMUNITY

On May 5, 2019, the residents of Niles, Illinois, woke up to the possibility of eighty-three non-credit learning opportunities in the following seven days. And this was not just for those with a Niles postal address. Their caregivers, nannies, and guests were welcome as well. Most of the learning programs were free. Some cost $5 for a ticket, applicable to a future purchase. The most expensive required a theater ticket, $25–$85. The range of learning included one-off talks, multiple-week classes or workshops, tours, film discussion groups, ESL instruction, book clubs, and maker rooms. They were offered by libraries, high schools, community colleges, alumni associations, and historical societies.

In smaller communities, in smaller metro markets, the offerings were similar, though scaled down. The common denominator was the diversity of audiences. The new audiences differ by age, interests, available time, day of event companion, attention span, and richness of learning options competing for their time.

AUDIENCE AWARENESS AND OTHER MUSEUMS

Two different museums reveal the range of audiences, one by its exhibits, the other by attendees at its conference.

National Postal Museum's objects, described in the Museum Highlights section of its website, encourage you to imagine the audiences they include. The U.S. mail reaches everyone.

- Airmail Beacon for night flying
- City Mailboxes
- Concord-style Mail Coach
- Door knocker
- Highway PO Mail
- Mail Crane for Railway Mail Service
- Mud Wagon for cross-country travelers
- Pneumatic Mail Canister—network beneath city streets
- Railway Service Car
- Screen Wagons—yesteryear's "last mile" service, between post offices

Also look at the conference participants enumerated in a newsletter from New Bedford (Massachusetts) Whaling Museum: "architects, artists, collectors, conservators, curators, historians and art historians, librarians, museum directors and staff, 360° photographers, researchers, scientists, spatial designers, and virtual and augmented reality specialists."

When it comes to discovering audiences, take a look at what they're coming to see.

YESTERDAY, TODAY, AND TOMORROW

The one sure thing about audiences is their enduring value to museums. They visited and learned a century ago and took their grandchildren. The respect of museums was passed along the generations, across cultures and geography by audiences accustomed to crossing borders. Today, they fearlessly cross other borders, some of which are your threshold. Tomorrow is an estimated guess, but museums will adapt because their audiences demand it. Writers: look around. Audiences are really interesting people to talk to.

REFERENCES

Cunha, Kyle J., and Curran, Elizabeth R., "A Brief Military Culture Overview," Springfield College Undergraduate Project, Spring 2013, https://www.co.grafton.nh.us/wp-content/uploads/2013/11/Military-Culture-PDF.pdf

Exhibitions, Museum Highlights, National Postal Museum, https://postalmuseum.si.edu/museum-highlights [accessed 8-27-21]

"Gender Pronouns," Lesbian, Gay, Bisexual, Transgender, Queer + (LGBTQ+) Resource Center, University of Wisconsin Milwaukee, https://uwm.edu/lgbtrc/support/gender-pronouns/ [accessed 8-19-21]

https://centerofthewest.org/our-museums/

https://www.sfmoma.org/artists-gallery/

"Module 1—Characteristics of Military Culture vs a Civilian Culture," Module Resource Material, https://www.veteranspatrol.org/module_1—characteristics [accessed 8-20-21]

Schaefer, Katherine, "The Changing Face of America's Veteran Population," Pew Research Center, April 5, 2021, https://www.pewresearch.org/fact-tank/2021/04/05/the-changing-face-of-americas-veteran-population/

"Virtual 30th International Panorama Council Conference," Museum Happenings—Late August 2021, *eNews from Johnny Cake Hill*, New Bedford Whaling Museum, https://myemail.constantcontact.com/Museum-Happenings—Late-August-2021.html?soid=1128002165729&aid=XIbPYnXDDV4 [accessed 8-27-21]

CHAPTER 2

Social Media

Social media has reframed the concept of audiences. Instead of targeting demographic, geographic, or behavioral segments, social media welcomes everyone who shares an interest. Although it is very inclusive, sending its messages around the world to all ages, backgrounds, socioeconomic positions, and devices, like all communications, it wins return readers and loyalty from only a very dedicated group of followers. Football fans and wheat farmers might enjoy learning about museums, but they must "follow" museums to be considered loyal.

This chapter will discuss writing for loyalty, writing to attract followers. It will show examples of museums that convey both a message and a magnetism—reasons to like the museum and also follow it.

Twitter plays a major role here because it favors brevity, the soul of good writing. It profits from having many readers, rather than many advertisers. It's ideal for museums because it favors messages that contain facts about objects and events of learning. The social aspect—retweeting—epitomizes the concept of ambassadors, engaged people who spread the word.

In brief, social media messages, especially the focused, concise, regular, date-appropriate, museum-referencing kind, achieve many museum goals:

Awareness
Audience building
Consistency and continuity
Retention
Inclusiveness
Involvement
Creativity
Mission

AWARENESS AND AUDIENCE BUILDING

Partnering with other arts organizations instantly broadens your audience. Anchorage Museum gets credit for its multi-culture hospitality:

> D.M. Aderibigbe joins Kirun Kapur and Lena Khalaf Tuffaha for Pièces de Ré-sistance, a series of talks with notable poets and novelists presented by Alaska Quarterly Review. 4–5 p.m. Friday, Feb. 11.

The National Quilting Museum's Block of the Month Club is a model of involvement. It uses a continuing, monthly event that has creative quilters waiting for the next idea.

Here's how the museum's Block of the Month explains itself and the museum: "Through the Block of the Month Club, The National Quilt Museum aims to challenge quilters to experiment with new techniques and styles while having fun connecting with quilters from all over the world, and learning more about the museum in the process!"

RISD Museum (@RISDMuseum) publicizes financial opportunities for students and makes good use of social media's immediacy and networking. Today's students mostly want to get through school, and financial help introduces them to museums in a program meaningful to them. Applause to RISD for explaining how these opportunities benefit all museums.

> APPLY NOW: Spalter Teaching Fellowship at RISD Museum is open to RISD & Brown students from all disciplinary backgrounds. Get trained as a museum educator, teach & work with children & youth ages 5 to 18, support learning from original works of art.

Milwaukee County Zoo delights viewers with the weekly photos of animals making charming animal faces and twisting into ever-new animal positions. Look for giraffes and chimps, otters and weasels at #Photooftheweek. Lots of other weekly photos compete for their time, but Milwaukee's photographers get up close and their photos stand out.

Asking viewers to send photos is as old as local television news, and still effective in drawing in readers. Here's a simple request from the Nat (@nhmsd), the Natural History Museum, San Diego, California: "Just thinking beautiful, tide pool thoughts this weekend. What's something you appreciate about our region?" The tweet accompanies a photo of a beautiful tide pool and it asks viewers to send their photos. It's a call to action that gets many responses and demonstrates how many followers the museum has. Human nature being what it is, a lot of other followers will follow suit.

Nevada Museum of Art (@nevadaart) gains the attention of STEAM educators and parents, merely by announcing another organization's conference on its Twitter feed: "Every year NV STEAM inspires innovation in education and inspires educators from across Nevada. Join us virtually for the 2022 NV STEAM Conference: Constructing Creativity, February 2 and 5, 2022."

By joining a community endeavor, working with creative thinkers outside one's own field of expertise, and generously sharing their information, a museum rises in awareness and the esteem of new audiences.

Writers: do the research on other institutions' names, dates, and contact information. Spell it right. They'll return the favor.

February in Akron, Ohio, may not seem the best time of year to attract new audiences to an outdoor zoo. Akron Zoo undertook the challenge by borrowing Summer the Groundhog for a Groundhog Day tweet and video. See the scene-stealing animal watch the movie *Groundhog Day* on a staffer's mobile device and be sure that awareness of the zoo is heightened, even if a visit doesn't immediately materialize. Awareness of Akron Zoo is aided by a camera move to the animal handler with a zoo logo-ed sweatshirt.

Writers: every calendar event is worth a tweet, if it's made relevant to the museum. Your skill is finding the connection. If there's no obvious affiliation to groundhogs, another popular day will pop up later.

Audience building continues throughout the year. When its outdoor tulip gardens aren't sprouting, Eastman Museum opens its auditorium with a film: "Dutch Connection is officially open! Join us in the Dryden Theatre, for the history and behind-the-scenes look at our annual floral display." For museums with an auditorium, this is a way to get people inside the museum in winter. However, the beauty of Twitter is its ability to insert a thought on just the right day, like tulips in February.

Writers: build a portfolio of videos to draw from when needed.

CONSISTENCY, CONTINUITY, AND RETENTION

Social media, especially tweets, offer museums retention because they appear regularly with reminders of the collection, the details of its objects, and the world-class maestros who created and interpret them. A consistent character on the scene at National Cowboy & Western Heritage Museum is Tim, #HashtagTheCowboy. Great guy! He welcomes readers every morning, and knows all about every item in the museum. He likes his followers, and the strategy is that they'll return the feeling—by returning.

Here's an example of how #HashtagTheCowboy welcomes virtual visitors every morning: "Morning! Our Western Wares exhibition is now open. Your weekend plans are set. Classic Western fashion, an Indian motorcycle, Dolly! See you this weekend! #HashtagTheCowboy Thanks, Tim."

Writers: discover what's most interesting, at the moment, in your museum and convey it in a few vibrant nouns and verbs. If several topics will interest followers, write several tweets that day.

"Morning! We're just putting the finishing touches on our newest exhibition, "Western Wares." Fashion, art, motorcycles, and more. Can't wait for you folks to see it. It opens on February 11th! bit.ly/WesternWares #HashtagTheCowboy Thanks, Tim (Nat'l Cowboy Museum@ncwhm).

Keep up the tweets, as Tim the Cowboy does.

Snuck into the vault to check out pieces from our upcoming "Western Wares" exhibition. This purse and beadwork is over 100 years old. Can you believe it? So much cool stuff for you folks to see starting Feb 11th! Learn more: bit.ly/WWBeadwork #HashtagTheCowboy Thanks, Tim

Tim the Cowboy is no fair-weather friend; he consistently shows up to spread the word about his museum: "Morning! The weather is looking rough for today so the Museum is closing at noon. Security is still working, and this guy on the mountainside is too. This is Clark Huling's 'Grand Canyon, Kaibab Trail' from 1973. #HashtagTheCowboy Thanks, Tim."

Weather is also on the agenda for @AnchorageMuseum: "A stroll through the museum's four floors of exhibitions is a great way to get through these cold, dark Friday nights. The Anchorage Museum is now open for extended hours 10 a.m. to 9 p.m. every Friday through April 2022." Words are good; actions speak louder, and Anchorage Museum gives the facts: "cold," "dark," "Friday," "nights," "extended hours," "9 p.m." "through April 2022."

Writers: when your museum undertakes magnanimous extra effort, tell that news in bold, unadorned words.

Nevada Art Museum (@NevadaArt) optimizes the human need for planning with: "Art Afternoons: Workshop and Social for Seniors" and "Hands-On! Second Saturdays." These ongoing programs with their brand names imitate holidays with a regular place on the calendar.

Naming a specific day in the week makes it a calendar event, one that can be planned and anticipated.

Happy Hands On! Second Saturday! Stop by today for free art activities.
    Draw like Picasso, create air-dry pinch pots . . . take a guided tour of the galleries.
    Happy Hands On! Second Saturday! Is a series. A program families can expect on a given day each month. And it will appear on Twitter each month. Happy retention!

Heard Museum (@HeardMuseum) in Phoenix reached out to a new group that has been praised, honored, and hired by museums, but seldom offered a workshop of its own: artists. "The Heard Museum Master Artist Workshop series offers Native artists access to mentorship . . . [with] a master-level artist. The in-person workshop will be instructed by Ho-Chunk artist, Melanie Sainz. More info here: bit.ly/3H8JrLL."

Social media can increase visitorship by addressing those groups that tried-but-not-so-true outreach programs don't reach. And, of course, artists have families; they'd also be visitors if they knew more.

EXPECTATION

Series of tweets give readers the expectation of more. These tweets become familiar and establish a reputation as sources of good stories and new information. Viewers look forward to them. Retaining readers on the screen obligates writers to fulfill the expectation. Nelson-Atkins Museum of Art (@nelson-atkins) does this with a consistent format:

- Two–three sentences
- An insight about the artist
- A short description of the artwork
- Context

Alison Saar was born #onthisday in 1956. Saar's piece Subway Preacher was inspired by a homeless man she often encountered on the subway. She is influenced by African, Haitian, and Creole folk art and spirituality. Currently on view in Contemporary Art bit.ly/3IHWjbW.

Fernand Leger was born #onthisday in 1881. This pristinely ordered composition recalls Léger's early training as an architect. The rectangular sections are overlaid with a precision-contoured vase and both circular and scalloped forms bit.ly/3H9P6kA. Not on view.

Paul Cezanne was born #onthisday, Jan. 19, 1839. Cezanne's work is said to be a bridge between the Impressionist and Cubist movements. Both Matisse and Picasso referred to Cezanne as "the father of us all." Quarry at Bibémus is on view in "Among Friends" bit.ly/31OXdUp

@Nelson-Atkins adapts the hashtag #onthisday by adding its specially formatted perspective on the artist of the day and the artwork itself. Each mini-bio is consistently brief, easy to read, a verbal miniature.

Writers: whatever the size of your museum, you probably have fifty-two objects to highlight in tweets. Find images and write twenty to forty words about each object or exhibit. For efficiency, edit the museum's labels or ask the education department for the suggested script it gives docents.

One short series of tweets from Nevada Museum of Art asks readers to guess the location of paintings in an exhibition:

Can you name the location of this Lorenzo Latimer painting? Post your guess in the comments below. Want a closer look? See this piece in "The Latimer School: Lorenzo Latimer and the Latimer Art Club."

Minerva Pierce titled this piece "Autumn Reflections." Can you guess where she was when she made this painting? Pierce was a member of the Latimer Art Club and an integral part of the Nevada Art Gallery, which would later become the Nevada Museum of Art.

When the curatorial and education people are enlisted, perhaps a word in support of social media is needed. Although tweets sometime get a bad rap for gossip and bombast, they should be valued as:

- intellectual
- informational
- educational
- institution-building.

They also unerringly:

- further interpretation goals
- attract readers who might also be scholars, donors, reviewers, and prospective hires, all looking for insights into the museum.

INCLUSIVENESS

Inclusiveness enfolds a lot of people and emotional territory. Museums enter into the lives of their entire community, geographic and cultural. Social media excels at welcoming the many, by name.

Noting both Black History Month and the historic occasion of the Cincinnati Bengals going to the Super Bowl (LVI, 2022) for the first time in thirty-four years, the Underground Railroad Museum and Freedom Center in Cincinnati covered two big events in February 2022:

> @FreedomCenter is celebrating #BlackHistoryMonth with events honoring liberators from multiple eras, music and culture.
> @FreedomCenter Go @Bengals!
> A few years ago the #CincinnatiBengals stopped by the #FreedomCenter to learn, grow and use their positions to enact real change in #Cincinnati and beyond.
> We're incredibly proud of our hometown team!

The tweets, in a few words, conveyed: hometown pride, the learning principle at work at the museum, activists, leaders, people in the arts, and football fans everywhere.

Pulitzer Arts Foundation (@PulitzerArts) wants to include non-conformists with a sense of humor:

This Sat, Jan 8 we are hosting the next session of Bad Drawing Club! 10am–noon CT, hang out, doodle, and chat on Zoom with other women, non-binary, trans, and gender non-conforming folks who like to draw.

Including girls reaches across diversity lines. With a calendar day devoted to girls in science and technology, as Pulitzer Arts Foundation does, museums are sending that message in many ways.

The associate curator of STEM Education at High Desert Museum (@High DesertMuse) uses the personal relations that social media establishes to tell girls: "On #WomenInSTEMDay, the Museum would like to remind girls everywhere to never let anyone tell you that you don't belong in STEM. Your voices, ideas & unique perspectives are vital to meet the challenges that the world faces."

Let's also include music for children who never carried tunes very far. Musical Instrument Museum (@MIMphx) asks parents to: "Embark on a musical journey with Musical Adventures (ages 6–10) to discover new cultures through music making, creating instruments, and exploring MIM's exhibits. Join the fun at bit.ly/3r7D0mq. #MIMkids." MIM picks up the tempo with a fifteen-second video that shows, close up, how to make a panpipe. Details for the parents combine with a short project for young children in a message that includes a new fringe group: children who aren't taught music in school.

Teenagers and younger occupy a large portion of the Metropolitan Museum of Art's (@MetMuseum) physical, calendar, and intellectual energy. It's large enough to devote a #hashtag to them.

How did ancient Egyptians create dazzling paintings? Explore the process with #MetKids—then try making your own tools for painting!

Hey, #MetTeens! Check out upcoming free classes and workshops designed to develop your skills, and allow you the opportunity to connect with art, new ideas, and other young people.

Although the Met is large enough to do almost anything, museums of any size can pinpoint new audience messages using the #hashtag approach.

INVOLVEMENT

While Inclusiveness is what museums do, involvement is what visitors do.

The rat-a-tat-tat of tweets gets the attention needed for involving visitors old and new. Tweets appear with forthright messages. Then they follow up with further details. When Crystal Bridges Museum of American Art, on the occasion of its tenth anniversary, asked viewers for their memories of the museum, they involved even more people by posting responses on Twitter:

Join us in reminiscing on our first decade by browsing meaningful memories submitted by members of our community.

The names of the contributors have been deleted, although they appear on the tweets.

My favorite memory was seeing the Hank Willis Thomas: All Things Being Equal . . . exhibition. I have never been so moved by art in my life. It really struck a chord with me as a Black woman seeing a part of my own cultural experience on display in an authentic way for the first time in my life.

I think my favorite Crystal Bridges experience was when I went on a school field trip in high school. My teacher made us sit and look at a painting for five minutes straight, which I had never done—this was when I discovered my love for art.

My favorite memory of Crystal Bridges is my first trip to the museum with my sister. We are 11 years apart in age and had never taken a trip together with just the two of us. This was such a fun and unique way to experience a new city and this beautiful museum together. Mixing our love of art, architecture, and nature, Crystal Bridges hit every sweet spot we were looking for! We will never forget that trip spending quality bonding time with one another. Thank you, Crystal Bridges!

By involving its large viewership, Crystal Bridges had a credible sample for a snapshot of the motivations and takeaways of its visitors. The museum asked a good question and got a rich response.

Writers: when working on visitor surveys, first learn the research goals. You might discover additional questions that will elicit meaningful responses.

Wing Luke Museum of the Asian American Experience used Twitter to ask for community participation in identifying a candidate for the leadership of their museum: "We are seeking nominations and applications for a dynamic #ExecutiveDirector to lead the next evolution of our community rooted and nationally recognized institution." Social media hiring that includes the community represents the Wing's community-rooted mission and identity.

Involvement is a form of flattery. When a respected institution requests reader input, it will get read. The Mark Twain House & Museum (@Mark Twain) tweets: "The #TwainHouse is looking for avid readers and literary enthusiasts to join the Selection Committee for the 2022 Mark Twain American Voice in Literature Award." The canny old storyteller has created a smart research project, asking to hear Americans' opinion on literature. The survey will provide valuable insights into American reading habits as it echoes the heart and soul of the museum.

Writers: offer your services in designing and writing the Selection Committee's guidelines. What looks like a simple form to non-writers in fact demands skill and experience in clarity writing.

Visitors and readers come to National Quilt Museum (@NatQuiltMuseum) in Paducah, Kentucky, to see and share and revel in the creativity of quilting. Its tweets are really love notes from loyal followers who talk about their blocks. Writers for the museum could never equal the warmth and enthusiasm of those who write to it.

"When I was 3 or 4, I was using watercolors & spilled some drops of paint on my paper. I kept painting & painted over the drops. My mom kept it to make into a quilt someday. I used that painting for inspiration." Quilting itself is involving, and the messages on Twitter amount to a virtual quilting bee. It's the perfect media for the museum and its mission to "to advance the art of today's quilter by bringing it to new and expanding audiences worldwide."

Hildene, the Lincoln Family Home in Manchester, Vermont, is part of a large community, the state of Vermont. It's a historic house museum, outside Manchester, and it closes for a few winter months. It appreciates its neighbors, and is diligent in involving Vermonters in its tweets:

> We practice "messy forest" forest management practices at @Hildene. This @ vermontbiz article by Ethan Tapper does a great job in explaining why messy is better than clean. Keep it messy, with intention. Learn why: vermontbiz .com/news/20.

> Announcing the 16th annual Hildene 8th Grade #Lincoln Essay Competition topic for Vermont residents and Vermont students. Applications, and more info available at: hildene.org/learning/linco . . . Submission deadline: February 12, 2022.

Writers: while keeping your words focused on museum objects, open your eyes to your region where there are many people just waiting to be involved.

If a museum has an involved following, it can ask for funds. To successfully compete at fundraising, Driehaus Museum also involved its staff, the people whose work in the museum would benefit from donations.

In a series of videos, shot at the entrance to the historic house museum, different staff members briefly described their jobs, and then gently broached the suggestion of supporting the work of the museum ending with: "On this #GivingTuesday, please consider supporting the work of the Museum and making a gift."

Writers: be prepared for holidays, national days, and popular days. All museums leverage them and your appeal must reflect your museum's needs.

CREATIVITY

Every human being is creative. Artists and scientists, historians and culture researchers, curators and educators and volunteers all create. Most imperatively, visitors are creative. It's one of the traits that draw them to museums.

At Lunar New Year 2022, starting Year of the Tiger, an impressive show of creativity burst from a tweet of Minnesota Museum of Science. The museum showed a painting of a tiger in a tweet about the science of tigers, and a cascade of beautiful artworks followed. Readers found their own visuals of tigers. They represented many cultures and genres. Viewers were inspired, just as museums hope they will be.

The communications that started this were successive posts about big cats. They followed the guidelines of being to the point, interesting, informative, and representative of the museum that posted them.

Science Museum of Minnesota (@ScienceMuseum) created this series of tweets to fire up the creativity of readers:

Happy #LunarNewYear! Are you shocked (like this tiger) that we're in week 2 of February? Let's dive into some big cat facts as we enter the #YearOfTheTiger.

Tigers would love it here in the land of lakes: they're some of the only cats that enjoy taking a dip!

They can live 20-25 years in the wild, and amazingly, underneath their furry stripes, their skin is striped, too.

While they might remind you of a giant housecat, tigers can't purr—like other big cats, they have a length of tough cartilage in their skull that allows them to roar but not rumble.

Should a museum prompt readers to send images of, say, tigers—give it a try. Don't just ask viewers to like you, though. Lead the way and persuade them to follow.

National Cowboy Museum, with its daily tweets, has established rapport with readers. And before Valentine's Day 2022 Tim #thecowboy tweeted a photo of a cowboy at a chuckwagon with: "Okay folks. Your turn. How would you caption this Cookie Valentines card? #HashtagTheCowboy Thanks, Tim." The photo was captioned with: "The cooks on the trail were called 'Cookies.' They weren't just the cook, they were also the barber, banker, veterinarian and doctor."

Tweets can get complex. The Cowboy Museum author had to locate the old west photo and a sample valentine, write a tweet, and elaborate on the legendary Cookies. Writers: he gave his audience a lot to look at. Everyone feels more creative when given some stimuli.

MISSION

Surprise—Twitter is revealed to be a model of mission communication. Mission statements are long and labored. Sometimes they're short and vague. Perhaps they're perfect and your museum collects unicorns.

Most mission communications actually play out in the History and About pages of websites, where there is space to reel out the remarkable enterprise of starting and nurturing a museum. In these cases, mission statements are scattered, fragmented.

On Twitter, museum missions are manifested clearly and organically. Twitter replicates that ever-moving process of collecting and interpreting according to a mission. Each tweet adds to the meaning of your museum. And it starts with the standing statement, the written profile that tops your feed when a viewer hits Search. Here are some examples:

Nelson-Atkins Museum of Art
@nelson-atkin
"Where the power of art engages the spirit of community."

Denver Museum
@DenverMuseumNS
"Be a catalyst! Ignite our community's passion for nature and science."

HancockShakerVillage
@HancockShaker
"Go back in time, forward in thought."

Crystal Bridges Museum of American Art
@crystalbridges
"Art, architecture, and nature in Bentonville, Arkansas."

TheNat
@SDNHM
"Explore the natural history of Southern California and Baja California—from past to present—at the San Diego Natural History Museum."

The Poe Museum
@PoeMuseum
"Illuminating Poe for everyone, evermore."

Old Stone House Museum & Historic Village
@OldStoneHouseVT
"Built by Alexander Lucius Twilight, the first African American to graduate college in the United States. We seek to preserve, educate and inspire."

Children's Museum SD
@CMSouthDakota
"Where imagination is as big as our skies! Play Along!"

Freedom Center
@FreedomCenter
"We reveal stories about freedom's heroes, from the era of the UGRR to contemporary times, challenging & inspiring everyone to take courageous steps for freedom."

EastmanMuseum
@EastmanMuseum
"World's foremost museum of photography and cinema located on the historic estate of George Eastman, the pioneer of popular photography."

The list is lengthy with purpose: compare the mission statements and realize how varied, compelling, and worthwhile museums are.

There's more to the mission than the words at the top of the tweets. It's ongoing. Here are examples of museums that, tweet after tweet, communicate their daily commitment to mission:

Planet Word Museum
@PlanetWordDC
"Planet Word is an interactive museum of words and language now open in Washington, D.C."

Join us Feb. 15 for the start of our new monthly series, Language &! We'll be sitting down with linguist Kathryn Hymes and cryptographer Hakan Seyalıoğlu, the masterminds behind @thornygames, to talk about the power and playfulness of language.

In our I'm Sold! gallery, you can find taglines from popular brands, all using techniques geared toward making their products memorable. "Plop, plop, fizz, fizz," "Mmm mmm good," and "Snap, crackle, pop" all use onomatopoeia. Do you know which products used these taglines?

The 2022 Winter Olympics are now underway! While we've been avidly cheering on the many talented athletes in sports as diverse as figure skating, luge, and skiing, we couldn't help but wonder about the origins of some of these sports' interesting terminology. #Etymonday

Mama T. Rex saw her shadow this morning! Do you know what that means? It means you should make time for play today.

Our Playful Preschooler classes start this Thursday! Play along.

Looking to fit in that holiday play? We are open New Year's Eve and Day!

We invite all families with children experiencing disabilities to our private sensory friendly playtime.

This museum boldly embraces what many children actually do to learn.

University of Nebraska State Museum, Morrill Hall
@MorrillHallUNL

Any guesses on our #FossilFriday today? An ancient softball? A fossilized grapefruit? No, it's actually the head of a femur from a 500,000 yr. old elephant! This epiphysis, aka "growth plate," had not fused to the rest of the femur yet, showing that this animal was still growing!

Collected from India ~1970s: silver owl and moon belt buckle. Owls have dual role in Hinduism–At times seen as a symbol of wealth, wisdom, & good fortune, owls can also = bad omens. This buckle = example of modern integration of owl imagery in Indian clothing. #anthroThursday

"Exciting news from our entomology collection: sharing Ardella magnaemirabilis (pic = top R), a new scarabaeoid species, genus & tribe named by our own Dr. MJ Paulsen. One of the smallest of 11,000+ species of "junebugs." #museummonday (digitalcommons.unl.edu/insectamundi/1)

These tweets come from an academic museum. The words flow from science and the museum dedicated to it.

SOCIAL BENEFITS FROM OTHER TECHNOLOGIES

Sociability isn't all virtual. It still occurs in the pre-meta world, inside your museum. In the spirit of social media, audio technology in museums encourages involvement. Eastman Museum in Rochester, New York, uses the interactive nature of stop labels to involve visitors in museum visits.

It's like an audio tour, but can be replayed from throughout the museum, allowing listeners to share ideas with companions in areas where talking is easier. It can be used to refer to compatible exhibits or parts of the museum, allowing different sharing opportunities.

An audio tour, narrated by Oscar-nominated actor Robert Forster, is offered throughout the historic mansion. Visit eastman.oncell.com or call (585) 563-3496 from your cell phone. Select exhibitions also offer cell phone tours. Look for symbols and stop numbers in the galleries. Service provider charges may apply.

Figure 2.1. Social media makes science a daily event, each post showcasing part of a collection or different aspects of a theme. Brainy!

Courtesy of Science Museum of Minnesota

Nevada Art Museum (@NevadaArt) suggests music for socialization, not to mention music for attracting different audiences to museums. It utilizes scan codes. "'People all over the world have problems. And as long as people have problems, the blues can never die.' —B.B. King. Come to the Museum and scan the codes on the wall to hear King play. nevadaart .org/summerofsoul."

Some basic rules of writing apply to stop labels and scan codes:

- Call them audio labels and think like a label writer. Keep the narrative short; keep the focus on the exhibit.
- Refer to the exhibit by name; these mini-talks may be replayed later in the museum visit.
- Point to specifics in work: colors, shapes, the size of the work, its position relative to other objects. This exercise in looking will energize museum-going. It's more than helpful to the vision impaired.
- Avoid generalities and scholarly words. They sound boring and aren't part of most people's listening vocabulary.
- Work the social angle and use phrases like: "Talk about this painting to the person next to you"; "look around and find the most popular object in the gallery"; "Discuss this work later in the café."

IN BRIEF

Writing for social media requires facts, nouns with better synonyms, ditto for verbs, repetition with variations on the theme, captions for photos and videos, and stamina to cut text.

REFERENCES

The examples in this chapter were selected for their skill in using social media strategically. These posts and tweets communicate the many singular aspects of their museum, including but not limited to: events, programs, collection, objects, exhibitions, creators, research, social initiatives, outreach, community partnerships, store, theater, archives, and mission. Social media, with its timely format, illuminates a museum's core values, every day—and like museums, then moves on to the challenges of the next day.

Readers are encouraged to visit the websites of the museums referenced in this chapter.

Akron Zoo
https://www.akronzoo.org/

Anchorage Museum
https://www.anchoragemuseum.org/

Children's Museum of South Dakota
https://prairieplay.org/

Crystal Bridges Museum of American Art
https://crystalbridges.org/

Denver Museum of Nature & Science
https://www.dmns.org/Driehaus Museum/

Eastman Museum
https://www.eastman.org/about

Hancock Shaker Village
https://hancockshakervillage.org/

Heard Museum
https://heard.org/

High Desert Museum
https://highdesertmuseum.org/

The Mark Twain House and Museum
https://marktwainhouse.org/

Metropolitan Museum of Art
https://www.metmuseum.org/

Milwaukee County Zoo
http://www.milwaukeezoo.org/

Musical Instrument Museum
https://mim.org/

The National Quilt Museum
https://quiltmuseum.org/

National Underground Railroad Museum Freedom Center
https://freedomcenter.org/

Nelson-Atkins Museum of Art
https://www.nelson-atkins.org/

Nevada Museum of Art
https://www.nevadaart.org/

Old Stone House Museum & Historic Village
https://www.oldstonehousemuseum.org/

Planet Word Museum
https://planetwordmuseum.org/

The Poe Museum
https://poemuseum.org/

Pulitzer Arts Foundation
https://pulitzerarts.org

San Diego Natural History Museum
https://www.sdnhm.org/

University of Nebraska State Museum/Morill Hall
https://museum.unl.edu/

Wing Luke Museum of the Asian-American Experience
https://www.wingluke.org/

CHAPTER 3

Inclusiveness

The challenges of Inclusiveness are:

Who?
Why?
What?

Who isn't being included? Why not? What should be done about that?

Overcome the first challenge and the problem recedes, but as the Art Institute of Chicago learned, we don't always recognize the excluded.

The Art Institute looks out over a great avenue, a great park, and a Great Lake. Its Modern Wing and sky bridge are as welcoming as its Beaux Arts frontage with the friendly bronze lions. But a caution: could this behemoth, built in 1893, be a walled fortress? On its facade are engraved names of artists like Fra Angelico, Botticelli, Durer, Raphael, Veronese, Rubens, Velasquez, Van Dyck, Rembrandt, Reynolds, Gainsborough, Murillo, and Turner.

Is this traditional elitism carved in stone?

The story continues with this message from the Art Institute:

Firmly rooted in Eurocentric tradition, the founding objectives of our institutional history did not consider gender, ethnic, and racial equity. When our early leaders carved the names of iconic artists into the building's neoclassical entablature, they branded the museum a temple of learning and paid homage to the essential roles that individual artists played in shaping the world's cultures and histories. While this list of names was entirely aspirational given our modest collections at that time, it was also very limited in scope—almost entirely white, Western European, and male. The omission of artists of color, especially Black artists, as well as female, Indigenous, and non-Western artists, is glaring. Despite our immutable entablature, we intentionally uncover new narratives in our galleries that allow continual, dynamic reconsideration in the present. We recognize the tension between our museum's history and the ongoing work of our present; we commit to critical self-reflection and participatory, recuperative action.

In short, it didn't realize.

Writers: as you read about other museums' initiatives and think, "I didn't realize that," be glad that, cumulatively, museums will comprehend the unknowns. Alerted, everyone can write words that are more inclusive.

Here are some of the once unforeseen areas to investigate:

Land acknowledgment
Native Americans
First Nation
Global museums
Refugees and other newcomers
Children
Safety
Reframing accessibility
English and language
Canada and America
Inclusions of citizen advisors
Unawareness
Other spaces
Programming with candor
Visuals and photographs—evidence of diversity, proof of inclusion

LAND ACKNOWLEDGMENT

To start the discussion at the beginning, museums are starting with land acknowledgment, because so many museums are built, from the ground up, on land originally owned, and not ceded, by indigenous people. Throughout North America, the term is variably: Native American, Native, First Nations (Canada), or American Indian. The Smithsonian, which recognizes all tribes and nations, uses "American Indian." Inclusiveness takes many forms!

Burke Museum, Seattle, exemplifies inclusiveness by acknowledging indigenous peoples' residency on every page of its website: "Land Acknowledgement: The Burke Museum stands on the lands of the Coast Salish Peoples, whose ancestors resided here since time immemorial. Many Indigenous peoples thrive in this place—alive and strong." Advising the Burke on its collection, exhibits, education, and research is the Native American Advisory Board. As has become practice with federal institutions, Native Americans are identified with their tribal affiliation following their name. The thirty-member board includes members of these tribes, communities and nations: Apsaalooke Nation, Colville, Lower Elwha Klallam, Lummi Nation, Makah, Muckleshoot, Nisqually Indian Tribe, Nuu-chah-nulth, Puyallup Tribe of Indians, Samish Nation, Snoqualmie Indian Tribe, Squaxin Island Tribe, Suquamish, Swinomish Indian Tribal Community, Tulalip, Umatilla, Unangan (Aleut), Wanapum, Yakama Nation, and Zuni/Tlingit. If this long list seems unwieldy, if the protocol of post-nominals is time-consuming, and if there are more people in this world than one has realized, welcome to inclusiveness and the reality that museums are embracing. The practice of stating tribe affiliation after a native person's name has become federal practice in all its departments' documents, much like post-nominals such as PhD, JD, MD, CPA, Esq., and USN have always been accorded.

Writers: take note. When writing a Native American's name, consider including his or her tribal affiliation. And, if possible, ask the individuals the terminology they prefer Native American, Indigenous People, First Nation, Native Peoples, Native, American Indian—all are choices. Then ask if they want any other affiliation noted. And no asterisks or endnotes. If it's important to the document, put in the main text.

NATIVE AMERICANS

Here's another inconvenient attitude in the North American narrative: indigenous people aren't a relic of history; they're your neighbor. They didn't disappear, and it's one of the subtle inequities that museums confront. It's a key message of Land Acknowledgement at Portland (OR) Museum of Art:

> The Portland Art Museum recognizes and honors the Indigenous peoples of this region on whose ancestral lands the museum now stands. . . . We also want to recognize that Portland today is a community of many diverse Native peoples who continue to live and work here. We respectfully acknowledge and honor all Indigenous communities—past, present, future—and are grateful for their ongoing and vibrant presence.

This statement appears on every page of the website—on Visit, Collection, Learn, Support—on every single page.

On the other side of the country, Parrish Art Museum in Water Mill, New York, uses this format: "Join Parrish Collection artist and fine art photographer Jeremy Dennis, member of the Shinnecock Indian Nation, for an evening-length program . . . to draw attention to the sacred land of the Shinnecock Hills."

Native Americans live in the present and are identified for their accomplishments, as well as their culture.

GLOBAL MUSEUM

Broadening out to the world is part of museums' DNA. They have always collaborated across borders with scientists, historians, artists, researchers, scholars, and speakers. Now museums are expanding this internationalism to the everyday life—visitors, staff, and volunteers. "Foreign" as a word has gotten a bad reputation. Many people crossing the threshold speak a language other than English, come from a country that isn't the U.S., and live a life heavily based on a culture from far and away.

The Musical Instrument Museum looks at inclusiveness globally, a collection of instruments from all over the globe, and a mission: "to develop a new kind of museum that would focus on the kind of instruments played every day by people worldwide . . . inspiring what we have in common."

Tenement Museum in New York City is based on the stories of immigrants to the United States, or as might be stated, emigrants from around the globe:

> At the Tenement Museum, we share stories of people who left where they came from, past and present, and look to understand refugee experiences within stories of why and how people move. In our *Your Story, Our Story* exhibit, a national project that explores identity and migration through stories of everyday objects and traditions, many participants shared their experiences as refugees and their descendants.

CHILDREN

Children are people, too, regardless of how they're usually categorized as Family—as in Family Day, Family Workshops, Family Tours. However, children are so smart, so complex, so different. Many museums give them the equity they need.

Tenement Museum, New York, uses children's toys as visual memories in its series, Your Story, Our Story. Across all cultures, images of book illustrations and stuffed animals, contribute to the fabric of American life.

One of the museum tours features that unsung heroine, the teenager, in Meet Victoria Confino, a tour of a 1916-period apartment and the way an Italian immigrant lived in a few rooms and a bathroom down the hall.

SAFETY

Safety means different things to different audiences. Insecurity abounds for those whose backgrounds include immigration, discrimination, a language not English, non-flexible work hours, and scant access to transportation.

The Museum of California looked at safety as what safety means to their diverse audiences:

> recognizing the disproportionate impacts of COVID-19 on communities of color. . . .
>
> Act with a mentality of abundance in order to find innovative solutions to ensure the physical safety and mental well being of all staff, partners, and visitors.
>
> Our Visitor Experience Team . . . including Visitor Experience Associates and Gallery Guides, expanded its safety risks analysis phase to include a pandemic social impact analysis, including research projects which brought to light a variety of disparate impacts, from negative bias towards Asian American communities to inequitable access to health care, to the digital divide. This research then fed into our DEIA Commitments which have been at the root of our policy decisions.

Note emphasis on mental well-being. Note also attention to all stake-holders—staff and partners as well as visitors.

Part of good writing is having courage to put internal discussions/thinking into words.

REFRAMING ACCESSIBILITY

Delaware Art Museum has a book club. Also movies in the garden. The museum captures audiences who like books, and it appeals to audiences who have never been to an art museum but do enjoy movies. It gives handicapped, out-of-town, working people another way to enjoy the museum, virtually. Hear the inclusive, welcoming tone of the website copy: "in addition to our interest in art and artists, we also seek to create a sense of community, conversation, and connection."

Accessibility and inclusiveness require getting from one place to another, to the museum and once inside.

Amon Carter Museum of American Art practices inclusiveness at an essential stage in the museum-going decision process. Many newcomers, of all backgrounds, are hesitant because they don't know the Wheres of:

- public transportation
- parking inexpensively
- locking their bicycles
- dropping off mobility-impaired visitors
- designated parking for vans with drop-down steps.

Amon Carter shows:

- bus routes that serve the museum
- distance from each museum stop to the main entrance
- number of bus route
- name of stop
- number of stairs to climb, handrails, dizziness factor.

Here's how St. Augustine Lighthouse & Maritime Museum, in a Q and A on its website, includes people with issues of stairs, heights, and small children: "For their safety, children must be at least 44 inches tall to climb. . . . There are 219 steps to reach the observation deck. There are also eight landings, one with a bench, where visitors can rest and let other people pass."

Accessibility is not just for the physically challenged. Visitors also need to access the restrooms without challenges. Here's how Burke Museum talks about what many people want to talk about first:

Restrooms are all-gender throughout the museum. Shared, multi-stall and private, single-stall restrooms are located on every floor. By offering restrooms that are all-gender, the Burke Museum seeks to minimize structural barriers to access and create a space that is welcoming to all.

Lactation Room: Mothers are welcome to nurse wherever they are comfortable within the building. A private lactation room is also available on Floor 2.

For smaller museums, multiple options may not be available. The Museum of Contemporary Photography at Columbia College Chicago says on its website: "If you require special accommodations for this event, please contact mocp@colum.edu."

State even the basics of access. Not only must a museum provide systems for access, but they are also required by the Americans with Disabilities Act to communicate accessibility throughout the museum. For example,

- Special elevators for accessibility—place signs throughout the museum.
- Signs usually in a certain place get moved—return them to the usual place.
- Information occurs at a certain place on your website—don't move it.
- Use alternative signage such as Braille, audio, assisted hearing devices, enlarged type, and closed captioning.
- Advertise a TTY number—instruct staff and volunteers how to use it.

And to prepare visitors for less-than-perfect accessibility, candor helps. A tour company specializing in cultural institutions offers a fitness test on its website:

- Sit in a dining chair, arms folded; stand and sit at least eight times.
- Raise each knee half way to hip height sixty times in two minutes.
- Be able to walk unaided at a pace of 3 mph for at least one hour.
- Stand unsupported for at least 30 minutes.

ENGLISH AND OTHER LANGUAGES

What can be done about visitors for whom English is a second language? Many websites include a drop-down menu for translation into 6–78 languages.

Queens Museum can translate Latest News into Arabic, Chinese (Simplified), Dutch (*"Laatste nieuws"*), French, German, Italian, Portuguese, Russian, and Spanish.

Burke Museum offers a choice of 78 languages, including Hmong and Zulu, along with Azerbaijani and Welsh.

Writers: the world's bounty of languages is a signal: people interpret words in 78 different ways. To get an idea of how your words are received, read them out loud. Insensitivity can't hide when it's spoken.

Depending on budget, museums can translate labels, printed pieces, handouts, and online material into the most common alternate language in your community. Also, remember the QR code and consider "Scan Here for a translation."

Writers: sometimes a sincere *"Celebracion!"* shows inclusiveness when your budget doesn't.

Colloquialisms and local dialects add diversity to an already diverse audience. All countries of the world embrace multiple languages, and it takes intuition and sensitivity to understand when your exhibition needs to speak more than plain English. For labels, panels, printed material, website text speaking of, or to, previously marginalized audiences, nuances can be mastered. National Museum of the American Indian, part of the Smithsonian Institution, publishes these guidelines under the heading titled: "The Impact of Words and Tips for Using Appropriate Terminology: Am I Using the Right Word?"

- Don't use the past tense. With Native Americans, it reinforces the notion that they're a vanished people or insubstantial. When you must use the past tense, include dates or "it may seem like Native cultures are no longer living."
- Use contemporary examples where appropriate.
- Beware of derogatory terms, even when it seems like clever writing. "Low man on the totem pole" may sound like stereotyping to Native Americans.
- The word "slave," even in an historic context, implies an inherent identity, rather than an imposed condition. Contemporary usage calls for "enslaved person."

Figure 3.1. Hayne Hudjihini, Eagle of Delight, Henry Inman (1832–1833), the Metropolitan Museum of Art, New York. On the Met website, its collection of nineteenth-century portraits of Native American leaders is enriched by links to "Read a Native Perspective," written by contemporary Natives.

Born into a prominent Eagle clan family of the Jiwere-Nut'achi (Otoe-Missouria) people, Hayne Hudjihini, Eagle of Delight, has a blue tattoo on her forehead denoting her royal status. Her marriage to Bear clan Chief Sumonyeacathee formed an Eagle-Bear union—a high honor among the Jiwere-Nut'achi people . . . in 1822 she and her husband traveled as ambassadors and protectors of Jiwere-Nut'achi sovereignty from their home in present-day Nebraska to Washington, D.C., to meet with President James Monroe. During this trip, Bureau of Indian Affairs superintendent Thomas McKenney is said to have fallen in love with her and commissioned her portrait. Despite Eagle clan members being known for their strength, health, and long lives, she died of measles shortly after she returned home. —Veronica, Rock, and Wolf Pipestem (Otoe-Missouria), descendants of Hayne Hudjihini

- Don't generalize with terms like "all Native Americans," or "the Indigenous culture." Native people comprise many different nations, tribes, and communities; each nation, tribe and community has its own culture. The *Inuit, Yup'ik,* and *Aleut* Peoples in the Arctic see themselves as culturally separate Indigenous people. In Mexico, Central America, and South America, the translated word for "Indian" has negative connotations. They prefer the word *"indígena"* or Indigenous, *"comunidad"* or community, and *"pueblo"* or people.

Importantly, sensitivity to the right word helps writers everywhere think more empathetically about their subjects and objects.

CANADA AND AMERICANS

Americans are not the only Americans. Canada is also part of the continent that's across the ocean from Europe, Africa, and Asia. Writers are learning to spot when North American might be a better phrase. There are over 2,000 museums in Canada.

First Nations, or First Nation people, are preferred usages in Canada. There are fifty-two different First Nation cultures recognized in Canada.

Sidebar: Amerigo Vespucci, the Italian explorer who explored the Amazon River in 1502, was the first person to realize that the land Columbus had discovered was not part of Asia. The continents that became known as North and South America were named after him.

Writers: to include people, dignify their diversity, and make equity work, just listen. Actually use the words, "we listened and this is what we heard." Face-to-face works wonders in finding the words you need.

UNAWARENESS FACTOR

Lurking in the corners of every institution is dusty unawareness. It means no harm but it often says, "Gee, I didn't know that."

A few of the more egregious examples of unawareness concern:

Repatriation
Phobias
Shift workers
Archives

Repatriation recognizes the difference between returning something and repatriating it with the culture that created it. The Burke Museum addresses the issue on the Collections and Research page of its website:

Q: Does the Burke repatriate collections?

A: Yes, the Burke Museum works closely with tribes throughout the U.S., meeting the letter and spirit of the Native American Graves Protection and Repatriation Act (NAGPRA). The Burke also works with other communities and countries to repatriate ancestors and sensitive artifacts.

Phobias are inexplicable fears, and in many cases are unknown by those who don't suffer from them. The Arab American National Museum says in an anti-oppression statement:

In alignment with AANM's commitment to creating an arts sector rooted in justice, we are committed to ensuring a space that is free of racism, transphobia, homophobia, Islamophobia, ableism, misogyny, classism or other biases. Our expectation is that all visitors will honor these ethics.

This statement has been graciously shared by the National Performance Network, of which AANM is a partner.

Diverse groups diverge when it comes to work schedules. Lower-income families, people of color, immigrants, those for whom English is a second language—many workers in this group work late, irregular shifts, work hours that continue when museums traditionally close.

Blanton Museum of Art, the University of Texas at Austin, actually asked its visitors:

If the museum were to stay open until 8 p.m. one night per week, which of these two evenings would you prefer?

Friday
Saturday
We appreciate your feedback

Many people, in and out of the museum, are unaware of its archives.

Inclusiveness is such a big word, one person could easily forget the people who work there. They oversee a lot of the language owned by a museum.

The Getty Research Institute archivists, working far in the back and away from the crowd, also help tell a story and, as one article says, "help shape the historical record . . . [with] reparative work that we can do as archivists to support communities fighting for justice."

And these are the words from the archives of the Oklahoma Historical Society:

Since 1934 the Oklahoma Historical Society American Indian Archives have housed American Indian records for numerous tribes. The records came to the Oklahoma Historical Society after Congress passed legislation giving the

OHS custody of the materials, . . . the archives include a significant number of records pertaining to the Five Tribes as well as other tribes.

The word "significant" matters. Deep in the archives, unknown to many good people, is information that supports and provides new insights on diversity and equity. Writers: watch your language when writing about the Archives, of less-known places like the Volunteer, Store, or History pages. Be on the lookout for uncomfortable anachronisms.

TALKING TO VISITORS WITH DISABILITIES

Royal Museums Greenwich, outside London, offers workshops, currently virtual, for people with dementia and their caregivers.

This group, including the challenged individual and their caregiver, cuts across all other divisions of age, background, race, and culture. It's inclusive and far-reaching.

MORE OTHER PEOPLE

Inclusiveness expands as museums' importance to their communities expands. Here are some people and spaces to think about:

Artists and other creators have special needs. They need special equipment to aid them in researching and creating. Artists, for example, often come to museums to learn by sketching and drawing. Burke Museum, like most museums, forbids pens and markers in the galleries, and realizes that not everyone who itches to sketch is a well-prepared with pencils; so they provide them at the front desk. Colored pencils, too.

Sketching & Drawing
Both regular and colored pencils are welcome in the museum galleries. Please leave your pens and markers at home or check them at the admissions desk on Floor 1.

Denver Museum of Natural Science relates "inclusiveness" to "good science" and, in so doing, enshrines it in the very DNA of its institution:

Active science takes place at the Museum every day. Our curators, collections managers, archivists, conservators, librarians, researchers, and lab assistants— along with 600 volunteers—are not only responsible for conducting research but also creating opportunities for citizens to become actively involved in science. The education staff creates compelling programs and experiences for millions of guests and schoolchildren.

This paragraph shows good writing about inclusiveness—details and specific language:

- Staff responsible for its mission are specified by title.
- Volunteers are not simply "loved, indebted to or appreciated"; they're specified in numbers. Six hundred—600!—is a fact not to be hidden behind hackneyed generalities.
- The opportunities for civilians are described in detail elsewhere in the site. They are numerous and impressive. Nice words are borne out by case histories and facts.
- A term is coined: Active Science. When you have a good idea, well-executed, give it a name, and make time to find one.

Part of the Museum's everyday concept of Inclusiveness is stated in its mission statement: "Science helps us understand that diversity in our natural world creates strength and nurtures life."

Some museums broaden inclusion to consultation. The Art Institute of Chicago compiles data that asks for hard looking at specifics:

- What factors actually drive attendance?
- Do local and tourist audiences behave the same way?
- Which objects in our collection are most popular with visitors?
- What audience segments are we reaching?
- How do we get more of our collection online?
- What are the strengths and gaps in our collection?
- How can we streamline the buying experience in the museum shop?

Tenement Museum also asks for visitor input, in this case for curatorial assistance in its Your Story, Our Story initiative to collect artifacts and memories from descendants of immigrants:

"Help us tell a more complete story of American immigration and migration by contributing a family object story to the collection."

Inclusiveness acquires different voices in the National Underground Railroad Freedom Center blog, Other Voices and blog posts such as:

In Teachers We Trust: Why We Oppose OH H.B. Nos. 322 and 327

And posts by white college professors on differing views on anti-racism: "I am researching the differences among anti-slavery positions, differences that often get glossed over when 'anti-slavery' is remembered only as a single position in opposition to slavery."

Equally important as the posts themselves is the inclusiveness of the forum, a blog open to a range of opinions.

SUPPLIER DIVERSITY

Forgotten but essential are museum suppliers, the companies and their people who supply products and services for everything from air quality systems to classroom chairs and photocopier repairs.

Here are some rhetorical questions to ask:

Are they local companies, small businesses, minority owned?
Do they hire the handicapped?
Do you include them in the same friendly chitchat you would an exhibition installer or publisher representative?

Writers: many visitors and supporters are your everyday tradespeople. And, by the way, they have families and friends who might like your museum, too.

PROGRAMMING WITH CANDOR

Eastman Museum, in the George Eastman House in Rochester, New York, shows films as parts of its many programs. Dr. Eastman invented moving picture cameras, as well as the Kodak hand-helds that became universally known. Films cover so many topics, in every corner of the globe; they're the perfect vehicle for showcasing underrepresented groups in professional ways.

Eastman Museum titled them "In Solidarity: Spotlighting Black Film Artists" and "In Solidarity: Celebrating Asian/American Directors."

> FREE FILM SERIES, In solidarity with the Black community—which continues to face pervasive discrimination, bigotry, and violence—the George Eastman Museum spotlights the contributions of Black film artists with this series of nine motion pictures from 1930 to the present.

Here, Inclusion is more than a goal, more even than an ongoing practice that has already begun. It's a statement of the problem in action taken.

Mariners' Museum and Park, in a newsletter in September 2021, set high standards for inclusivity. The titles announcing each event and the fact-oriented text announced programs rooted in diverse and inclusive topics:

Find your connection at The Mariners' Museum and Park!

From histories about the Civil War and the Hampton Roads regions to contribution of the U. S. Coast Guard, the Mariners' will share incredible stories that show how we are all connected through the world's waters.

National Hispanic Heritage Month Celebración!

Select Museum team members and special guest speakers will be available in our galleries to share fascinating stories of the people, history, and geography of Latin America and the Caribbean.

Writers: including everyone takes practice. And sometimes it shouldn't happen. For example, when speaking to a hearing-impaired person, should you talk to the ASL signer, as well as to the student? No! Ignore the student in favor of the interpreter? That would be exclusion.

PHOTOGRAPHS

Remember the messages that photos send. They document the way things really appear to the viewer. Of course, photographers select and frame their shots. And museums can select the shots they want to use. The goal is to visualize diversity where it occurs, and then to make sure that happens.

Parrish Art Museum projects a good example with a photo of its Kids Summer Camp and an art class. The first thing one notices is the zigs and zags of height. Kids come in all sizes, and that's an instant signal of diversity. Then there's skin color, and hair color, and this is important because persons of color want their children to see people like them. In reality, this is a great photo of diversity and equity: all the children hold up the same shape piece of paper, but each child has drawn their own picture.

REFERENCES

"About the Arab American National Museum," About, Arab American National Museum, https://arabamericanmuseum.org/

"About Your Visit," Visit, Burke Museum, https://www.burkemuseum.org/visit/about-your-visit [accessed 1-23-22]

"All Aboard Reminiscence Workshop," What's On, Royal Museum Greenwich, https://www.rmg.co.uk/whats-on/online/all-aboard-reminiscence-workshop [accessed 1-23-22]

"Black Authors, Black Directors," Dryden Theatre, Eastman Museum, https://www.eastman.org/solidarity-spotlighting-black-film-artists [accessed 1-23-22]

Bottomley, Amy, "In Teachers We Trust: Why We Oppose OH H.B. Nos. 322 and 327," Other Voices, National Underground Railroad Freedom Center, October 26, 2021,

https://freedomcenter.org/voice/the-power-and-pitfalls-of-white-anti-racism-ange
lina-grimke-yesterday-and-today [accessed 1-20-22]

Ceja, Samantha, Sara McGillivray, and Helen Kim, "How Getty Archivists Support
Racial Justice: Inside the Ongoing Work to Reexamine Thousands of Records to
Create Better and More Equitable Archives," Featured News, Getty Research Center, June 16, 2021. http://Blogs.Getty.Edu/Iris/Getty-Archivists-Support-Racial-Jus-
tice/ [accessed 1-21-22]

Film & Workshop | An Evening With Jeremy Dennis, Parrish Art Museum, Janu-
ary 14, 2022, https://parrishart.org/event/film-workshop-an-evening-with-jeremy
-dennis/ [accessed 1-21-22]

"Fitness," About Us, Martin Randall Travel, https://www.martinrandall.com/about-us
[accessed 1-21-22]

"Frequently Asked Questions by Lighthouse Visitors," Visit, St. Augustine Lighthouse Museum, https://www.staugustinelighthouse.org/2019/04/30/%ef%bb%bf
frequently-asked-questions-by-lighthouse-visitors/ [accessed 1-20-22]

"Glossary of Terms," Canadian Race Relations Foundation/Fondation canadienne
des relations raciales, https://www.crrf-fcrr.ca/en/resources/glossary-a-terms
-en-gb-1? [accessed 8-26-21]

"History of the Denver Museum of Nature & Science," About Us, Denver Museum
of Nature & Science, https://www.dmns.org/about/about-us/museum-history
[accessed 1-23-22]

https://www.burkemusem.org/about/our-work [accessed 1-22-22]

https://queensmuseum.org/?utm_source=QMail&utm_campaign=07f9e3d904
-EMAIL_CAMPAIGN_2020_04_04_03_36_COPY_01&utm_medium=email&utm
_term=0_32b24c670e-07f9e3d904-246122589

https://yourstory.tenement.org

"Identity," About Us, Art Institute of Chicago, https://www.artic.edu/about-us/iden
tity [accessed 12-22-21]

"The Impact of Words and Tips for Using Appropriate Terminology: Am I Using the
Right Word?" Native Knowledge 360. National Museum of the American Indian,
https://americanindian.si.edu/nk360/informational/impact-words-tips [accessed
1-22-22]

"Inclusivity Statement," Mission and Vision, About Us, Denver Museum of Science
& "Your Story Our Story," Tenement Museum, https://yourstory.tenement.org

"Henry Inman, Hayne Hudjihini, Eagle of Delight," Pipestem, V., Pipestem, R.,
Pipestem, W. (Oboe-Missouria), Native Perspective, The Metropolitan Museum
of Art https://www.metmuseum.org/about-the-met/collection-areas/the-ameri
can-wing/native-perspectives [accessed 4-4-22]

"Learn," Portland Art Museum, https://portlandartmuseum.org/learn/pro
grams-tours/ [accessed 12-23-21]

"Maintaining Accessibility in Museums," *Disability Rights Section*, Civil Rights Divi-
sion, U.S. Department of Justice, https://www.ada.gov/business/museum_access
.htm [accessed 1-23-22]

"Meet Victoria: 1916," Building Tours, Visit, Tenement Museum, https://www.tene
ment.org/tour/meet-victoria-1916/ [accessed 1-21-22]

"National Hispanic Heritage Month Celebracion," September 18, 2021, https://10123 .blackbaudhosting.com/10123/National-Hispanic-Heritage-Month-Celebra cion?mc_cid=d80545c983&mc_eid=f3b56802e0 [accessed 1-23-22]

"Native American Advisory Board," Leadership, About, Burke Museum, https:// www.burkemuseum.org/about/leadership [accessed 1-21-22]

Nature, https://www.dmns.org/about/about-us/ [accessed 1-23-22]

"New discoveries await when you visit the Mariners' this month!" e-mail 9-1-21 [accessed 1-20-22]

"Our Commitment to Re-Opening Through the Lens of Diversity, Equity, Inclusion, and Access," Blog, Oakland Museum of California, https://museumca.org/blog /our-commitment-re-opening-through-lens-diversity-equity-inclusion-and-access [accessed 1-22-22]

"Our Story," About, Musical Instrument Museum, http://mim.org/our-story/ [accessed 1-3-22]

"Photos at Zoom Discussion Session: Wardell Milan," Museum of Contemporary Photography, August 13, 2021, https://www.mocp.org/events/event?id=3679479 5956026 [accessed 1-23-22]

"The Power of Applied Data for Museums," Alliance Blog, Alliance of American Museums, January 17, 2017, https://www.aam-us.org/2017/01/17/the-power-of -applied-data-for-museums/ [accessed 1-20-22]

"Repatriation," About, Burke Museum, https://www.burkemuseum.org/about/our -work/repatriation [accessed 1-22-22]

"The State of Museums in Canada," Canadian Museums Association, June, 2016, https://museums.in1touch.org/uploaded/web/docs/Advocacy/CMA_Recommen dations_CHPC_2016_EN.pdf [accessed 1-22-22]

Suchland, Jennifer, "The Power and Pitfalls of White Anti-Racism: Angelina Grimké Yesterday and Today," Freedom Center Voices, March 19, 2021, https://freedomcen ter.org/voice/the-power-and-pitfalls-of-white-anti-racism-angelina-grimke -yesterday-and-today/ [accessed 1-20-22]

"Summer Camps 2022," https://parrishart.org/summercamp/ [accessed 1-20-22]

"Virtual DelArt Readers: Book Club," Programs & Events, Delaware Art Museum, July 2021, https://delart.org/event/virtual-delart-readers-book-club-2021 -06-24-2021-07-29/ [accessed 1-23-22]

"We Want Your Input," e-mail January 19, 2022, Blanton Museum of Art, https:// mailchi.mp/blantonmuseum/august20-181358?e=1cc1747e31 [accessed 1-23-22]

"Your Story, Our Story," Tenement Museum, https://yourstory.tenement.org/ [accessed 1-21-22]

CHAPTER 4

Collaborations

Relationships with the Community

Back in the day, public relations was a one-way street. Institutions sent notifications about membership programs and fundraising events to the public; there was scant realization of how many publics were out there. Institutions relied on the media—print and online—until the media became a two-way street between thousands of publics and the institution.

When the publics changed, and the media changed, and even the one-way street changed, relationships pivoted to collaborations. This chapter will look at how institutions all over the country collaborate.

Theories won't work because the soul of collaborating is You and Me. Just Us, my friend, figuring out how to make this work.

THE PARTNERS OF THE COLLABORATION—THE MUSEUM

Museums have been collaborating a long time because they listened to experts, considered context, and truly cared about the makers and caretakers of culture. The question was, and is, what does the museum have to collaborate about? Why would a group in the community want to partner with a museum? Fortunately, there are very good reasons.

Before you start seeking out these potentials partners, know how much museums have to offer. The community will learn quickly why museums make successful collaborators, for all the following reasons.

WHO COLLABORATES—THE COMMUNITY

This is a much bigger group, but it doesn't make the museum's job any easier.

WHAT MUSEUMS OFFER AND WHY THE
COMMUNITY WANTS TO CONTRIBUTE TO IT

When writing a document for a collaboration, whether a grant request or proposal outline, the writer must connect the commonalities between the two parties. There are reasons a community institution wants to partner with a museum, and here they are:

Collaboration Advantage: Experience with issues of the day
Collaboration Advantage: Planning and budgeting expertise
Collaboration Advantage: Expertise with scholarly topics
Collaboration Advantage: Education skills and track record
Collaboration Advantage: Visibility
Collaboration Advantage: Meeting spaces

Case in Point

Chickasaw Cultural Center, Sulphur, Oklahoma, exemplifies tribes being "the first voice" to share their stories. Emerson Vallo (Acoma Pueblo) of the Alaska Native Tourism Association, said: "More tribes are now seeing the advantages of having a cultural center or museum, so that they do their own interpretation of their own people." With so many tribes in the United States alone, collaborations empower individual museums. Diversity that is at the heart of Native American culture is changing the parameters of all American museums.

Writers: know the culture of your partner (for example, Native Americans privilege their tribes and custom now requires that all individual names be followed by their tribe). If the partner is a business, educational institution, or government, listen for facts and terminology and ask at least three questions.

EXPERTISE

Scholars don't always get PhDs and teach in universities. The ones who gravitate to museums and cultural institutions understand dealing with the publics, and working with museums in many countries, languages, and cultures, in addition to the intricacies of subject. Scholars have areas of inquiry; they reach out and listen.

Case in Point

Citizen Science fills museums' needs to gather data of all sorts, from watching "the arms of spiral galaxies" to counting migrating birds. Few budgets in any institution can afford unlimited hours of staff time.

At North Carolina Museum of Natural Sciences in Raleigh, programs have included projects to "trace the arms of spiral galaxies to measure the windings," training to "identify blood cell types before you classify the cell types from photos of monkey blood smears," and digitizing documents.

The collaboration serves both scientists and citizens by teaching professional research skills to amateurs. It assumes a high level of learning that's possible for the average citizen and, in so doing, inspires a new generation of scientists. It also reassures the current generation of museum supporters that its mission is in good hands.

Writers: you're writing for amateurs who will be working with the pros. Use words like this from North Carolina:

- With your help, we can preserve . . .
- Whether you are a researcher or not!
- That's where you come in! Your sightings help scientists at the Museum and around the world learn more about the biodiversity . . .
- . . . and it only takes a few seconds of your time to help.

RESPECT FOR THE ECOLOGICAL WORLD

Queens Museum broadened its expected activities when it went to its border with Brooklyn on a volunteer landscaping project. The purpose was to protect the Ridgewood Reservoir and water conservation and the ecology of the region, and along the way it found: hard-working new volunteers; new learning for existing volunteers and staff; new opportunities for more joint ventures; a new (pop-up) venue; and new branded merchandise.

Writers: position collaborations as explorations for new information and skills, updating of processes and management, strengthening finances, and implementing strategy. Where appropriate, stress reinforcement of both partners' missions. Remind participants to tell friends and family about the venture. Add the experience to your institution's credentials document.

VISIBILITY

Look at your buildings and grounds. Large or small, Main Street or neighborhood, museum buildings are known and are improving their curb appeal so visitors find them easily. Tourism and economic development bureaus give them more visibility.

Example: Shaker Village of Pleasantville, Harrodsburg, Kentucky, became the perfect partner for a two-day Jazz Festival because Shaker Village is "Kentucky's largest National Historic Landmark."

Figure 4.1. Shaker Village existed as an agricultural community, devoted not only to its way of life, but also to the cultural and economical success of the region. Producing and selling its products benefited everyone. Writers: reference your town and community where relevant. Interconnectedness is everywhere.
Courtesy of Shaker Village of Pleasant Hill

Writers: the museum development office and event planners did their job; here's yours:

Mention the generosity and name of the sponsoring partner before you write up the attractions of the museum half of the partnership.
Thank the sponsoring partner several times.
Mention every name that is capitalized, like National Landmarks, and Heritage Jazz Festival. Museums don't survive and thrive alone.

CHILD-FRIENDLY

The Education Department is filled with masters of youth programming and execution. School boards, teachers, children, and caregivers love them. Museums stretch far beyond their starting point to meet children more than halfway. Remember that children rule, with parents as regents, and that both parties will mature into important new audiences.

Example: Collaborations with K–12 are established, and the teamwork needn't be only two-way, as Cranbrook Art Museum demonstrates. It developed a multi-school partnership built on elementary schools joining in the planning stage, sharing in the follow-up discussions, and joining the analysis of the results.

Writers: in writing about collaborations based on long-honored models, listen for what's different. If your museum, like Cranbrook Art Museum, takes a different approach, underscore that. Also, the analysis partnership gives you material you need to summarize the concept.

SAVVY BUDGETERS

Museums operate on budgets that are carefully made and kept—scholarly souls with accountant-sharp minds. Wide-reaching collection and exhibition contracts are part of a day's work, and major donors with tough questions are another part.

SOMETHING SPECIAL TO OFFER

Museums know what they have to offer, and they leverage it wisely. They're past masters at interacting with experts in their field of collecting, with other museums,

Example: Wing Luke Museum of the Asian-American Experience, in Seattle, and the Tenement Museum of the Lower East Side, in New York, connect Asian Americans across the country, via their oral histories told in recorded stories and memories. It's part of a virtual series, "Your Story, Our Story." The stories come from descendants of Asian immigrants to the West Coast. The platform for telling the stories is provided by the Tenement Museum. Oral storytelling uncovers incidents and details formerly unrealized, almost forgotten; they beg to be told and safeguarded for future history seekers. This collaboration is a brilliant example.

Writers: sometimes good writing means letting other people talk. Your job is not done, however. Listen to their words, look at the speakers, if possible, and hear the heart of their story for which they've provided the text. You may have to edit for length, and you don't want to lose a syllable of the meaning.

EXPERIENCE WITH TOPICAL ISSUES

Museums are addressing inclusiveness and equity with professionalism and heightened sensitivity. They draw on deep wells of awareness of world cultures and audiences. They also realize there's a lot to learn and different pathways to understand. Museum people at all levels, in all departments, are listening.

"Collaboration is in fact critical to the ways in which we push back against 'expertise' as a manifestation of inequitable hierarchies in our museums and in the broader landscape of teaching and learning," Sarah Boyd Alvarez, Senior Director for Students and Educators in the Department of Learning and Public Engagement at the Art Institute of Chicago, says.

ROOTS IN THE COMMUNITY

Museums are respected members of the community. They have long local histories and staff who live in and know the territory.

Case in Point

The Oral History Lab of the Wing Luke Museum of Asian-American Experience encourages individuals in the Asian community to record their memories for future exhibits. These recollections provide the detail, context, and authority to complement museum scholarship. The Oral Lab works with various schools' Asian Pacific American history projects to provide recording and transcribing equipment, and housing for the resulting recordings and any of the projects' photographs, documents, and objects that were assembled as part of the classwork. The partnership results in new connections with schools, new networks, and a new generation of community engagement.

Two Western museums connect to their small communities through books. They become a more visible member of the community with which they share different audiences.

Northwest Montana History Museum in Kalispell tells about its gratitude for being a member of a large community on its Bookstore page: "Thanks to the hard work . . . [and] generous contributions" of supporters at all levels, the bookstore could now "become a less-kept secret."

And there's a wider community, with a tourist audience, that also benefits from the partnership: "Visitors to Glacier National Park and locals alike can spend a relaxing and informative afternoon in the Schoolbell Bookstore."

COLLABORATIONS WITH BUSINESS—CORPORATIONS

Both small and large businesses like to partner with cultural institutions. Museums are perfect because, in addition to their cultural repute, they are tangible. They have a building that's visible and known as part of the community. Many people have been inside the building, so they know it personally. Museums have objects to show, programs to attend, and events for children. If a business wants a successful partner, museums look successful. Museums collect with a purpose. Their collections and interpretations distinguish them. Museums' adherence to detail, policy, inclusiveness, and accessibility, not to mention their withstanding public scrutiny every day, resonate with public corporations. Beauty and wonder, coupled with professionalism, target museums for corporate collaboration. When corporations need to manifest their own missions, museums provide a platform.

Case in Point

Equity and economic opportunity are part of Bank of America's mission and it has a long-standing partnership with Harvey B. Gantt Center for

African-American History + Culture, in Charlotte, North Carolina. One partnership was an initiative, "Masterpiece Moment," consisting of a series of videos devoted to artworks in twenty-five museums across the United States. The art tells a story, and so does the breadth of the program, which demonstrates diversity of cultures and audiences, as well as accessibility, thanks to the format of five- to seven-minute videos.

Writers: when writing about collaboration, represent both partners equally, not just the museum. It might take extra research.

EXPLAINING COLLABORATIONS TO THE FINANCIAL DEPARTMENT

At some point, in this chapter or in an actual collaborative effort, museums need to explain to the Finance Department, once again, what they're doing and why. Collaborations, like anything new, take extra resources of time, staff, and budget. So, here's why collaborations are worthwhile:

- Enable museums to fulfill their mission
- Result in funds or in-kind help to expand, maintain, or repair
- Achieve their goal, thanks to fresh eyes, diverse ideas, and inspired talent
- Reduce or replace reliance on outside staff
- Enlarge your audiences and mailing lists
- Build networking contacts
- Connect to ever-changing business community, government resources, and scholars
- Realize the impossible dream

COLLABORATION WITH GOVERNMENT

Cultural institutions get plenty from their governments, at all levels, and when the collaboration is balanced and mutually advantageous, cultural institutions remember their manners and say so. For example, Parrish Art Museum states in its credits that support comes partly from "the property taxpayers from the Southampton Union Free School District and the Tuckahoe Common School District."

This is an extra line of text to fit into all communications, down at page bottom with all the other partners. Look at that section on an e-mail newsletter, Events page, or About Us disclosure. Ask if the local government has a logo or signature, to place next to the corporate supporters' logos. Expand on the credit line, space permitting, with an explanation of the contribution.

COLLABORATION WITH INSTITUTIONS OF HIGHER LEARNING

A decade ago, research conducted by Crystal Bridges Museum of American Art in Bentonville, Arkansas, announced the "Results of a Study on Culturally Enriching School Field Trips." Among its findings were that field trips increased analytical thinking, recall, empathy, and interest in things cultural. They had the greatest effect on rural, poverty-level, and minority students. Its data indicated "the value of cultural field trips in an era of budget cuts & decreased arts funding." With these findings in mind, many museums might see the advantages of this kind of research for their own purposes.

There are so many ways to collaborate with colleges and universities; that proactiveness counts. Here are some mentioned in this book's chapters on education (chapter 7), research (chapter 18), volunteers (chapter 19), and some others, too:

- Internships
- New categories of volunteers
- Guest lectures by sports team leaders and coaches
- Guest lectures to the schools' lifelong learning program
- Technical support for exploring new platforms
- CCTV space, or bulletin boards, to announce programs
- Facilities for commencement or other large events that want to include larger audiences
- Contacts for thesis research
- Speakers for Commencement
- Artwork for analytical thinking in non-art departments

COLLABORATIONS WITH OTHER CULTURAL INSTITUTIONS

In Birmingham, Alabama, the Birmingham Civil Rights Institute teams with seven major museums and the library for an after-school program. The goal is not only student achievement, but also family participation. A diversity of institutions, at different places in the city, offers diverse families better access.

Writers: when it comes to equity and education, plus additional goals of families with their complex schedules, plus the involvement of other diverse institutions, get the facts exactly right. Generalities won't help families plan their time and energy.

The Parrish Art Museum partners with library staff and patrons to increase community inclusiveness and accessibility. Library card passes, available at the museum, are a tangible symbol of the connection.

Pulitzer Arts Foundation, St. Louis, has partnered for twenty years with the St. Louis Symphony, for its long-running chamber music program. Strong synergy has durability. Two different tastes—one oral, one visual—are fulfilled. The concept of diversity also applies to learning styles.

Writers: take a cue from the announcement in the Pulitzer's e-mail newsletter where, above the proprietary name of the program, appears the word "series" and below the name appears the word "ongoing." The stability of this and any partnership deserves mention.

DO THE RIGHT THING

Look at museums' sturdy buildings, their heritage, the honor wall of supporters through the generations, the constant comments on social media: all attest to a museum's place of importance in the wider community. Most people count on museums to respond to topical issues and expect them to do the right thing.

Example: Land acknowledgment. One of the most ancient of collaborations is that between museums and the Native lands they sit on. Unlike the ideal museum collaboration, this one is unbalanced, of uneven benefit, and historically unfair—a good example of how not to structure an enduring relationship.

Example: "The use of land acknowledgements to start gatherings and events is becoming increasingly common. At the Burke Museum, we do this practice before every meeting and program." Staffers take turns saying what being part of Indigenous peoples' land means to them.

Many museums, of all sizes, sit on lands that once belonged to Native Americans, or Indigenous Peoples. Many have instituted land acknowledgment, not as a gesture, but rather as a part of their life.

Writers: if your institution is considering ways to acknowledge the original owners of the land under your man-made foundation, some suggestions will keep the process from becoming token. Land acknowledgment should:

- Involve all staffers—all their jobs start with the land—in writing their own land acknowledgment.
- Occupy a regular part of your written routine—in your mission, or a disclaimer, in environmental graphics, in digital and print materials.
- Don't romanticize Native Peoples—they aren't history; they're no more romantic than you are.
- Include Native Peoples from the start, in understanding the meaning and then in writing statements.
- Recognize and use correctly the terms "nation," "tribe," and "band."

- Use tribal names, in parentheses, after given names, where appropriate. It's not a title, by the way, like PhD or Editor. It's a Native usage.
- Involve children, Native children, so they see their culture being included, and all other children, so they see other cultures not their own being included.
- Ask and learn the local terminology of the Native Americans and Indigenous People in your region. Minnesota and Washington and Alaska and North Carolina are different. Actually, there are 567 federally recognized tribes in thirty-five of the United States.
- Know that federally recognized tribes reside in the following states: Alabama, Alaska, Arizona, California, Colorado, Connecticut, Florida, Idaho, Indiana, Iowa, Kansas, Louisiana, Maine, Massachusetts, Michigan, Minnesota, Mississippi, Montana, Nebraska, Nevada, New Mexico, New York, North Carolina, North Dakota, Oklahoma, Oregon, Rhode Island, South Carolina, South Dakota, Texas, Utah, Virginia, Washington, Wisconsin, Wyoming.

HOW TO FIND A COMMUNITY COLLABORATOR

To discover where you need help, look outside and see who you admire. It doesn't have to be a current or even prospective collaborator, just an organization or person, podcast, or streaming show that you admire. Build from there.

Collaborations start with collaborators who extend themselves—extend their open hours, their translation and closed captioning capabilities, their family events, and the radius of their usual sphere of influence.

Be ready to state exactly, distinctively what you stand for:

The School of Fine Arts offers a world-class professional education that focuses exclusively on the success of the emerging fine artist. Our priority is the quality, comprehensiveness, and relevance of a fine arts education to develop and pursue an artistic vision wherever it may lead.

Here are some of the community groups to investigate as partner material. What they have in common is roots in the community, institutionalized structure, and experience in client service.

- Businesses, local and regional
- Educational institutions—community colleges, four-year colleges, certificate programs
- Lifelong learning programs
- Local sports teams

- Other cultural institutions such as libraries, landmarks, lifelong learning programs
- Travel and hospitality
- Funders—people who invest in organizations they admire
- "Formers"—people once affiliated with you in a specific role who left that role, but are still loyal ambassadors and insightful partners
- Scholars—who understand your discipline

How does one start a conversation with a person they've identified as a prospective collaborator? Here are some icebreakers:

What was your year like?
We need help in some areas and thought maybe you could give us some advice.
We had a great intern this summer you might be interested in.

THE BALANCE OF POWER

Relations with an institution's community are a delicate balance between all parties, not because it's a power struggle, but because the partnership can be so powerful for all. The goal is to acknowledge the power of a business's acumen, the power of an educator's influence, the power of curiosity inherent in a museum. With a collaboration:

All sides realize the advantages, all sides are seen
All are included, there is no fringe
Differences disappear
All voices are heard.

Writers: as with parties involved in a collaboration, learn to say: How are things going?

REFERENCES

"Alaska Native Tourism Association Visits the Chickasaw Cultural Center," News & Media, Chickasaw Cultural Center, https://www.chickasawculturalcenter.com /news-and-media [accessed 9-16-21]
Alvarez, Sarah Boyd, "Collaboration, Expertise, and Museum Education: Reflections from a COVID-era Furlough," Blog, RK&A, June 23, 2021, https://rka-learnwithus .com/collaboration-expertise-and-museum-education-reflections-from-a-covid -era-furlough/?utm_campaign=Sarah%20Boyd%20Alvarez%20blog%20

posts&utm_content=170542427&utm_medium=social&utm_source=linked in&hss_channel=lcp-1628112 [accessed 9-16-21]

"Bank of America Announces 'Masterpiece Moment' Video Series to Celebrate Museum Partners and Important Works of Art," Press Releases, Newsroom, Bank of America, January 18, 2021, https://newsroom.bankofamerica.com/content/news room/press-releases/2021/01/bank-of-america-announces—masterpiece-mo ment—video-series-to-c.html [accessed 9-17-21]

"Birmingham Cultural Alliance Project," For Children, Birmingham Cultural Relations Institute, https://www.bcri.org/for-children/ [accessed 9-16-21]

"Crystal Bridges Museum of American Art & University of Arkansas Department of Education Reform Announce Results of a Study on Culturally Enriching School Field Trips," Newsroom, Crystal Bridges Museum of American Art, https://crystal bridges.org/news-room/crystal-bridges-museum-of-american-art-university-of -arkansas-department-of-education-reform-announce-results-of-a-study-on-cul turally-enriching-school-field-trips/ [accessed 9-16-21]

"Current Projects," Citizen Science, Research & Collections, North Carolina Museum of Natural Sciences, https://naturalsciences.org/research-collections/citizen -science [accessed 9-12-21]

"Discover the Finest Museum Bookstore in Montana," Bookstore, Northwest Montana History Museum, https://www.nwmthistory.org/bookstore/ [accessed 1-2-22]

"Harvey B. Gantt Center Announces Masterpiece Moment, featuring Folding Sheets, in partnership with Bank of America," News, Harvey B. Gantt Center for African-American History + Culture, August 12, 2021, https://www.ganttcenter.org/about -the-center/news/2021/219/ [accessed 9-17-21]

"Initiative for Equity + Innovation," Public, Assets, Gantt Center for African-American History + Culture, https://www.ganttcenter.org/public/assets/IEI-Fact-Sheet-Web.pdf [accessed 9-16-21]

Kentucky Heritage Jazz Festival, https://t.e2ma.net/message/82p5ng/0gb1mcfb

"Learn More About the Museum's New Library Pass Program," Join and Give, Parrish Art Museum, e-mail September 10, 2021, https://parrishart.org/join_give/

"Next at the Parrish | Exhibition Opening & Landscape Pleasures," Parrish Art Museum, Sept 1, 2021, https://mailchi.mp/parrishart.org/landscape-pleasures-sand futures-justin-bealju-13388559?e=cfd343c158 [accessed 9-2-21]

Olsen, Polly (Yakima), "Acknowledging the Land, Building Deeper Relationships," News & Stories, Burke Museum, August 24, 2021, https://www.burkemuseum .org/news/acknowledging-land-building-deeper-relationships?utm_source=news letter&utm_medium=email&utm_content=Read%20the%20article&utm_cam paign=IL-sept-9-2021 [accessed 9-12-21]

"Oral History Lab," Wing Luke Museum of the Asian American Experience, http:// www.wingluke.org/programs/ [accessed 9-15-21]

"Picture Yourself at PAFA," School, PAFA, Pennsylvania Academy of Fine Arts, Fall 2021, https://www.pafa.org/school [accessed 9-14-21]

Saenz, Martha, "Federal and State Recognized Tribes," National Conference State Legislatures, March 2020, https://www.ncsl.org/legislators-staff/legislators /quad-caucus/list-of-federal-and-state-recognized-tribes.aspx [accessed 9-12-21]

"St. Louis Symphony Live at the Pulitzer, Programs, Pulitzer Foundation, https:// pulitzerarts.org/program/st-louis-symphony-live-at-the-pulitzer/

"Teacher Advisory Group," Cranbrook Art Museum, https://cranbrookartmuseum
.org/learn/teachers/education-partnerships/ [accessed 9-15-21]

"Terms to Use and/or Avoid," Indigenous Terminology and Land Acknowledgement:
A Guide for the Queen's Community, Queen's University, https://www.queensu
.ca/indigenous/sites/oiiwww/files/2021-03/QU-Indigenous-Terminology-Guide
.pdf [accessed 6-18-22]

"Toolkit: Mutual of America Museum Leadership Series," The Association of Midwest Museums, Summer 2021, https://files.constantcontact.com/d87f37a9001/41
be0a94-46f2-449d-8fba-bb8221999594.pdf [accessed 9-14-21]

"Volunteer Landscaping at the Ridgewood Reservoir (Offsite)," Events, Queens
Museum, November 2020, https://queensmuseum.org/events/volunteer-land
scaping-at-the-ridgewood-reservoir?utm_source=QMail&utm_campaign=bdf
cfd4bfb-EMAIL_CAMPAIGN_2020_04_04_03_36_COPY_01&utm_medium
=email&utm_term=0_32b24c670e-bdfcfd4bfb-246122589 [accessed 9-16-21]

"World-Class Jazz Performances in an Iconic Setting," 2021 Kentucky Heritage Jazz
Festival, https://shakervillageky.org/events/ft-harrod-jazz-festival-at-shaker-village/

"Your Story, Our Story, Tenement Museum, https://yourstory.tenement.org/part
ners/wing-luke [accessed 9-15-21]

Zuroski, Dr. Eugenia, "Academic Land Acknowledgment for Settler Scholars: A Guest
Post by Dr. Eugenia Zuroski," HYPERLINK "https://asecsgradcaucus.wordpress
.com/" Graduate and Early Career Caucus, American Society for Eighteenth-
Century Studies, HYPERLINK "https://asecsgradcaucus.wordpress.com/2020/02
/25/academic-land-acknowledgment-for-settler-scholars-a-guest-post-by-dr-euge
nia-zuroski/" February 25, 2020, https://asecsgradcaucus.wordpress.com/2020/02
/25/academic-land-acknowledgment-for-settler-scholars-a-guest-post-by-dr-euge
nia-zuroski/ [accessed 6-18-22]

CHAPTER 5

Speaker Events

When a speaker starts to talk, and people gather to listen, it's engagement. The spoken word reaches out, people to people, in satisfying ways no other aspect of a museum can provide. Think of the applause at the end of any spoken event, including Zoom meetings. With speaker events, the focus is on the person at the podium. The goal of this chapter is connecting the respected speakers with the reputation of the museum presenting them.

DEFINING THE EVENT

Do you know if your speaker event is a talk, lecture, speech, conversation, or discussion? These terms have become somewhat fungible, but the format for each is solid. Once the format is settled, you can begin calibrating communications. This chapter deals with speaker events that require a registration and, sometimes, a fee. Gallery talks are covered in chapter 9, "Tours."

TALKS

A talk is a flexible term that is used for many speaker events. By any other name, a talk is still a genial discourse given by a speaker who is knowledgeable, respected, and fluent with words and maybe even a storyteller. This person has mastered a subject, as well as riffs on that subject. Often the speaker brings slides.

Speakers: explain how your interests mesh with the museum's and the curiosity of your audiences. Rapport with the audience is a feature of talks.

Historian Leslie Goddard, PhD, engages audiences by putting historic women, such as Louisa May Alcott, Georgia O'Keefe, and even Betty Crocker, in context with their times. In introducing America's First Ladies, she asks, as an educator: "Who do you think was best or worst? Why were some so vilified? And what might the future hold for the role of American First Lady?" Those three questions serve as a template for summarizing many talks.

Writers: emphasize what the speaker is known for, where the renown originates. Then you can connect that renown to the museum. In announcing the talk in newsletters or posts, borrow some of the expert terms or phrases used by the presenter; they're vivid.

Battleship New Jersey Museum and Memorial titles one of the talks, "The 5-inch Guns of USS Olympia."

LECTURE

A lecture is a structured, long talk, given by a speaker whose credentials—title and associations—add gravitas to the host museum. San Diego Museum has a monthly guest lecture series relating to its permanent collection. In October 2021, for the lecture titled "Día de Muertos 1987–2021: How an Annual Exhibition Unites Community & Museum," the lecturer was Cesáreo Moreno, Chief Curator and Visual Arts Director, National Museum of Mexican Art. His name, title, and affiliation don't need elaborating. The title of the lecture signals its relevance.

Speakers: your name, title, and affiliation speak volumes for you. State them so audiences can see their value and relevance to your museum host. Many speakers who incorporate slides into their presentations put their name, title, and affiliation on every frame.

Writers: lecturers take pride in their scholarship and the museum is proud to host them. Often, good writing means letting the name of the lecture and the lecturer's title do the talking.

Museums don't need to book big-name lecturers; they have unique access to many experts whose areas of inquiry represent the museum's interests. Here's what the Mariners' Museum writes: "Love all things maritime? Hear from select Mariners' Museum staff and experienced volunteers within our Speakers Bureau program."

LECTURE SERIES

When a lecture is part of a series, it moves across the line from event to program. Series bespeak continuity and commitment to a broader community of intellectual exploration. If a museum-goer can't attend one lecture, there's a whole menu of coming lectures to take its place. A series of lectures fortifies the connection to the museum. The San Diego Museum of Art puts it this way: "The Museum's lecture-based programs offer curators, educators, artists, and guest speakers the opportunity to present a wide variety of perspectives on the Museum's exhibitions and collections."

SPEECH

Speeches are shorter than lectures, and they intersperse factual stories with personal anecdotes. They sometimes are found in the category keynote address. The speaker is prominent and eminently qualified, often hired through a speaker's bureau. The speech should be positioned as topical and relevant to the museum's collection, mission, or place in the community.

Speakers: in addition to greeting the museum and the people in the audience, state one of your credentials or areas of inquiry that link your expertise to the museum. For example, "as a visiting professor, I was learning history from a new perspective, a viewpoint this museum promises in every gallery."

Writers: stress the speaker's credentials that validate the connection to the museum and the importance of the topic. List the speaker's salient accomplishments, especially those that are "awards," "honors," "professor of," and "prize." Also mention "anecdotes," because some of the best speeches are a full slate of personal stories that humanize the connection.

America's National Churchill Museum in Fulton, Missouri, used the title of one book to illustrate the connection between the keynote speaker and the museum: "The keynote speaker for the evening was historian and Pulitzer Prize–winning author, Doris Kearns Goodwin. Ms. Goodwin was awarded the Pulitzer Prize in history for *No Ordinary Time: Franklin and Eleanor Roosevelt: The Home Front in World War II.*

For museums who book less stellar speakers, play up the connection between the speaker and the community; it demonstrates the scope and outreach that your museum is so adept at developing.

CONVERSATION

This informal, two-person chat is a smart way to convince eminent persons to speak at a museum event; the question and answer format means that they don't have to prepare a talk in advance. The burden is on the questioner to structure a scintillating conversation by scripting scintillating questions.

Main Speakers: if you're the named attraction, some background information on your interlocutor will help you answer questions with spontaneity. It will demonstrate your connection to the museum if you are comfortable with its representative on stage with you.

Questioning Speakers: if you're asking the questions, help your guest relate remarks to the museum with phrases like:

"As you know, the museum's current exhibitions feature . . ."
"You're renowned for your writing about one of our favorite topics . . ."

Writers: You need plenty of information about the "in conversation" main speaker before you write the e-mail announcement, website story, or follow-up blog. For example, in the description of "A Conversation with Artist Diedrick Brackens," presented by Blanton Museum of Art, Austin, it's important to know that Brackens "honors Black and queer histories through textiles" and that his weavings reference sources such as European tapestries, quilts of the American South, and popular culture like the film *Moonlight.* Inclusiveness and diversity are here, as are topics for the conversation, and accompanying web stories and blog articles. By the way, this conversation is part of a series—smart continuity for the museum—so mention upcoming conversations in the series.

WEBINAR

This neologism describes a wonderful new phenomenon that virtually combines the text of a talk or lecture with a discussion. Audience Q-and-A and chat comments are also key to the concept. This open format makes it inclusive and interesting, and helps relate the speaker to the museum community. Webinars usually register fifty or more attendees, a large field of small faces that swings the event toward a lecture. To maintain the colloquial feel, encourage attendees to identify themselves by city on their screen ID, and to join in chat comments during the course of the webinar. Most speakers stop midway through the talk so the comments can be passed along and addressed, where appropriate, during the rest of the talk.

Speakers: introduce yourself with one credential plus its relevance to the museum that is sponsoring your webinar. This will help attendees understand its focus and have "permission to believe" your expertise and leadership. This is critically important if the discussion veers off course and you have to pull rank to get it back on track.

Writers: in a newsletter announcement or website Events page, the lecture aspect deserves a full description. You don't know how the discussion parts will unfold, but you can help define the topic. Don't shy from long descriptions.

New Bedford Whaling Museum described one webinar in its Portuguese Lecture Series in depth: "Portuguese Lecture Series: The Eruption of Insular Identities: A Comparative Study of Azorean and Cape Verdean Prose with Brianna Medeiros."

DISCUSSIONS

Discussions are frequently used in classroom contexts, such as a series of current events groups. Although not considered scholarly, many participants are well-versed in the subject and they make their points expertly via virtual versions, which accommodate forty to sixty people from all over the world and can produce an ever-larger pool of well-informed contributors. In any discussion, stress the level of expertise that's expected in a discussion and simply say, "The announcement for this discussion stated that no special expertise is required to enjoy participation. Let's keep the discussion at a level that accommodates everyone's expectations."

The featured speaker in a discussion is a facilitator, but the real speakers are the participants around the table. The group might be amateur historians or film critics, but everyone is an equal among equals.

Speakers: virtual discussions typically begin with a short introduction by you, as the facilitator, that connects your experience to the museum's collections and exhibits. It's your job to invite all participants to use video-conferencing features such as chat, comment, questions and answers. Stress that participants' questions and comments are welcome. You might start by asking everyone to introduce themselves by putting their name and location on screen—"Joan M., Atlanta"—or introducing themselves in chat. It demonstrates diversity and inclusiveness, and underlines the participatory nature of discussions.

Writers: in announcing a discussion in newsletters or posts, explain how discussions work, how facilitators lead the discussion, and how the value lies in each participant's contribution. Underscore how free and open the discussions are, that the range of comments will enlighten, and that they aren't intended to be lessons.

STRUCTURE OF MESSAGES

Talk or lecture, speech or conversation, there's a structure for communicating them to museum audiences. The speaker is the main draw, whether from renown, credentials, or reputation for being spellbinding. The topic always matters, because charming words alone don't fulfill curiosity. The date and venue count a lot, because people's lives are a constant competition for time, effort, and benefit.

NAME AND TITLES OF SPEAKER

The name and title of the speaker tell the readers that this is a speaker event. This may sound obvious, but a person headlining an event is different from a nameless docent tour or education class. If the name is well-known, the writer's job is half done. The subject and importance of the lecture is clear. However, few museums book boldface names, so speakers' titles clarify the importance of the event.

Speakers: in the bio that you send the museum planners, expand on your titles; they are understood in the circles where you made your name, but may not strike a chord with museum event audiences. Make your experiences the first paragraph of your bio. If you're a paleoanthropologist, tell where you last found a hominid fossil.

Writers: get the speaker's name—including title, position with company, honorifics, middle initials, and Jr.—spelled correctly. "Getting" includes e-mailing them or their assistants to be certain. Review the speaker's bio and edit for meaning, brevity, and, particularly, interest. The challenge is not to validate this person; that's a given. Your job is to make them interesting and pertinent to the museum's goals. Research the speaker.

Figure 5.1. Lectures, talks, and presentations reach diverse audiences wherever there's a podium and a microphone.
luckat/iStock via Getty Images

TITLE OF TALK OR LECTURE

Most speakers have a title for their talk. Here's a great title the Western Museum of Mining and Industry wrote: "Some of the Hidden History of Cripple Creek."

And the opening sentence of the lecture description explains that it will "focus on what many authors of books on the mining district have missed over the years."

Writers: some titles need absolutely no further explanation, and if your task is coming up with titles, take a cue from the writer at the Vesterheim National Norwegian-American Museum.

"The History of Norwegian Sweaters"
"Rocks and Hard Places: Emigration through the Lens of Knud Knudsen"
"Ruth Meier: The Anne Frank of Norway"
"In Trunks, Hands, and Hearts: What Norwegian Immigrants Brought to the United States"

These titles are a master class in vivid nouns.

Writers: If a title needs a stronger connection to the museum, work with the speaker and diplomatically strengthen it with a description that follows the colon:

"History of Book Clubs" becomes, "History of Book Clubs: Recollections from our Archives."

After-the-colon editing also distinguishes one lecture from others in a series, as this from the Driehaus Museum.

"Virtual Story Time at the Museum: Exploring Architecture."

CREDENTIALS

Pour them on because titles and letters after a name don't tell the whole story; they don't explain relevance to the museum. Institute of Contemporary Art in Miami, in its lecture series, connects artists and their credentials with the goals of the museum:

"ICA Speaks" creates a forum where members of our museum community engage with our collection by hearing from the artists themselves. We are proud that this series features today's leading artists, and figures whose works advance important and inclusive narratives of contemporary art.

DATE

The date is never just a detail. It could be an anniversary, a local commemoration, an annual festival, or tied to the weather. The date helps connect the speaking event with the museum.

Speakers: find out the significance of the date and mention it in your opening remarks.

Writers: highlight the date if it's an annual event, part of a series, linked to a community undertaking, related to the season, or important to the speaker or their field of expertise. Then connect that to the museum.

Mention the day of the week with the date. Not everyone plans by the number on a calendar page. Also, the day of the week reminds readers of a continuing series.

Here's how Asian Art Museum, San Francisco, describes one speaker event: "This beautiful and provocative 15th-century gilt bronze sculpture of the deity Guhyasamaja—meaning 'secret union'—can be read as a cosmic mandala. Docent Bill Kinsey discusses the symbolic features of this sacred Buddhist image and its power in Vajrayana Buddhism."

What puts a rather arcane subject in context is the heading: "Tuesday Take Out Lunch Series."

TOPIC

The topic of a talk is infused with a little marketing. It indicates the audiences that would love it, promotes community involvement, and highlights the diversity and inclusiveness in its content. Importantly, it promotes the museum's accomplishments, goals, and sustained exploration of knowledge. Whether writing a brief e-mail announcement or an Event on a website home page, explain what the speaker event is all about.

Writers: topicality is a big order. Here's how Discovery Museum in Acton, Massachusetts, encompasses it:

> The Discovery Museum Speaker Series presents expert voices on matters of importance to our communities, free of charge and open to the public. Researchers, educators, best-selling authors, and field experts bring national perspective to pressing topics underscored by the Discovery Museum's three-pronged emphasis on science, nature, and play.

If a speaker event is part of a topical series, make that clear. This deep delve into a topic is something museums do well; flaunt it. If it's a virtual event, state whether it will be closed-captioned. If the museum is making signers available, say so.

VENUE

Where will the speaker speak? Location matters. It's the stage set for the main attraction. An auditorium with a podium and a wall-mounted screen establishes a different tone than chairs in the demonstration kitchen of a botanic garden. Establishing the connection between the speaker and the venue previews the event and makes audiences feel welcome.

Here are some familiar museum venues; when museums open these doors to audiences, a connection is implicit. Writers will spell it out.

> Conference room—the noontime lunch series is held Thursdays in our conference room.
> Makerspace—join the artist for a creative hour in our Creative Lab.
> Outdoor terrace—the program starts at sundown on our terrace overlooking the rose garden.
> Lobby after closing hours—the talk will be held in our Art Deco lobby.
> Auditorium—enjoy the presentation in our beautiful new auditorium.

The George Eastman Museum in Rochester, New York, hosts many talks in the Dryden Theatre, one of the few theaters in the country equipped to project original nitrate film, films in their original, historic nitrate format. This is how the connection to the George Eastman Museum—in case one doesn't remember Eastman-Kodak's role in all things film—is made: "The 500-seat Dryden Theatre is the premier exhibition space for the art of cinema as championed and interpreted by the George Eastman Museum."

TIMING OF YOUR COMMUNICATIONS

There are specific stages of announcements leading to a participant's registration and attendance at a talk, lecture, or discussion.

Follow the decision-making steps people take when making a decision, including freeing up time to attend a speaker event.

- Announcement—Send an early e-mail, three weeks ahead, announcing the name of event, title, speaker, date, time. Include a Register link.
- Persuasion—In an e-newsletter two weeks before the event, provide insight on the speaker, connect the museum to the importance of topic, and review earlier appearances by the speaker. Include a Register link.
- Prep—One week in advance, acclimate audiences to the topic and speaker of the event. Additional persuasion might include a preview of the talk and quotes or comments from previous audiences. Include a Register link.

- Reminder to ticket-holders to actually attend the speaker event—highlight the date, day of week, time, and length of talk. Add a link for "More Information and Register."

THANK-YOU NOTE

Everyone has been taught to write one, but they might not have been taught how to do it.

First, acknowledge what the gift looks like. "Thank you for attending the museum's lecture about . . ."

Tell what that gift of attendance means to the museum. "Your contribution supports our new . . ."

If the talk was part of a series, add a reminder. "Thank you for attending our Thursday Lunch & Lab talk. Next month's talk is . . ."

Send your follow-up thank you with a follow-up remembrance, as the Driehaus Museum did: "Thank you for attending the Driehaus Museum's Presentation, 'A Tale of Today: A Slice of Culinary History—Betty Crocker Celebrates 100.' This YouTube link to the recording of the presentation will be available until July 27, 2021."

REVIEW OF TOOLS

Writers: line up your tools. Know what's available to you as you write about the speech to come. Here, in brief, are the primary advantages of the various media that connect the speaker event with the museum:

E-mail newsletters—Subject line makes the connection immediately

Website—Space to expand on the talk and speaker and their connection to the museum

Social media post—Popular endorsement that spreads the connection wide and far

Blog—Part of a knowledgeable series that shows the ongoing connection between talks and the museum

Signage—Point of sale announcements of a speaker event that reaches prospects while they're inside the museum itself

Environmental graphics—Directions to the event that guides attendees through the wider museum before arriving at the talk

QR code in galleries and store—Additional knowledge about the speakers and topics, near the exhibits or bookshelves, that (1) visualize the connection to the museum and (2) sell related information

Print material—Fold-out, pass-along, stick-around announcements give recipients plenty of time to think about the museum

Postal code invitations—Sent to the recipient's home to establish a more personal connection

E-mail—Best way to target audiences that have already established a connection with the museum

Closed captioning—Connects the speaker and the museum to millions of people who have been left in the silence up to now.

IN PRAISE OF SPEAKERS AND WRITERS

The human voice reaches out to people really well. It's a time-proven platform that adapts to every idea that needs proclaiming. Voices make noise, people listen, and speakers frequently steal the show. It's the writer's job to let them talk, but only after their connection to the museum is written. With so many speakers speaking, and virtual events giving them more podiums, the challenge of connecting them to one specific museum grows. Writers who identify that spark of rapport between speaker and museum and the museum's bounty of many audiences are valuable; thanks to them, the museum owns the show.

REFERENCES

"About the Dryden Theatre," George Eastman Museum, https://www.eastman.org/about-dryden-theatre [accessed 10-10-21]

"America's First Ladies," Lectures, Leslie Goddard, 2021, http://www.lesliegoddard.info/lectures.html [accessed 10-8-21]

"Battleship New Jersey," https://youtu.be/TZJpWEg7Ed0 [accessed 9-26-21]

"Dia de Muertos 1987–2021: How an Annual Exhibition Unites Community & Museum," Guest Lecture Series, San Diego Museum of Art, October 15, 2021, https://www.sdmart.org/talks/ [accessed 10-8-21]

"Discovery Museum Speaker Series," Education, Discovery Museum, https://www.discoveryacton.org/education/discovery-museums-speaker-series [accessed 10-9-21]

Gartenfeld, Alex, quoted in, "Institute of Contemporary Art Speaker Series Returns," Aventura Magazine, August 17, 2021, https://aventuramagazine.com/institute-of-contemporary-art-speaker-series-returns/ [accessed 10-9-21]

"Guest Lecture Series," Talks, San Diego Museum of Art, October 2021 [accessed 9-26-21]

"Monthly Lecture Series," Western Museum of the Mining Industry, www.wmmi.org [accessed 10-7-21]

"Portuguese Lecture Series," Programs, New Bedford Whaling Museum, October 19, 2021, https://www.whalingmuseum.org/program/portuguese-lecture-series-medeiros/ [accessed 10-8-21]

"Request a Speaker," Programs, Vesterheim National Norwegian-American Museum, https://vesterheim.org/wp-content/uploads/2021/02/Vesterheim-Presentations2021.pdf [accessed 10-9-21]

"The Secret Union of Enlightenment," Takeout Tuesdays: Lunchtime Conversations About Art, Event, Asian Art Museum, https://calendar.asianart.org/event/takeout-tuesday-october-5/ [accessed 10-1-21]

"A Tale of Today: A Slice of Culinary History—Betty Crocker Celebrates 100," Programs & Events, Driehaus Museum, https://driehausmuseum.org/programs/archive-detail/a-tale-of-today-a-slice-of-culinary-history-betty-crocker-celebrates-100-years [accessed 9-28-21]

"Talks," San Diego Museum of Art, October 2021, https://www.sdmart.org/talks/ [accessed 10-14-21]

"Think History's Boring? Think Again," Leslie Goddard, http://www.lesliegoddard.info/ [accessed 9-26-21]

"Tragedy on the Mississippi," Maritime Topic Lectures, Mariners' Museum, October 27, 2021, https://marinersmuseum.org/maritime-topic-lectures/?mc_cid=c9d08a1f9a&mc_eid=f3b56802e0 [accessed 10-6-21]

"Virtual Event: Artist Talk with Diedrick Brackens," Blanton Museum of Art, November 17, 2021, https://blantonmuseum.org/events/artist-talk-diedrick-brackens-in-conversation-with-blanton-curator-veronica-roberts/ [accessed 10-8-21]

"Watch: Virtual Story Time at the Museum: Exploring Architecture," Programs, Driehaus Museum, July 9, 2021, https://driehausmuseum.org/programs/detail/virtual-story-time-at-the-museum-3

"Winston S. Churchill Leadership Medal," Programs & News, March 5, 2021, America's National Churchill Museum, https://www.nationalchurchillmuseum.org/churchill-leadership-medal.html

CHAPTER 6

Performance Spaces

The Museum on Stage

All a museum needs is a raised stage and auditorium seating and a whole new audience can appear. A lectern and fifty folding chairs will also do the trick, as will a demonstration kitchen with overhead mirror, conference room with a screen, and tables with floral arrangements. You can't underestimate theatrical setups in drawing new audiences. Regardless of the intended audience for a film or concert, demonstration or private gathering, note the collateral consequence: many new people as yet unfamiliar with your museum. Bright lights and a little staging don't dilute the museum's brand one bit. Illuminating new ideas is what museums do.

This chapter will follow museums as they annex spaces that serve new audiences: Each one attracts—and has the power to retain—new audiences.

Writers: this chapter surveys not only the writing needed to publicize performances, but also the ways to connect them back to the museum. Performances last a few hours; museums are forever.

STAGE PERFORMANCES

With a stage and equipment, museums are positioned to offer scheduled performances and charge for a ticket. And there are many ways to get out the word. Existing e-mail lists can be more finely targeted with e-newsletters and follow-up e-mail. Audiences with focused interests will be reached with social media. And everyone will be able to get full information on the website.

Let's raise the proverbial curtain on Eastman Museum's advanced-design Dryden Theater and its regularly scheduled film screenings. The films are presented for the pleasure of any audience but, of course, they reflect perfectly the Eastman brand and George Eastman's fundamental significance for the camera and film industries. Descriptions are geared to the general audience, but film aficionados will appreciate the language of film scholarship.

For example, the website description for *The Yearling* reads:

> Lush color, fine acting, and a first-rate script make this classic tearjerker a must-see for adults and children alike.

The writer writes for every possible audience, from film buffs to wildlife lovers of all ages. Writers: for performances and gatherings of any kind, direct your words to at least two different audiences. Performance spaces welcome everyone and you can count on that!

This description of *Underworld* talks more directly to students of film, and also intrigues any crime and thriller audience:

> Silent Tuesdays . . . despite the fact that movies about organized criminals date back as early as D. W. Griffith, this film is the start of . . . the gangster genre. Live piano accompaniment by Dr. Philip C. Carli.

Where appropriate, add interpretation and context to descriptions of a performance. Pack lots of museum-oriented facts into paragraphs as well-written as this one. In the above paragraph, the reader will learn about the Eastman Museum's knowledge of film and the entertainment history. The piano player in the theater is a wonderful little performance in itself, recalling the days of movie palace glory.

Because museums, like Eastman, offer programs regularly, use social media posts to announce popular events when their tickets go on sale, like this:

> DrydenTheatre, @ DrydenTheatre, Dec 6
> Nitrate film fans! Today's the day. Tickets are now on sale for the 6th Nitrate Picture Show, June 2-5, 2022! Head to our website for details and to get your passes http://eastman.org/nitrate-picture-show

And you can also post ticket reminders the day of:

> "DrydenTheatre @DrydenTheatre 1h
> *It's a Wonderful Life* (1946) 35mm TONIGHT, December 7, 7:30 p.m. Series: Holidays | Best Picture Nominees of 1946 | Special Guests (Frank Capra, US 1946, 130 min., 35mm) "Every time a bell rings . . ." head to the Dryden Theatre! BUY TICKETS https://bit.ly/3ybNMdu

PERFORMANCE IN THE PARK

Architecture critic Herbert Muschamp, writing about park design, told of "'desire lines' to describe tracks carved into the grass by those who don't follow the paths."

A spectacular use of annexed space is Pulitzer Arts Foundation's partnership with the St. Louis Symphony for performances in the museum's adjoining transformed empty lot, Park-Like. Visitors are invited to walk and listen. One concert, John Luther Adams's "songbirds," was a fitting choice. The text said:

> American composer John Luther Adams lived for 40 years in the wilds of Alaska, and his works are inextricably linked with the natural world, giving voice to nature's beauty, danger and fragility.

Writers: if there's room on a web page for longer descriptions of a performance or concert, write a version of program notes. Talk about the creator; explain the museum's mission and goals in performance programs; give some details about the performance itself.

There are no stages outdoors—nature doesn't need man-made elevation—but the unexpected presence of special events equates to a performance. And that leads down the path to the way to the Chicago Botanic Garden in suburban Glencoe. It hit gold a few years ago with its "Lightscape, an after-dark illuminated trail," a sell-out. The illuminated exhibits spaced along a roped trail lit up the dark in ways that challenge a writer's vocabulary.

A few words of advice: Writers, brush up your captions. For visual performances like a light show, your website should splurge on photos, and each

Figure 6.1. On museums' grounds, in historic house parlors, and in the lobby after hours, concerts add another way to appeal to many audiences.
Page Light Studios / iStock via Getty images

one will need identification that differs one from the other. The Garden titled some of its exhibits:

"Find your Zen moment."
"Bask in the light's warm glow."

More than a superlative example of expanding the museum footprint, holiday shows open doors to different audiences at different seasons. For botanic gardens, it's also a means of visitor retention in off seasons.

Another kind of bright and shiny show expands the museum footprint throughout historic locales.

Shaker Village of Pleasant Hill, Harrodsburg, Kentucky, lights up when daylight saving time ends, and a stroll through the historic, brightly lit town is a spectacle in itself. For four weekends in November it also talks as it walks, one presentation featuring a docent recounting the Civil War's impact on the steadfastly pacifist Shakers. The requirements of a museum performance are met with a scripted story, a lighted set of a village, and a large audience. The presentation is interpreted so its connection to the museum is clear. Shaker Village includes a description of the tour talk so that if tickets sell out, disappointed viewers can be intrigued enough to watch the calendar for next year's event:

> The Shakers were committed pacifists but were unable to fully avoid the nation's deadliest war. Soldiers camped in the village, marched on its roads on their way to the Perryville Battlefield and traded control of its vital ferry on the Kentucky River.

Writers: the one example of performance prose you don't want to use is "Sold Out." Always add a positive paragraph to that, for example:

- Other events during the season
- Coming events
- The date of next year's performance.

PARTIES

There are two sides to parties that need good writing: one announces the fun and festivities, the other tells date, time, and place.

E-newsletters excel in announcements with inviting words, full descriptions, and fun-loving visuals. (See chapter 12, "E-mail Newsletters.") However, social media is unique in dealing with time sensitivity. A museum can time its announcements and reminders to the day. Here's what Milwaukee County Zoo does:

Milwaukee County Zoo. Wild Lights @MilwaukeeCoZoo Dec 1
Step into our illuminated world and enjoy a starry stroll under sparkling lights & animal displays during Wild Lights, We Energies, opening tonight!

The connection to the museum comes with the daily posts that show lions, penguins, and cows walking in the snow.

COMMUNITY SPACE: PEOPLE TAKE THE STAGE

Community spaces come in all sizes and visions. In small towns, where many museums reside, local libraries are repurposing their spaces by redefining what "learning" can mean. For example,

- film discussion groups
- community meetings
- recipe tastings
- genealogy research
- armchair travel
- makerspaces.

Any museum can do the same, bringing new learners through the door.

Harvey B. Gantt Center for African-American Arts + Culture resides in a larger neighborhood, and is part of an arts complex. It fosters local connections through an assortment of facilities overlooking the museum's galleries.

Writers: the following are taken from the Harvey B. Gantt Center, which has a selection of sophisticated rental facilities designed to dazzle and link.

The Mezzanine overlooks the Harper-Roddey Grand Lobby . . . giving you and your guests the advantage of being surrounded by our two feature exhibitions.

The Harper-Roddey Grand Lobby and Mezzanine together create a loft-like ambiance, where guests are able to experience the culture of the museum.

The Learning Center, a state-of-the-art classroom, is perfect for hosting creative workshops, seminars, training programs, and lectures.

The terrace is an added bonus feature in the Rooftop Pavilion [that] . . . provides a scenic view of the Carolina Panthers Bank of America Stadium.

LOBBY: THE STAGE IS SET

The Franklin Institute in Philadelphia has two performance spaces, and one is kind of a pop-up in the main atrium. Literally, a lot of pops, bursts, and controlled explosions as Live Science Stage presents ten-minute demonstrations all day long. What makes this a spectacle is the surprise factor of entertainment in the lobby while waiting to get one's entrance ticket. The murals and architecture of the atrium are works of art in themselves.

Lobbies outside of museum theaters should hold a special place in membership's heart. That's where visitors congregate and talk, engaging with the museum while they're thinking about the art of performance. At the Museum of Contemporary Art Chicago, the lobby outside the Edlis Neeson Theater is spacious; art is displayed on the walls; there's a spiral staircase leading to and previewing the museum lobby above.

And the MCA theater performances reflect museological convictions. The online text for "In Progress: Amir George" says: "In Progress is a series designed to give artists, thinkers, and curators a platform for developing new works with input from audiences, and to give patrons a glimpse into the creative process."

Writer's note #1: dance with the one that brung ya. For every creative theatrical performance there's a museum that provided the theater lobby. Encourage audience members to congregate and discuss the show during intermission.

Writer's note #2: talk to twosomes. Most people go to theater with a friend, so develop lobby signage and table cards that include two people. It could be a Friends Drink Free, or Discussion Topics for Two.

Writer's note #3: while on the subject of twosomes at the theater, remember these Rules of Two:

- Two spaces for names on web order forms
- Two spaces for e-mail addresses in e-newsletters
- Use "you and your theater partner" as an alternative to "you" wherever appropriate in any written material.

HISTORY'S STAGE

Museums are history books—multiple iterations of an event or era. Sometimes their exhibitions envelop many interlocking stories within one set of walls, and they occupy a very large stage. Such is the multi-gallery permanent exhibition at the Illinois Holocaust Museum. The first stop on the exhibition tour is the amazing film and hologram presentation at the entrance to the Take a Stand Center, devoted to people who stood up for human and civil rights, past and present, and engage today's citizens in societal issues. There's a small theater that introduces people who took a stand, and it shows holograms of Holocaust survivors being "interviewed" by the audience. Artificial Intelligence, AI, has converted a set a pre-filmed answers by the survivors to a long list of questions posed by curators and educators. The survivors' (members of an increasingly small group of European Jews interned in concentration camps in World War II Germany) answers are collected in a database that is capable of sorting and projecting them to real-time questions from the live audience in the theater. The hologram technology is spectacular in itself, but its power is human. Coupled with a short film about the survivor's life, it's a performance for history.

Real-time questions, asked spontaneously by the audience: "What was your family life before the war?" "Where did your father work?" "Do you have brothers or sisters?" "What happened to your family?"

Prompt questions that can be written in advance for the docent/facilitator to ask for the audiences that view the film:

- Tell us about the city you lived in
- What did your parents do
- What did you do as a child
- Any memories from your early life that you'd like to share
- What camp were you transported to
- Any experiences from the camp you can tell us

These prompt questions could also be prepared for the docents' use with the audience in the theater.

Holograms are a format all museums can consider, budget permitting. The Q-and-A format with a real hologram is a teaching tool for school groups and prospective donors, as well as visitors.

Is this a performance? Yes, in all aspects. It has a lectern, a screen, a theater, an audience, and a schedule that can be announced in advance. It has novelty. And the stars! They shine a light for the ages.

PERFORMANCE ART

Hoop dance is a performance art created by multiple Indigenous communities throughout the U.S. and Canada to celebrate and honor their traditions. At the Hoop Dance Contest, held annually on the grounds of Heard Museum in Phoenix, dancers incorporate new and creative designs and intricate footwork into the framework of four to fifty hoops moved in patterns representing animals, insects, and changing seasons. Performers are judged on creativity, precision, showmanship, speed, athleticism, and art. The museum's lawn is the stage, and the large number of competitors and their audience, not to mention the longevity of this annual event, makes it a spectacle.

For writers, the goal is describing new kinds of art, which these spontaneous performances always are, and connecting them to the mission and collecting philosophy of the museum. Here are some connecting themes:

- Learning
- Creativity
- Reflects the objects in the museum
- Employs techniques used in the works in the museum
- Performed by artists who share the goals of the museum.

As the Heard Museum says: "With roots in healing ceremonies, traditions and practices, today hoop dance is shared as an artistic expression."

FACILITIES RENTAL

Advantages of renting out your spaces are just short of spectacular. New audiences are not only invited but retained, thanks to connection to the galleries, networking spaces for meetings, screens, and Wi-Fi and technical assistance; air conditioning; photo settings; novelty. New Bedford Whaling Museum makes the point this way:

> Depart from traditional venues and give your guests an experience they'll never forget at the New Bedford Whaling Museum. Nestled among 18th and 19th century homes and cobblestone streets, with unparalleled harbor views.

Weddings, big-ticket performances with unique stars, could steal the show away from the museum. Not necessarily, if you offer a doorway to the museum: "Shake up your guests' curiosities with access to our changing galleries or a tour through our award-winning USS *Monitor* Center." This from the Mariners' Museum in Newport News, Virginia, 600 miles south of its coastal colleague in Massachusetts.

CONFERENCES AND MEETINGS

Call them Businesspersons Theater. Conference rooms have a large screen, video conferencing tools, and a techie to handle the details. Wall and floor coverings are attractive. And that long, gleaming conference table! That in itself is a signifier of new audiences: the dozens of inquiring minds who are inside your museum, perhaps for the first time, ready to learn something new. Sell yourself.

Here are some written materials you can produce to leverage the meeting without overwhelming it:

- Handout sheet describing current exhibitions
- Brochure, to be arranged on a side table
- Inexpensively printed sheet headed "Welcome [name of meeting]" that features the museum's calendar for the month and a QR code connecting to the website calendar page.
- Notepad with image and caption of object in the museum
- Tabletop cards that use the same image and caption as the notepad
- Event-specific membership form with "Scan for discounted membership form"
- Discounted family tickets to encourage businesspeople to return on weekends
- Counter card—on a side table—with the title of a meeting-congruent book available in the museum store. Add a QR code to "Scan for other titles" or "Scan for discount."

ROAD SHOWS

There are two Mark Twain museums, one in Hartford, Connecticut, where he lived his adult life as a legend; the other, his boyhood home, marked by the legendary white picket fence in Tom Sawyer and Huckleberry Finn, in Hannibal, Missouri. The latter has, in addition to Twain's family home, that of his friend, the real-life model for Becky Thatcher.

Hannibal also claims "Tom and Becky," Twain's fictional characters based on the time when he was still Sam Clemens. In Hannibal, there's an annual Tom and Becky contest. There, also, one will discover that actors can be hired to portray Tom and Becky at parties.

Writers: when writing about performances tied to well-known people and events, tautly tie the characters and performance to the museum sponsoring it. Here's how Mark Twain Boyhood Home Museum outlines that tie-in in the Request Form:

To those requesting an appearance by Tom & Becky actors, the Mark Twain museum asks that this short form be completed:

The Name of Event
Purpose of Event
Requesting Organization
Perform Engagement Scene?
Presentation with Engagement Scene?

Part of a writer's assignment is protecting the museum's brand. When a third party hires actors or other representations of a museum, both museum and the requesting organization need to know if the:

- name of the event reflects the character and personalities of the original presentation, in this case the fictional characters Tom Sawyer and Becky Thatcher performing the fictional engagement scene.
- purpose of the event is consistent with the purpose of the museum
- organization requesting the museum performance has the same values and goals as the museum
- intellectual property of the museum—such as a scene in a museum performance—is credited and/or paid for
- organizer of the event wants an introduction added to the requested performance. This must be scripted scrupulously to mesh with the museum's intent.

Lending a performance or performer is bigger than just a loan of intellectual property; it's sharing the museum's identity. Writers: be circumspect.

SPACE NAME

Space is generic. A museum's specific performance spaces—theaters, meeting rooms, terraces, gardens—demand their own identity. When museums give a room a name, that room becomes a serious part of the museum. Without a name, there is no long-term importance to the museum that, of course, carries a proud name of its own. These are generic names: theater, conference room, visitors lounge, dining room, café, and store. Here are some gathering spaces and their non-generic names:

The Boardroom—the conference room at Gantt Center: "The boardroom is our executive suite that can seat up to 20 at its elegant wooden conference table."

The Meadow View Barn—a venue at Shaker Village of Pleasant Hill, Kentucky Meadow View Barn is a restored, open-air tobacco barn with stunning views of the rolling Shaker Village countryside.

SUMMING UP SPACES

Performance spaces serve purposes large and small: hosting a major speaker; refilling the coffee pots for a business meeting; opening your doors for a book discussion. Each space broadens horizons for these reasons:

- Welcoming new audiences
- Showcasing new ideas
- Shaking hands with the community
- Burnishing the museum's purpose.

Where there's a stage, there's a call for a writer to explain why events there are a level above the ordinary. Some words to remember as you describe the above-the-ordinary:

- Unusual nouns
- Unexpected adjectives
- Active verbs
- Words that sound like the museum talking
- No words that clash with the museum's attitude and personality
- Any expressions that aren't trite or used elsewhere on the page or post.

Writers: when dealing with performance spaces, be bright, descriptive, and brief. Pretend you've got a mic and ten seconds to command the attention of the audience. Your words represent the museum, and they're part of the show.

REFERENCES

"Café Fledermaus," Dine, Neue Galerie, https://www.neuegalerie.org/cafefleder maus [accessed 12-8-21]

"Daily Live Science Demonstrations," The Franklin Institute, https://www.fi.edu /live-science-demos?utm_medium=email&utm_source=marketing&utm_cam paign=General%20Interest%208.18.21%20SK%20Copy

"Dining at Otium," Visit, The Broad, https://www.thebroad.org/visit/dining-otium [accessed 11-28-21]

"Distinctive, Unforgettable Events," Venue Rentals, New Bedford Whaling Museum, https://www.whalingmuseum.org/about/venue-rentals/ [accessed 11-15-21]

"Events," Eastman Museum, https://www.eastman.org/event/film-screenings /union-pacific [accessed 11-27-21]

"Facility Rentals, Harvey B. Gantt Center, https://www.ganttcenter.org/public/assets /FacilityRentals_RevOct2021.pdf [accessed 11-28-21]

https://www.ganttcenter.org/?utm_source=Friends+of+The+Gantt&utm_campaign =444d6916ae-Unmasked+May+26+%28D1%29_COPY_01&utm_medium =email&utm_term=0_931a2bacb4-444d6916ae-401774176&mc_cid=444 d6916ae&mc_eid=b9dc85c20f [accessed 11-17-21]

"Get Ready for Some Holiday Joy," Chicago Botanic Garden, https://www.chicago botanic.org/lightscape [accessed 11-20-21]

"Hoop Dance Contest," Upcoming Events, Heard Museum, February 12 and 13, https://heard.org/event/hoop/ [accessed 11-17-21]

https://bit.ly/3ybNMdu [accessed 12-7-21]

http://eastman.org/nitrate-picture-show [accessed 12-8-21]

https://pulitzerarts.org/program/st-louis-symphony-live-at-the-pulitzer-sep-27-28 2021/

https://www.artnews.com/art-news/product-recommendations/essential-books -performance-art-1234608015/

"In Progress: Amir George," Museum of Contemporary Art Chicago, https://mca chicago.org/calendar/2021/12/in-progress-amir-george [accessed 12-8-21]

"Interactive Holograms: Survivor Stories Experience," Events, Illinois Holocaust Museum and Education Center, https://www.ilholocaustmuseum.org/?s=Hologram [accessed 11-17-21]

Muschamp, Herbert, "A Mountaintop Temple Where Art's Future Worships Its Past," *New York Times*, December 1, 1997, https://www.nytimes.com/1997/12/01 /arts/a-mountaintop-temple-where-art-s-future-worships-its-past.html [accessed 11-20-21]

"Rental Information," Facilities Rental, The Mariners' Museum and Park, https:// www.marinersmuseum.org/rental-information/ [accessed 12-13-21]

"Request for Tom & Becky Appearance," Mark Twain Boyhood Home & Museum, https://i0.wp.com/www.marktwainmuseum.org/wp-content/uploads/2016/04/

"St. Louis Symphony: Live at the Pulitzer," Programs, Pulitzer Arts Foundation, September 27–28, 2021, https://pulitzerarts.org/program/st-louis-symphony-live -at-the-pulitzer-sep-27-28-2021/ [accessed 11-18-21]

"Underworld," Film Screenings, Events, Eastman Museum, https://www.eastman .org/events/film-screenings [accessed 11-20-21]

"Venues," Shaker Village of Pleasant Hill, https://shakervillageky.org/venues/ [accessed 2-15-22]

"War Comes to Zion: Pleasant Hill & the American Civil War," Events, November 5, 6, 12, 13, 19, 20, 26, 27, 2021, Shaker Village of Pleasant Hill, https://shaker villageky.org/events/war-comes-to-zion-pleasant-hill-and-the-american-civil-war/ [accessed 11-26-21]

"Welcome to the Library," Wilmette Public Library, September–October 2021, https://www.wilmettelibrary.info/media/document/425 [accessed 12-8-21]

"Wild Lights at the Milwaukee County Zoo,"@MilwaukeeCoZoo, December 2021 [accessed 12-7-21]

"Wild Lights at the Milwaukee County Zoo," Milwaukee County Zoo, December 2021 https://twitter.com/search?q=milwaukee%20zoo&src=typed_query [accessed 12-7-21]

CHAPTER 7

Education

Queens Museum in New York offers family classes for parents and children:

> Year of Uncertainty: Family Programs . . . on weekends at the Queens Museum . . . include adult engaging activities, curated exclusively for parents while children are working in parallel.

North Carolina Museum of Natural Sciences in Raleigh invites high school age students to volunteer as interns: "One required monthly meeting with Living Collections staff. Two required monthly group meetings with guest scientists, researchers and Museum curators to explore a variety of natural science."

Tamástslikt Cultural Institute in Pendleton, Oregon, created a video showing how foreigners, like the Lewis and Clark Expedition and Oregon Trail pioneers, affected Native people's lives: "The experience of newcomers entering and crossing those homelands, including how those events impacted life for Native people and how those foreigners' experiences in the plateau contrasted with the goals they had set when leaving their homes."

The tides of change that bring ever-new audiences and attitudes into museum communities also generate life-changing education programs. The ingenuity astounds and inspires.

This chapter looks at museums and their educators who have met new audiences and new expectations with sound plans and grace. It aims to help writers describe newly inclusive programs with their diverse outlooks and voices.

FIRST, MAKE AN INVENTORY OF AUDIENCES

In writing about one's education department and education programs, the first task is knowing the audiences involved. There are so many of them, often overlapping. These are the audiences of learners that educators serve.

- Children
- Their caregivers
- Underrepresented minorities
- Immigrants and migrants
- People with English as a second language
- Learners with different educational backgrounds
- Adults
- Teachers
- Newcomers
- Lifelong learners
- Professionals and amateurs in many areas of inquiry
- The curious

Writing a program's description includes the main beneficiary. Writing to newcomers, talk about the program's benefit to them. Think about your audience as you write. You'll naturally write differently to, for example, adults in the general Adult audience and adults in the Lifelong Learner audience. Where a program aims for several audiences, pick an individual to address.

SECOND, MAKE AN INVENTORY OF CHANGES

Educators who create programs respond to external changes and audience needs. Writers must articulate them. These are the changes that help define educators' tasks that writers can mention.

- School schedules
- Year in school
- Diverse learning styles
- Jobs and work schedules
- Family responsibilities
- Finances

When writing about education programs, something so important to so many audiences, be sensitive to diverse goals and also diversity of impediments. Part of a program's description should include the date, day, time, length; whether it is part of a series; whether it will be repeated at other dates, days, and times; if there will be simultaneous translation or closed captioning; if supplies will be provided; possibility of central places to get broadband service. This will require concise wording and organization; keep program descriptions small bite-size.

Here's how Nevada Art Museum communicates to different audiences:

> Looking to . . . [prepare] for applying to a college, or a future career? The . . . Museum School is a great place to continue your education in the arts. . . . Need-based scholarships and state-approved professional development hours are available.

> [exploring] . . . a team building activity with your staff . . . [or] co-workers? Contact . . .

THIRD, MEMORIZE THE INVENTORY OF MUSEUMS' UNIQUE EDUCATIONAL ADVANTAGES

With all the institutions offering education, museums stand apart. They're not encyclopedic; they're special, with one-of-a-kind ways to inspire curiosity and learning. Here's a short list of how museums engross learners:

- Visual literacy
- Innovation
- Cross-cultural ideas
- Jobs and careers never before thought of
- Working with adults
- Staff and visitors that embody diversity

Good writing boasts a little. Along with accurate information, provide a little one-upmanship. Learners reach out for learning because they want new advantages so badly. Take an audience-eye view of the museum and add one of the above items to program descriptions on websites, e-mail announcements, and posts. Develop a special advantage into a blog topic or hashtag.

WRITING FOR CHILDREN

Displays that entertain excel at engaging children. The life-size figures at the Abraham Lincoln Presidential Library and Museum in Springfield, Illinois, encourage younger children to enter the world the museum displays and relate the historic story with their own experience, and then discuss it:

ALPLM's historians specialize in the life and times of Abraham Lincoln and the Civil War Era. . . . After touring the museum, students are invited to participate in a 30-minute "Q&A" session with one of our historians . . . to ask questions about their museum experience, dive deeper into the Civil War Era . . . and learn more about how the historians do their important work at . . . the museum.

Writers: consider a short discussion at the end of a program. Educators know the value of comparing notes. As the Western Museum of Mining & Industry says about its STEM camp: "Fabulous take-aways and stories to share."

WRITING FOR CHILDREN PLUS PARENTS AND CAREGIVERS

Children come to museums with adults, in person or virtually. Writers must talk to all those audiences. Which is the primary audience is a question that has puzzled marketers for generations.

Burke Museum developed BackPack Boxes for preschoolers and they're full of interesting little learning tools. Children and caregivers both would be charmed by them. But which audience do you write to? Burke tells the adults how to use them.

Backyard Scientist Burke Box (6 backpacks)

Best for preschools, after school programs, community organizations or events serving multiple young learners simultaneously when you have lots of curious young learners to serve . . . .

Individual Backyard Scientist Backpack

Best for caregivers and families serving one or two young learners over a short period of time . . . .

Looking for a fun weekend activity or something to enhance a park visit? An individual Backyard Scientist Backpack is a great fit! Bring this backpack into your home environment . . . .

Writers: when writing to parents and caregivers, remember to say your children, your children's experience, your children will explore. Your children's class starts at . . . Explore.

TEACHING OUTSIDE THE EDUCATION DEPARTMENT

Anyone who visits a museum, virtually or in person, is a learner. Included in this unintended audience of learners are other museum professionals, scholars, donors, prospective sponsors and suppliers, as well as visitors. One writes to them in mission statements on all platforms, support and donation pages, and research sections. When writing to these audiences, use words and terms of the reader. They could be scientific terms, academic terms, or language of the business and financial community.

Milwaukee County Zoo has stepped classes for children ages three through eleven. The descriptions use science-specific vocabulary and mature topics like ecosystems: "As students grow in our programs, our classes go deeper into animal behavior, zoo careers, ecosystems and conservation concepts."

COMMUNICATING CROSS-CULTURAL IDEAS AND FOREIGN WORDS

Museums translate concepts, discoveries, and cultures with visuals. It's visuals and objects that are in their collections. Learning activities that revolve around images, as well as words, work well for audiences of limited English skills, or audiences whose learning style is visual. Children who speak English can use these activities online with the help of their parents who don't speak English easily. Diverse audiences appreciate that your museum speaks foreign languages like they do. Remember, also, that

Figure 7.1. Beginning potter learns techniques and professional terminology in Racine Art Museum's six-week class of Handbuilding With Clay.
Courtesy of Racine Art Museum

museum audiences could be anywhere in the world. Museums are global whether they know it or not.

The highly visual learning exercises taken from the website of the Pompidou Centre in Paris cited in the references is a good example of a child's exercise that can work across all time zones.

ESL INSTRUCTION

Tenement Museum terms its English Language Workshops for "learners of English as a new language." It builds on its building tours, and the stories of immigrants who lived and worked there, to start conversations with the learners, helping them converse with strangers, talk about their own experiences, and learn English.

That format works for many museums that want to create programs for diverse audiences.

Writers: use short words and short sentences. Don't avoid multisyllable words or professional terms; just use them in shorter sentences. Explain a word or term that might reside outside common usage. Simply say, "That means . . ." Use words that make sense written and spoken and translated into closed captioning. Watch out for homonyms.

WRITING TO AND FOR YOUNG PEOPLE
WHO WILL BE LEARNING WITH ADULTS

Many children grow up knowing few adults except parents and teachers. There's a paucity of age diversity in their lives. Mentoring adults are a scarcity that afflicts many children of all backgrounds; they're spending more time with their families than outsiders, and many don't talk one-on-one with an adult until their first college or job interview. Utilize the adults in your museum to demonstrate working on an equal basis with older people.

When writing about a program or activity designed for young people, writers need to emphasize the adult in the process.

In this activity, you'll assess fossils side by side with working professionals.

Or

Your grade school children will learn about old farm tools from area farmers.

Or

Young coders will shake hands with some of the top computer scientists in the area.

A subset of working with adults is adults working with adults. Meeting new people is difficult for many people who struggle with English, different cultures, and the fatigue that comes with newcomer learning loads. When writing about education programs that might appeal to this audience, use adult words, and adult sentences. Also write to the occasion:

- For on-site programs, write a little less, so the speaker can speak slowly and there's time for the audience to read the slides.
- For websites, take a second look at the tabs. "Education" communicates better then "Learning."
- For e-mail announcements and newsletters, put the program name or titles first in the Subject line. Don't start the Subject line with "new for fall."
- For social media posts, start with the name of the museum, then the title of the program. For example, "Smith Museum offers global cooking at home."

GET SERIOUS. GIVE YOUR PROPRIETARY PROGRAMS A NAME

When professors propose a new course, they give it a name. These courses are intellectual property, and a name is part of their identity. Names also sell a new course to the committees that approve it and the students who sign up for it. Just as new courses—and their names—add to a professor's CV, a new course title is shorthand for expert when professors discuss consulting gigs or speaking engagements.

It's the same with a museum's intellectual property, of which Your Education Programs are an example. This isn't a legal issue, but a matter of reputation. Your creativity and professionalism undergird them, and you're putting your name and the program on the line. Actually, until they have a name, your education programs shouldn't be capitalized.

A named program is also a marketing advantage. Burke Museum, with its Backyard Scientist Burke Box and Individual Backyard Scientist Backpack, has more value than a generic take-home box.

WRITING FOR TEACHERS

Professional development classes need good writing because of the effort obstacle: teachers need the courses; they don't necessarily want them. Courses take place during vacations. Courses are rigorous. They may require a learning curve, which teachers are more accustomed to giving than undergoing.

This example of a professional development course from Crystal Bridges Museum of American Art in Bentonville, Arkansas, makes a course approachable and relevant.

Your students are affected by the news, too . . . this session will show you how to incorporate art and current events into your existing curriculum.

Consider the title of this six-hour-a-day, five-day course: "Summer Teacher Institute: Being Present in the Moment." This course has a reasonable tone, appropriate to a time-intensive program. It sounds new, not newsy.

Use quotes. Teachers are like everyone else who reads: they like it short and to the point, and maybe with a little humor. Quotes do that; otherwise they wouldn't have been quoted in the first place. Note: teachers actually have a sense of humor.

Here's a comment on the Burke Museum web page about their summer field work program, DIG, for teachers. "The number one thing I plan on taking back is telling my students about what doing science is actually like in the field . . . [It's not just] being inside wearing a lab coat."

WRITING ABOUT THE FIELD TRIP

School trips carry the burden of meeting state academic requirements. These should be explained on the web page with the same rigor the longer document spells out the details. The Western Museum of Mining and Industry describes its academic "components" as three-part, a good model for education objectives that all teachers respect.

- Explore the exhibits
- Interpret their meaning
- Analyze their impact

The museum adds another benefit not usually offered to children: "A trip to the museum . . . introduces students to a lifelong learning resource in their community."

Writers: writing to teachers is really writing to two audiences, the teacher and the student. Explain programs with both audiences in mind, such as "Classes will explore the exhibits with plenty of time to point out the details of each, and then give students the opportunity to investigate them on their own."

ADULTS' VIRTUAL LEARNING

Adult learners aren't as easily categorized as child learners. They range widely in age, zip codes, and amount of prior education. They never bonded over a shared classroom, teacher, or recess. Adults are independent operators. Several key thoughts govern writing for them:

- Titles—Make the subject of the program worth their time.
- Compensate for the monotony of postage stamp–sized faces with participants' first names or city names. The class will cohere better if they know something about the face of John, Atlanta and Jenna, Minneapolis.
- Detailed descriptions—Familiarize busy adults beforehand with what their hour will entail.
- Length of program.
- Learning outcomes—what you hope class participants will take away.
- Credentials of speaker.

Driehaus Museum in Chicago writes wonderfully informative blog articles and even the titles teach:

"A Tale of Today: Up from the Ashes—Pullman Porters and the Great Migration."

"Tragedy & Brilliance: The Life of Henri de Toulouse-Lautrec."

For learning outcomes, Wing Luke Museum in Seattle provides this example from a conference on heritage sites partnered with the National Forest Service:

Why participate?
Learn more about the Study and explore its purpose to tell and acknowledge diverse stories
Learn about the National Historic Landmark process and benefits
Connect with others passionate about Asian American Pacific Islander heritage sites in the Pacific Northwest.

COMMUNICATE THE CONNECTIONS BETWEEN EDUCATION AND THE BUILDING AND GROUNDS

When writing about education programs and classes, add a quiet shout-out for the study spaces provided by your nooks and crannies.

- Add a paragraph, "quiet study spaces," under the Education tab.
- Talk up your rooms that let learners of all ages use workstations and tables for studying at their own pace.
- If you have a library, emphasize it as a learning environment. Talk about your research center's inspiring view, as the National World War I Museum and Memorial site does: "the Edward Jones Research Center . . . also offers an intimate, ground-level view of the symbolic poppy field."

Writers: describe the museum and surrounding landscape as quiet spaces, serene, conducive to individual research, a calm retreat away from home.

MUSEUM SCHOOLS

School. The word has gravitas. Children like school; it's where they learn stuff and where their friends are. Adults respect schools. People who have been marginalized trust schools to equalize that situation.

Diversity of classes reinforces the concept that there's a school program for everyone appropriate to their needs and resources of time and energy. Imagine the many audiences who could benefit from the classes announced by the Nevada Museum of Art, in Reno, which offered classes in *En Plein Air* painting, pigment mixing, glass bead-making, and textile marbling in scarves. The museum's website tells readers: "Looking to build a design portfolio in preparation for applying to a college or university?" Portfolio is a promise parents and students alike pay attention to.

When writing about a museum school's courses, be prepared to articulate each course, and its desired outcomes. This might require second interviews with the educators and extra research. Students and their families know that museum school programs are costly but worth it. The writing must match the weightiness and incorporate words like:

- This program prepares students for . . .
- The class lasts twelve weeks and each class lasts four hours
- Credits earned in our courses are transferable
- Students have access to state-of-the-art labs
- Courses are designed to lead to professional certification and college degrees
- Each class costs . . .

Writers: use specific words, numbers, and dates. Use terms the professionals use. Listen to the pros carefully because their jargon flows casually as they talk. Use professional terminology where possible, defining it if necessary. Stretch students' vocabulary with highest common denominator language.

OUTREACH EDUCATION

Many audiences are neither schoolchildren, nor adults, nor educators. They aren't already in the museums or its programs, so museums need to find them. Birmingham (Alabama) Civil Rights Institute knows where: "BCRI Outreach programs reach an audience of 20,000 people annually in area schools, churches, club meetings and other venues."

Follow-up keeps an outreach program in participants' minds, long after an actual or virtual session ends. "Thank you for visiting our museum. We hope you enjoyed the experience and will come back soon with your family. Just use this code for free entry."

Museums also reach out to scholars and researchers. It's an important part of museums' mission to constantly interpret their collections in light of the present and future. At Crystal Bridges Museum of American Art in Bentonville, Arkansas:

> Crystal Bridges fosters scholarship in the fields of American art and art history, as well as research that expands our understanding of the power of art experiences to positively impact lives. [The museum's Learn page] features reports from research projects, symposia, and reports, as well as results from studies by other institutions regarding art in education, distance learning, and quality of life in our region.

EDUCATION GOING FORWARD

Educators know that acknowledgment of the past is needed to properly move forward. This foundational message from Brooklyn Museum has relevance for all museums:

> The Brooklyn Museum stands on land that is part of the unceded, ancestral homeland of the Lenape (Delaware) people. As a sign of respect, we recognize and honor the Lenape (Delaware) Nations, their elders past and present, and future generations.

Writers: learn the language usages of different cultures. Be sensitive to other people's way of talking. Be sensitive to your way of talking. You may want to listen to educators talk. When it comes to writing about education, writers are teachers, too.

REFERENCES

"Backyard Scientist Backpacks," Burke Boxes, Educators & Families, Burke Museum, https://www.burkemuseum.org/education/educators-and-schools [accessed 9-15-21]

Blog, Driehaus Museum, https://driehausmuseum.org/blog [accessed 9-15-21]

Brooks, David, *The Social Animal*, New York: Random House, 2012

"Buildings and Belief," Coach Tours at Shaker Village, Explore, Shaker Village, https://shakervillageky.org/coach-tours/ [accessed 9-8-21]

"Burke Boxes," Educators & Families, Burke Museum, https://www.burkemuseum.org/education/educators-and-schools/burke-boxes [accessed 9-6-21]

Conner, Bobbie and Bill Lang, "Video Presentation: Foreigners in Native Home-lands: Lewis and Clark and the Pioneers," Tamastslikt Cultural Institute, https://www.tamastslikt.org/video-presentation-foreigners-in-native-homelands-lewis-and-clark-and-the-pioneers/

"Découpe comme Matisse | Tuto," [cut out like Matisse/Tutorial] Centre Pompidou, https://www.centrepompidou.fr/en/videos/video/decoupe-comme-matisse-tuto [accessed 9-15-21]

"Engage the Historians," Enhance Your Experience, Learn, Abraham Lincoln Presidential Library and Museum, https://presidentlincoln.illinois.gov/learn/educators/enhance-your-experience/ [accessed 2-15-22]

"English Language Workshops," About Us, Tenement Museum, https://www.tenement.org/about-us/ [accessed 9-2-21]

"Experience History Like Never Before," Abraham Lincoln Presidential Library and Museum, https://presidentlincoln.illinois.gov [accessed 9-23-21]

"Field Trips & School Tours," Western Museum of Mining & Industry, https://wmmi.org/education/school-trips.html [accessed 9-2-21]

Henry, Jill, Comments, DIG Field School, Educators and Schools, Education, The Burke, https://www.burkemuseum.org/education/educators-and-schools/dig-field-school [accessed 9-15-21]

https://mailchi.mp/nevadaart/enroll-for-in-person-summer-classes-144499?e=db5836b8f1

"Individual Backyard Scientist Backpack," Backyard Scientist Backpacks, Burke Museum, https://www.burkemuseum.org/education/educators-and-schools/burke-boxes/backyard-scientist-backpacks [accessed 9-15-21]

"Interactive Map," Explore, The Franklin Institute, https://www.fi.edu/map?field_floor_value=2 [accessed 9-6-21]

"Junior Curators," Teens, Audiences, Learn, North Carolina Museum of Natural Sciences, https://naturalsciences.org/learn/junior-curators [accessed 2-15-22]

"Lenapehoking: Land of the Lenape," About the Museum, Brooklyn Museum, https://www.brooklynmuseum.org/about [accessed 9-6-21]

"Many Histories and a Shared Future," Our Values, About the Museum, Brooklyn Museum, https://www.brooklynmuseum.org/about [accessed 2-15-22]

[Name withheld] "Outstanding and Unique Presentation!" Reviews, August 2021, Trip Advisor [accessed 9-6-21]

"National Park Service AAPI Theme Study," Training + Workshops, Education, Wing Luke Museum of the Asian Pacific American Experience, https://www.wingluke.org/education/ [accessed 9-8-21]

"Offering Helping Hands to Paws, Fins and Hooves," Conservation, About Us, Milwaukee County Zoo, http://www.milwaukeezoo.org/conservation/ [accessed 9-6-21]

"Onsite School Visits," Learn, Tenement Museum, https://www.tenement.org/teacher-resources/ [accessed 2-15-22]

"Outreach," For Children, Learn, Birmingham Civil Rights Institute, https://www.bcri.org/for-children/

"Plan Your Field Trip," Explore, Shaker Village, https://shakervillageky.org/student-groups/ [accessed 9-8-21]

"Queens Museum Family Programs," Education, Queens Museum, Fall 2021, https://queensmuseum.org/families [accessed 2-15-22]

"Research and Scholarship," Learn & Engage, Crystal Bridges, https://crystalbridges.org/reports-and-research/ [accessed 2-15-22]

Rogers, Bob, Middle School Magic," Abraham Lincoln Presidential Library and Museum, 2015, https://youtu.be/osXm4AP0nZI [accessed 9-6-21]

"Summer Teacher Institute: Being Present in the Moment" Calendar, Crystal Bridges Museum of American Art, https://crystalbridges.org/calendar/virtual-summer-teacher-institute-being-present-in-the-moment/ [accessed 9-6-21]

"Virtual Field Trips," Learn, Tenement Museum, https://www.tenement.org/teacher-resources/ [accessed 2-15-22]

"Where Appreciation and Conservation Go Hand in Hand," About Us, Milwaukee County Zoo, http://www.milwaukeezoo.org/about/ [accessed 9-6-21]

"Zoo Classes," Education, Milwaukee County Zoo, https://www.zoosociety.org/education/zoo-classes-camps/ [accessed 2-15-22]

CHAPTER 8

Stores

The Shopper and the Visitor

Stores are a gift to museums. They attract not only shoppers, but also visitors and curious prospective visitors. Counters of merchandise, shelves of books, every inch of space entices diverse audiences to linger longer and make another connection with the museum. Inside the museum or virtually, the store sells the museum, too.

Museum stores welcome so many different kinds of audiences, it's essential to make them connect more deeply and more often, for the shopper to see references to the museum in every purchase. Here's an example from the online store at Musical Instrument Museum in Phoenix: "MIM's special exhibition Congo Masks and Music: Masterpieces from Central Africa . . . reflects the diverse settings of masquerades." The text appears next to photographs of the masks and instruments; the store web page is a summary of the gallery. Connection made.

This chapter will show how to connect the museum with the purchase, in the museum itself, at the store, and online. Varying sizes and footprints of museums present different challenges. Certainly, one doesn't write the same way for a science museum as for a historic house. And a store, by definition, stores all manner of things.

Writers: channel the talents of curator and merchandiser to find the apt connection. Learn the merchandise, learn the exhibit goals, and write how they meet.

CONNECTION POINTS BETWEEN MUSEUM AND STORE

The following are just some of the places for the written word, and sometimes the spoken word, to link a shopper to the museum and the gallery visitor to some takeaway memories.

- E-mail announcement
- Website
- In the store
- Community
- Learning
- Brand
- QR codes

E-MAIL

E-mail announcements provide the first opportunity to connect the museum and the store because e-mail reaches your entire mailing list. Only a percentage will open the mail and respond, but that's a percentage of a huge number. And the connection, museum plus store, equals a larger audience than either one on its own. Diverse groups, who haven't made the decision to visit, might be tempted to shop.

E-mail is timely, and Racine Art Museum leverages the timeliness of winter in the e-mail announcement: "The RAM Museum Store is stocked with everything you need to prepare for the impending winter weather."

New Bedford Whaling Museum borrows the timeliness of the holiday season in its e-mail store announcements; however, it astutely understands that although every museum sells holiday merchandise, only the Whaling Museum has ships and whales. Here's what the e-mail announcement says: "Sail about for a little while with our collection of Moby-Dick products! From books to pillows to apparel, there is something for every Melville fan on your holiday shopping list to enjoy." And: "Land Crafted. Sea Inspired. Evoke your favorite coastal destination this holiday season with a range of high quality lotions, soaps, and bath bombs."

Holiday appeal is good. Connection to the Whaling Museum is better. Good job, writer.

WEBSITE

Visitors to a museum website have already made one decision—to learn more about the museum. They may be planning a visit, returning for a class or talk, enrolling their child in a program, donating money, or spending money. The lure of shopping and the tab, often right at the top of the screen with other main-line tabs, attracts newcomers and returnees alike. These shoppers are about to enter your museum. Welcome them.

Burke Museum writes: "The Burke Store offers something for everyone as part of the museum's mission to foster a better understanding of the world and our place in it. Our diverse selection of gifts and books is guided by the museum's exhibitions and our natural history and cultural heritage collections."

Once inside an online store, visitors like to roam the aisles. Roaming the virtual aisles of a website saves shoppers many steps and Denver Art Museum saves even more by this simple organizational technique: The museum titles its online tab "Holiday Gift Guide." It positions the store as informative, not just mercantile. Once arrived at the shopping page there are further classifications:

"For kids and grand-kids."
"Artist-related gifts."
"Exhibition-related gifts."

Smart to remember the role of grandparents in museum visits and gifts. And don't be shy about connecting store purchases and museum exhibitions.

Writers: add to the Gift Guide concept with items particular to your museum:

- For history buffs
- For young astronomers
- Trees, wetlands, and rose gardens

A similar taxonomy can be printed as Gift Guide signs in the actual store, or as a Scan Me code printed on cards throughout the store.

IN THE STORE

Now that the visitor is in the store, in person or online, the ties that bind start to work harder. Shoppers have seen the exhibits and want to learn more; they want to own a memory to keep for them or show others. If the store is located physically near the entrance, many people drop in there first for a preview of what's ahead. Just like previewing a museum online via its store.

The Legacy Shop, store of the Illinois Holocaust Museum & Education Center, literally knits one of the museum's exhibits into a store item. One of the education exhibits is a little red dress, knitted by a grandmother who had escaped Germany for Shanghai in 1939. A copy of the dress is displayed in the store, and a pattern is for sale. Surprising in its charm, beauty amid danger, it's a powerful connection to the positivism that informs the museum's exhibits.

Another connection between the store and museum is more surprising. What, the visitor might ask, are books on Nelson Mandela, Dr. Martin

Luther King Jr., the Armenian Genocide, and LGBTQ doing on the shelves? With the books' covers facing out, they strikingly proclaim many of the injustices throughout the world. The museum tells a great deal about its mission right in the store.

On its website, these connections preview and summarize the philosophy of the museum. In-person visitors are directed through the store as they leave the museum. It's a powerful way to reinforce a guiding philosophy one last time.

Counter Cards

Use the immediacy and physical nearness of a counter card or shelf talker to remind museum store shoppers:

- All jewelry designed by local artists
- Proceeds benefit community STEM projects
- Books on contemporaries of Brunelleschi
- Scan here for articles and essays about the current and past exhibits

Virtual Shelf Talkers

Typical shoppers want to browse and peruse. Lingering benefits museums because visitors who stay longer make stronger connections to the museum. There's time for their memories to sink in. In-store or online, there are techniques writers can use to encourage shoppers to linger.

The Museum of the City of New York gives online book shoppers reason to stay longer with this simple link: "Filter." Visitors to the Books section click on "Filter" and they're hooked with a tempting list of forty categories of books, from Architecture to Rebel Women. It's hard not to virtually window shop through this large virtual bookshelf.

Store Personnel

Some of the people in the store don't shop; they sell. They add uncountable value to the store by listening to questions, answering them with merchandise knowledge, talking about the museum itself.

The Alliance of American Museums suggests in-store or virtual events to interpret its collection in a different setting, one with real people:

- Trunk show
- Product demonstrations
- Meet-the-maker videos

Writers: the allure of store events is so strong, you need only a few words to connect them to the museum. Think of a small counter card near the object, or a short caption underneath its photograph.

- Open the trunk and hear the story of our collection.
- Ever wonder how real people used this implement? Our curator shows you how.
- These beaded objects are the work of artisans using traditional tools. Watch them explain their art.

Writers, don't forget captions. Different viewers read different meanings into visuals, and a few words strengthen the communication.

A word about that word—hybrid. The concept will endure comfortably and usefully if institutions find ways to refresh it, as did Nelson-Atkins Museum of Art in Kansas City. The museum created a virtual drawing class, a reproduction of a famous artwork for students to order online, and an included-in-the-price tool kit of drawing supplies to be picked up inside the museum in advance. Online + virtual + inside real museum. It's a novel way to be a museum today, and the connection is made clear on the website:

Countless artists have sharpened their skills by copying famous works of art. Here is your chance to do the same . . . a museum Teaching Artist will introduce

Figure 8.1. Stores connect visitors to the museum across miles, as well as across the counter, with information as well as memories.
monkeybusinessimages/ iStock via Getty images

a work in the Nelson-Atkins collection, then guide participants as they create their own works of art.

Here's another shopper benefit that links online shoppers to the physical museum. Mississippi Museum of Art in Jackson offers "curbside pickup. For service, simply call to place your order. We will wrap and deliver to your car when you arrive. If you need additional gifts, we are available to help as your personal shopper!"

COMMUNITY

Towns large and small take pride in their arts, and the community aspect of museums imbues the store, as well as the gallery, lecture hall, and classrooms.

Delaware Art Museum connects its monthly DelArt Readers group to the store by stocking the titles on the group's reading list. It's nice cross-merchandising, and connects the museum with the community in a tangible sociable way.

The DelArt Readers, a community-led book club, meets monthly to discuss, debate, celebrate, and share both works of fiction and non-fiction. Our selections are focused on art, artists, and/or the artistic process either in general or in response to the Museum's collections or exhibits. In addition to our interest in art and artists, we also seek to create a sense of community, conversation, and connection.

Cooperstown, the community, is synonymous with National Baseball Hall of Fame Museum, and now the museum store makes the connection by selling—marketing—a visit to the town itself in the same column as it sells souvenir pins, baseball cards, and reproduction photographs. Described as "an unspoiled repository of America's heritage, rich in history, art, architecture and natural beauty," Cooperstown is a big destination for diverse audiences. The store page links to travel and lodging information, a smart tactic to encourage visits, especially since part of its mission is to collect, preserve, exhibit, and interpret for a global audience.

Community causes occupy a large part of Queens Museum mission and its foundational philosophy. Its store is a partner in that mission, donating proceeds to local charities and the people.

The August Tree . . . partnered with Queens Museum, to become the Queens Museum Gift Shop. Curated with the celebration of Queens in mind, products feature the Queens urban lifestyle, art, history, diversity and of course, Queens Museum merchandise.

Other Communities

Community is a complex concept: neighborhood, culture, family, town, colleagues, and fellow volunteer for causes. The Illinois Holocaust Museum & Education Center views its community broadly in defining its mission: "preserving the legacy of the Holocaust by honoring the memories of those who were lost and by teaching universal lessons that combat hatred, prejudice, and indifference."

Its store bookshelves, covers facing out, vividly manifest this worldview. One looks at the books and wonders why a Holocaust museum encompasses so many world injustices. Books prompt thoughts, and that's a philosophy in itself.

Writers: stores, historically, have been central to their communities. People gather to shop, sharing news and ideas and stocking up for the future. Hold this thought when writing about the store.

Writers: another way to include the community when connecting books to the museum is to borrow from commercial bookstores: solicit short statements from the staff about specific books in the store. The personal reviews help lift the book off the shelf and into the real or virtual shopping cart. Give the staffer's name or initials and position at the museum; individuals make the link even stronger.

Where's the Store?

Some museums site them in the lobby, where visitors coming and going can't miss them. Others have satellite stores in the galleries. And all stores grapple with the overarching issues of visitorship and connection.

Parrish Art Museum, Water Mill, New York, addresses the location of the museum store and its special place as a destination store. Location: "Tucked just inside the main lobby of the Museum, the bright and spacious Museum Shop . . ." Merchandise/collection synergy, Parrish Art Museum explains that it's a "destination store . . . for creative shoppers . . . with objects that are inspired by the museum's collection . . . and one of a kind."

And in a nice prelude to the store, Musical Instrument Museum, on its website, shows a welcoming photograph of the entrance to the MIM Store. The Shop page also has words of welcome: "Thank you for shopping the online store of the Musical Instrument Museum. We offer a selection of items from around the world that educate, inspire, and entertain."

The Illinois Holocaust Museum & Education Center directs visitors through the store as they exit the museum. They leave with additional learning beamed from all four walls.

Writers: visitors need directions to the museum. Usually it's verbal, within the top-line tab Visit. Sometimes a small locator map is included. However, it can't be repeated too often: pictures speak louder than words. You'll still need to write a caption to the photo, and "thank you for visiting" is a good start.

LEARNING

Museum stores are extensions of museum learning. Some museums put that teaching in writing.

The Petersen Automotive Museum Store connects to the museum in everything it sells, from $5 Ferrari exhibit posters to $200 signed prints of cars and drivers. And then, of course, all those 1:18, 1:24, 1:43 and 1:64 scale models.

And then there is this description of a photograph in its "Featured Artist" drop-down menu:

Hector Cademartori's motor racing artwork depicts some of the greatest Grand Prix racing moments in History. Born in Buenos Aires, Argentina, Cademartori was first influenced in racing in the mid-1960s by the European tradition and great drivers such as Dan Gurney, Jackie Stewart, Pedro Rodriguez and Graham Hill.

Writers: incorporating researched knowledge with standard store item descriptions demands scrupulous attention to details like names, dates, and ratios. With visitors to websites like Petersen Automotive Museum's, you can be pretty sure your reader will know more than you. You have the advantage of rigorous museum curators behind you, and their knowledge will be appreciated.

Another rule: watch the balance between researched and anecdotal information. Both aid learning. Here's what can be read on the Petersen website:

inevitably, a car came along that was so extreme—with supernatural performance and outrageous luxury—that it outshone all supercars to date: the Bugatti Veyron of 2005. With its 4-digit horsepower, 7-digit price tag, quad-turbocharged 16-cylinder engine, and top speed greater than 250 miles per hour . . .

This kind of precise writing is found on blogs authored by researchers who also have personal observations. It's a forward-looking example of extending museum rigor through the store.

Anchorage Museum store lists its large selection of merchandise in categories like Alaskan Native Art, Northern Collection, and this stand-out: Learning & Family Engagement. It's unexpected for a museum store, and compelling. Kudos to Anchorage Museum and this corner of a store that has morphed into a new business. "The Anchorage Museum has curated a collection of products that encourage imagination and creativity, foster learning, and deepen the understanding of our collective world."

The Getty Museum, renowned for its research as well as its collection and exhibitions, puts centuries of research into its online book store. Click on any of the twenty-seven pages of books and find information like this from *Issues in the Conservation of Paintings*:

> Some are classic and highly influential writings; others, although little known when first published, in retrospect reflect important themes and issues in the history of the field. Many appear here in English for the first time, including translations of . . . Victor Bauer-Bolton's treatise from 1914, *"Sollen fehlende Stellen bei Gemälden ergänzt werden?"* (Should Missing Areas of Paintings Be Made Good?).

Destination Store

Although books are expected at museum stores, Northwest Montana History Museum upgrades its bookshelves to a reading room. "Visitors to Glacier National Park and locals alike can spend a relaxing and informative afternoon in the Schoolbell Bookstore [and its] . . . fiction and nonfiction books that highlight Montana's rich history." The connection to the museum is strong. It's a new kind of museum store, and its emphasis on learning adds to the museum's mission.

Tacoma Art Museum also offers a reading room for kids and families. "Curl up in the Betty Gene and John Walker Reading Alcove with a great book. TAM Studio's family library includes a complete collection of Caldecott Medal-winning picture books and a rotating selection of books related to works of art on view at the museum."

Like the above-mentioned Parrish Art Museum store, destination is a wonderful descriptor when the information inside is worth it.

BRAND

Exemplary exhibitions, educational projects, and learning events, not to mention the collection itself, all contribute to defining a museum's brand. Seldom, however, is a museum's identity made manifest in the store.

Enter the Dali Museum in St. Petersburg, Florida, and Museum of Glass in Tacoma.

The store of the Dali Museum in St. Petersburg, Florida, is, to use the vernacular, surreal, filled with objects in the shape of melting clocks and teardrop eyes. The museum fulfills the goal of reflecting and continuing the museum experience. The web page says: "Our Dalí-inspired Museum Store merchandise serves as a memory of the Dalí experience and reflects a surreal attitude and spirit of our collection, the most comprehensive in the world outside of Spain."

Writers: the Dali Museum Store captures the personality of Salvador Dali, as well as that of the museum. When the ideals of one person are so rigorously applied to merchandise, part of your job is to depict the person. It's one more chance, on the website or in the store, to expound the museum's story.

Two categories of merchandise distinguish the store at Museum of Glass, in Tacoma, Washington: items made at the Hot Shop of the museum, priced from $100 to $1,200, and fine art glass pieces priced up to $14,000. The prices prove the rarity of these objects and the singularity of the museum. Glass is a fine art; its creators are artists and traditionally skilled artisans; the museum is noteworthy for its large, traditional glass-making hot shop on premise. The connection between singular museum and its store is symbiotic.

Writers: when store merchandise is so pertinent to a museum's identity and personality, give extra space to the latter, a little less to the items with the price tag.

For science museums with a strong research commitment, books define the store. At San Diego Natural History Museum, books are sold separately from apparel and souvenirs and on their own separate website as publications that are "authored by museum staff and volunteers along with other notable books that support The Nat's mission." The Mission that the publications support says, in part: "To interpret the natural world through research, education and exhibits."

Writers: everyone knows what a book is, but in a merchandise setting, give them a further description. Just listing the categories of books strengthens their link to the museum and its mission: "Deserts: California & Southwest"; "Geoscience"; "History/Lore/Native Americans."

QR CODES

Best new invention of the Hybrid Twenties? The little Scan Here icon has power to bring museums to real life, and visitors out of their shells. Wherever one appears, readers know there's a bigger world at their fingertips. Called "a barcode on steroids" by an Asian government agency, QR codes let visitors viewing an exhibit in a museum's gallery learn more by connecting to a book in the museum store. Or the reverse: a shopper who finds a small telescope in the store can connect back to an exhibit at the planetarium.

QR, which stands for Quick Response, is well named; it allows the web to respond to the curiosity of a reader who wants to "scan here and learn more." Places a museum might place a quick response to visitor curiosity:

- Next to an exhibit label
- Near a wall panel introducing an exhibition
- At the entrance to a gallery
- Information desk
- Coat room
- Lecture hall
- Throughout museum grounds
- Lecture program
- Countertop in store
- Bookshelf
- Stationery shelf
- Check-out counter
- Handout at talk
- Printed piece
- Community poster

Store merchandise is only one kind of connective purchase. Selling experiences is a powerful way to connect a shopper to the museum and its knowledge. Travel is a bounteous learning purchase. The National World War II Museum, in New Orleans, is selling five tours to World War II sites—Pacific Theater, European Theater, and "The Home Front," the museum itself. The vehicle is a costly, four-color mailer sent to a mailing list by postal service. What makes it cost effective is a QR code for every tour, and it takes a wide audience right to the website. Mail in one's mailbox is individual, personalized. The World War II Museum on the Mississippi River has just expanded its audience to Puget Sound and Hampton Roads, with a printed piece that will stay around for awhile plus a page on a smartphone that's ready for action.

EXIT

Once visitors have entered the store, the learning continues. Visually, audibly, and tactilely, messages are interpreted for each person, in their own way. Imagine the most diverse group of shoppers, all exploring your galleries, rooms, and objects. Talk to them in the store and don't forget to thank them for coming. A sign by the exit door is a good start.

REFERENCES

"2022 Book Selection & Schedule," What's On, Delaware Art Museum, https:// delart.org/event/delartreaders/ [accessed 1-18-22]

"The All-New Burke Store Is Open!" Store, Visit, Burke Museum, https://www .burkemuseum.org/visit/store [accessed 1-15-22]

Bomford, David and Mark Lewis, ed., "Issues in the Conservation of Paintings, paperback," Books to delight the eye and nourish the mind, Getty Publications, Getty Museum Store, https://shop.getty.edu/collections/getty-publications ?page=11&sort_by=title-ascending, page 11 of 27 [accessed 1-17-22]

"Books Authored by The Nat," The Nat, San Diego Natural History, Sunbelt Publications, Museum, https://sunbeltpublications.com/shop/thenat/ [accessed 1-16-22]"

"Categories," The Museum Store, Museum of Glass, https://museumofglassstore .org/collections/collections [accessed 1-16-22]

"Congo Masks and Music Magnets," Online Store, Musical Instrument Museum, https://www.themimstore.org/collections/personal-accessories/products/congo -masks-and-music-magnets?variant=32329796485186 [accessed 1-11-22]

"The Dali Museum Store," Visit, The Dali Museum, https://thedali.org/visit/store -cafe/the-museum-store/ [accessed 1-16-22]

"Discover the Finest Bookstore in Montana," Bookstore, Northwest Montana History Museum, https://www.nwmthistory.org/bookstore/ [accessed 12-31-21]

"Educational Travel Programs," Brochure, The National World War II Museum, mailed January 2022

"Featured Artist: Hector Cademartori," Museum Store, Petersen Automotive Museum, https://petersenstore.org/collections/featured-artist-hector-cademartori [accessed 11-26-21]

Getty Publications, Museum Store, Getty Foundation Research Museum, https:// shop.getty.edu/collections/getty-publications [accessed 1-17-22]

"Holiday Shopping," The White Whale, New Bedford Museum, December 15, 2021, https://myemail.constantcontact.com/Don-t-Delay—Last-Day-for-Christmas-De livery.html?soid=1128002165729&aid=JwAZ8R2Ukk4 [accessed 12-15-21]

https://shop.getty.edu/products/issues-in-the-conservation-of-paintings-978-089 2367818 [accessed 1-17-22]

https://shop.mcny.org/collections/books-and-prints [accessed 12-31-21]

"Hypercars: The Allure of the Extreme," Featured Exhibits, Museum Store, Petersen Automotive Museum, https://petersenstore.org/collections/super-car-exhibit-col lection [accessed 1-18-22]

"Learning & Family Engagement," Anchorage Museum Store, Anchorage Museum, https://anchorage-museum-association.myshopify.com/collections/learning [accessed 1-16-22]

"The Legacy Shop," Home, https://illinois-holocaust-museum.myshopify.com/ [accessed 1-13-22]

"The Little Red Dress Knitting Pattern by Melissa Shinsato," The Legacy Shop, Shop, Illinois Holocaust Museum, https://illinois-holocaust-museum.myshopify.com /products/the-little-red-dress-knitting-pattern-by-meilissa-shinsato?_pos=1 &_sid=2d158f49b&_ss=r [accessed 1-11-22]

"Mission," About, Illinois Holocaust Museum & Education Center, https://www
.ilholocaustmuseum.org/about/mission/ [accessed 1-18-22]

"Museum Shop," Parrish Art Museum, https://parrishart.org/visit/museum-shop/
[accessed 12-4-21]

"The Museum Store," Shop, Mississippi Art Museum, https://www.msmuseumart
.org/shop/ [accessed 1-18-22]

"Museum Store Sunday—Five Years and Going Strong!" Alliance Blog, American Alliance of Museums, November 4, 2021, https://www.aam-us.org/2021/11/04/mu
seum-store-sunday-five-years-and-going-strong/ [accessed November 14, 2021]

"Our Mission," https://www.sdnat.org/ [accessed 1-16-22]

"Petersen Store," https://petersenstore.org [accessed 11-26-21]

"Plan Your Visit," Visit, National Baseball Hall of Fame and Museum, https://base
ballhall.org/planyourvisit?mc_cid=4d10ddf36b&mc_eid=0d70ef97d8 [accessed
10-30-21]

"The QR Code Is Everywhere, But Where Did it Come From?" *TechNews*, GovTech,
September 24, 2020, https://www.tech.gov.sg/media/technews/2020-09-24-the
-qr-code-is-everywhere-but-where-did-it-come-from [accessed 1-11-22]

"RAM Museum Store," Recommended, Racine Art Museum, October 26, 2021,
https://myemail.constantcontact.com/Learn-from-Notable-Area-Artists.html?so
id=1101481332095&aid=bHr2CVfJxAo [accessed 10-27-21]

"About the August Tree," Queens Museum Shop by the August Tree, Queens Museum, https://theaugusttree.com/pages/about-us [accessed 9-24-21]

"2021 Holiday Gift Guide," Denver Art Museum, December 2021, https://www.den
verartmuseum.org/en/blog/2021-holiday-gift-guide [accessed 12-18-21]

"2022 Book Selection & Schedule," What's On, Delaware Art Museum, https://
delart.org/event/delartreaders/ [accessed 1-18-22]

"Virtual Adult Programs," January 22, 2022, Nelson-Atkins Museum of Art, https://
cart.nelson-atkins.org/29001/32135 [accessed 11-29-21]

"Welcome to the MIM Online Store," About Us, MIM Online Store, https://www
.themimstore.org/pages/about-us [accessed 1-11-22]

"Welcome to TAM Studio," Tam Studio, Tacoma Art Museum, https://www.tacoma
artmuseum.org/visit/tam-studio/ [accessed 1-18-22]

CHAPTER 9

Tours

Charting the Curators' Path

Faithfulness to a plan is something good writers understand: anything less is sloppy. For museum writers and docents who script and lead tours, the challenge is staying faithful to the curators' planned path through an exhibition. Every museum exhibition has a theme: objects within an exhibition, exhibits within a gallery, all relate to the theme. Tours have a mental roadmap that must be communicated. These tours are, as the Museum of Contemporary Art Chicago says on its website: "designed to help you navigate the many concepts, methods, materials, and ideas that contemporary artists incorporate in their work. Join the conversation by taking a tour."

Writers and docents work toward the same tour guidelines, and in this chapter, they are treated interchangeably. They follow the same museological landmarks, albeit sometimes in a different order, and they abide by the same script, although docents can ad-lib where necessary. Here's what to point out:

- Created output—point to the artifact, display, features of a historic room, specific detail in a large object.
- Creators (name usually on wall label)—artist, craftsman, historic-homeowner, Mother Nature.
- Era—when the exhibit first appeared.
- Context—what else was going on then.
- Implications—Start with, "so," or "therefore."
- Gallery neighbors—what is next to what in the room. Curators adeptly mix objects of seemingly different purposes and tour leaders must connect them to the theme.
- Wall text and digital adaptations—although you probably didn't write the label, know what it says and be prepared to paraphrase it.

That's a lot to learn as you guide visitors along the curated path. A unifying theme helps everyone stay on track. Many exhibitions will already have a title that encompasses its theme. For other tours, the curator and education department work with tour guides and writers to develop a theme. Virtual tours, with their variety of formats and the added variable of at-home distractions, are especially needful of unifying themes.

THEMES

Themes help writers/docents organize the stops on a tour. A good theme relates to each object so that a tour leader could say (doesn't have to say) this is a good example of our theme. Tenement Museum in New York repeats it mission with each tour because each is a story about the immigrant families who lived in its tenement buildings from the 1880s to 1950s. Its tours have themes such as:

"Hard Times: 1880"
"Tenement Women: 1902"
"Day in the Life: 1930s"
"Everyday Chinatown: Stories of Ordinary Artifacts"

Here are some tips for finding a theme:

- Write a list of "why these objects were selected to show you."
- Find one word or phrase in your list that captures the essence of the tour—the theme.
- Identify one object on your list that is particularly distinctive and base your theme on that.
- After your first tour, heed the questions group participants asked. You may want to change your theme.

VIRTUAL TOUR ADAPTATION

Tenement Museum of New York is the world master in the alchemy of turning everyday objects into treasures of information about the lives of the immigrant families that lived on the Lower East Side. The museum owns a huge collection of artifacts, memoirs, photographs, documents, and official records that curators mine to create themes for their virtual tours like:

"From Orchard to Essex: Street Peddlers and Market Vendors of the Lower East Side"

"Everyday Chinatown: Stories of Ordinary Artifacts"
"Kitchen Liberation: Immigrant Home Cooking and Women's Rights"

The value of themes is keeping tours on topic as they move from object to object. Docents can call upon the theme when visitor questions and comments stray off topic: "That's an interesting question; I'll have to think how that relates to the theme of this tour. We can talk after the tour."

Writers/Docents: know the curatorial or education objective. Know the objects and why they were selected for the theme of the tour. Be able to point to an object and say, "this is a good example of [title or theme of exhibits] because. . . ." To get to that level of knowledge and comfort, there's a timeline of preparation.

TIMELINE FOR WRITING A TOUR SCRIPT

Curators need six months to several years to plan an exhibition and how they want visitors to view it. Writers and docents don't have that much time, but should plan on about four weeks to learn the tour and write about it. Here are the stages:

1. Introductory talk from curator and/or education department, including statement of theme.
2. Walk-through of exhibition and attendant labs, library, or demonstration galleries to view the exhibition in person. Led by museum curator or educator.
3. Second walk-through for docents, on their own, to develop their own tour plan.
4. Outline of the objects to be covered on each tour—12 is probably tops in 45–60 minutes.
5. Research of any details not covered in the introductory talk, but of personal interest.
6. Writing an outline—a list of tour stops and why you selected that item to talk about.
7. Connective narration to fill in the outline.
8. Another walk-through, this time of the 12-object tour to see if the outline works.
9. Review or research of any stops on the tour that need practice so they can be narrated spontaneously.
10. Personal additions to your planned tour. Keep eyes open for material learned along the way from other media. If, in your additional research, you find an interesting visual, save it on your tablet to show the group.

11. Lead the tour and learn from experience.
12. Ask end-of-tour wrap-up questions (formulated in advance).

INTRODUCTORY TALK FROM CURATOR
AND/OR EDUCATION DEPARTMENT

Several weeks before a docent's new tour is scheduled to begin, the exhibition and its theme, goals, individual artifacts, creators, and context will be
communicated. It could be a large visiting art exhibition, a new story at a
historic house, or a changing season at a botanic garden that needs learning.
    Writers/docents: ask these three questions of the curator:

- Is any object in this exhibition new or newly researched?
- Why is this exhibition timely?
- Should I highlight any artist or creator in this tour?

Writers/docents: ask these three questions of other docents:

- What input from previous tours bear on this tour?
- What questions might a tourer ask that I can prepare for?
- Does anyone have an insight you'd share with me?

Writers/docents: listen to other docents' questions since they reflect accu-
mulated knowledge from previous tours.

WALK-THROUGH FOR DOCENTS,
LED BY MUSEUM CURATOR OR EDUCATOR

Just as it sounds, this is a boots-on-the-ground experience of the tour route.
It is led by the curator or educator, and it's your opportunity to look and
ask questions that will get an informed answer. These tours last an hour and
simply outline the tour. Writers will need to fill in the gaps.
    Writers: now's the time to learn how to ask questions. Many people go
to presentations and think they can lean back and listen. Don't be one of
those people. Write a list of ten questions in advance. At least one of them
will elicit an answer you can use in your tour script.

- What's your favorite object?
- Why this time period?
- Any objects here that are especially timely?

- Give an example of two objects shown near each other, and why.
- Point out something humorous.
- What will visitors find surprising?
- Put another way, what will new audiences to the museum find surprising?
- WHY? At any point ask why the curator made the selections you're seeing.

SECOND WALK-THROUGH BY WRITER/DOCENT ON OWN TIME

Plan on spending an hour to select the objects you like, understand, and can do justice to. If something stumps you, chances are visitors will wonder about it, too. For example, "What other animals are we going to see?"

Here's how Milwaukee County Zoo answers questions like that: "The animals on exhibit may change from day to day, based on weather conditions and necessary veterinary procedures . . . a variety of animals will be in their outdoor habitats including elephants, giraffes . . . grizzly bears, harbor seals and alpaca."

Writer/Docent: bring a tablet, if you have one, for on-the-spot research. If you've found a photo or short piece of information to share, have it saved on your tablet. Additional knowledge on a hand-held device is not superfluous in a museum. When appropriate, and used judiciously, they add value to a formal presentation and engage visitors in a different way. Show one or two in the course of the tour, or even at the beginning for context. Save photos on your tablet for future use in virtual tours.

You can also use a tablet to look up answers to questions that you can't answer. Small tablets are professional. Don't use your phone.

WRITE AN OUTLINE

Map out the objects and exhibits to be covered on your tour. After the second walk-through, you will be immersed in the exhibition and familiar enough with it to select objects to present on your tour. Select twelve, which is more than enough for a forty-five-minute tour. One way to confront your narrative is using the first person.

At Pennsylvania Academy of Fine Arts, a virtual tour of a photography exhibition was led by the photographer, Shoog McDaniel, who spoke in the first person throughout. It was informative and charming—the tour as seen by the creator of the works.

Writers/Docents: you can pare down the number of items on the tour during the tour itself. Nobody will know what you've omitted.

VIRTUAL TOUR ADAPTATION

An outline of stops is even more necessary for a virtual tour because the visitor can't see ahead. Battleship New Jersey, with its 887-foot length, has so much to show—from teak decks (non-slippery when wet) to 123-pound anchor chains and forward enlisted berthing area—that a tour must be plotted in advance.

And with its multiple levels you need a walk-through just to time the tour. Together you can select the windlasses and capstans, cage towers and decks to feature.

Virtual tours have a very wide lens; so many actual objects loom larger when captured by a camera, rather than the human eye. St. Augustine Lighthouse & Maritime Museum sidestepped that obstacle by utilizing two narrators; one talked about the larger picture, the other pointed out details. Very effective.

FILL IN THE OUTLINE WITH CONNECTIVE NARRATIVE

Each tour is held together differently. A rule of thumb is: "Here's where we are now, there's where we're going. This is the first thing you'll see when you get there."

St. Augustine Lighthouse & Maritime Museum connects one segment of its tour with: "These are the kinds of things that soldiers and sailors would have on board . . . coming from Charleston . . . evacuating loyalists . . . mix of things . . . military and civilian . . . we've got some of them over here [shows display cases] like rigging elements."

WALK THROUGH THE TWELVE-OBJECT TOUR
TO SEE IF THE NARRATIVE WORKS

To ascertain if your narrative makes sense, mutter to yourself as you walk through. You must talk out loud (softly) to get the timing right. Adjust as needed. Go through the same drill with virtual tour scripts.

Docents, sometimes you forget what you want to say. It happens to the best. Here's a memory tool: "The reason I want to show you this is . . ."

SHOWTIME

Let the tour begin! Writers/docents: now that you have (1) an outline, (2) a narrative, and (3) a theme, you have all the words you need to lead the tour.

However, don't fear spontaneity. Enthusiasm counts in energizing a tour and spurring learning.

First, get to the "Tour starts here" sign ten minutes early and be ready to chat with visitors; they frequently line up early. Conversation starter: "Where are you from?"

Before the tour actually starts, especially if it's virtual, hold up a sign with The Theme. Writers have already written a theme for the tour itself, and with few or no revisions it will communicate in text.

Preview briefly the point of the tour. Milwaukee Zoo announces a series of "Wild Connections" tours that are highly scientific as expected from a zoological garden:

> "Learn what it's like to care for the animals, their unique adaptations and behaviors."
> "Learn about habitat design and zoo planning."
> "Learn why their white feathers that resemble a mustache are so important, and what you can do to help them thrive in the wild."

Second, start on time with a welcome and an introduction to what the tour entails. Tell tourers how long it lasts, if there are stairs or an elevator, and if there are benches.

Third, preview what's ahead. At the Lincoln Home in Springfield, Illinois (the house where Abraham and Mary Lincoln lived, not the encyclopedic presidential library and museum), the docents are Rangers, and they wear the Ranger uniform, so they're a visual introduction that this will be informative. In the virtual tour, the Ranger informs visitors that this is a weekly

Figure 9.1.   Guided tours point out what to see and why, often in real time. Leave space in the script for questions.
Lingbeek / E+ via Getty images

series, with a different tour every week, and that to kick things off, "We'll explore what it was like to be 'At Home with the Lincolns.'" This kind of introduction works for virtual and in-person museum tours.

Some museums start the welcoming process on their websites. Tenement Museum in New York highlights: "how Black and African Americans shaped Lower Manhattan as they made homes, businesses, and communities there over the centuries . . . from the story of Sebastiaen de Britto, one of the first Black residents of the area in the 1640s, to Studio We, a musicians collective in the 1970s."

The Tenement Museum even invites prospective viewers to write the tour text for them. It started the process in an e-mail announcement by inviting readers to ask questions about past tours and e-mail them for a future Q-and-A talk: "Have you ever wanted to know something about life in the tenements that wasn't addressed on a tour?"

The writers wisely suggested some questions, just to get things started:

- "Where did everybody sleep?"
- "Did immigrants really have their names changed at Ellis Island?"

Questions from visitors are eye-opening: they employ words spoken by real people, different people who aren't curators; they show involvement in the museum's tours; they demonstrate how different age groups, cultures, and backgrounds react to an exhibit.

Another way to prep visitors for a tour is on your website, especially if you're in an area visited by tourists with many choices on their agenda. The Postal Museum in Washington, D.C., provides before-you-go advice on its website:

- A floor plan to familiarize the family before they start out and
- Accessibility information

"Sign language, oral interpreters, assisted listening devices, and descriptive guide experiences for the visually impaired may be requested with advance notice for tours and events."

And here's a surprisingly simple idea: A basic definition of what a tour actually is. Nevada Art Museum states it on its website, and it's worth paraphrasing at the beginning of a tour: "Experience an in-person guided tour or virtual presentation of the current exhibitions with one of the Museum's volunteer docents. . . . A volunteer docent will guide you through the galleries, offering insight and history to the artwork on view."

The website explanation continues its explanation with the all-important word FREE.

On in-person tours, you might want to say, "Please, no tipping." Many museum newcomers think it's expected.

LISTEN AND REMEMBER THE QUESTIONS ASKED

When one has a script to write and follow, one important topic is missing: listening. Tour leaders learn a lot about scripting a tour by listening to questions from the tour group. The epitome of Talk and Listen is expressed by Great Basin Museum, a small treasure in Delta, Utah, in advice for volunteer tour guides on its website: "You will find that our friendly docents love to relate experiences from their early years in our Valley and even more interested in hearing about your more memorable life events."

Writers: Listening helps you pick up new language for everything you write because, of course, nothing about a museum is routine.

Lincoln Home calls the pre-tour list "Highlights," but it's really a fundamental outline to familiarize newcomers with what could be a strange experience:

- Formal Parlor
- Sitting Room
- Dining Room
- Guest Bedroom
- Abraham Lincoln's Bedroom
- Mary Lincoln's Bedroom
- Boys' Room
- Hired Girl/Hired Help's Room
- Kitchen

At the beginning of a tour, assure the group they can ask questions at any time. Find out early where viewers want more information. You'll also get people talking, and when they do, they learn more deeply. If the questions pile up, say so and ask the group to wait for the end.

St. Augustine Lighthouse & Maritime Museum understands the importance of connecting memories of the tour to the mission of the museum itself. The following description is a template for any museum tour, at the Welcome Connection to Museum.

On a Dark of the Moon Ghost Tour you not only hear spooky stories based on real history in the lighthouse at night, you also help us investigate our maritime past. Ghost Tours support both maritime archaeology and historic research discoveries at the Museum. Stepping up to shiver down your spine helps save our underwater heritage!

Every educator knows, learners have questions that have nothing to do with the topic and everything to do with location of bathrooms. So, throughout the in-person tour, be prepared to intersperse questions before they're asked:

- At the beginning of the tour, state the duration in minutes, the number of galleries to be visited, the availability of elevators and the location of exits (part of accessibility, some visitors get tired or claustrophobic).
- If there are no-touch, no-talk, no-pens, no-photo requirements, say so loud and clear at the beginning. Use the exact same wording during the tour, if you need to repeat.
- During the tour, depending on your location, ask if everyone can hear and see properly.
- During the tour, if there's a place to sit and observe an exhibit more carefully, give tourers the opportunity. Tell them in how many minutes the tour will commence.
- During the tour, point, then talk briefly; point, then ask a question and wait for responses; talk, then listen.

Delaware Art Museum builds one tour around visitor participation and their individual experience with the arts. "Participants will take a deep dive into viewing and discussing selected works of art from the Museum's collection. Each person is encouraged to bring their personal experiences and reflections to the conversation."

Commonly Asked Questions will soon become clear. These can be collected, assembled, and answered with Q-and-A text on your website; in a video; or accessed with a QR code posted along the tour route. This is especially useful if your tour covers a lot of territory, through a garden or multi-building campus.

THE TOUR WRAP-UP

Tours are like lectures and speeches: they're too informative to end with "that's all I have." Many amateur speakers end their talks with a whimper. Museum tour guides end their tours with a shout-out.

First, thank the tour group for their interest and good questions.

Then relate the tour to the museum that made it possible.

At the end of the tour, ask memory-making questions. Here's how Ranger Roger, Ranger Jorge, Ranger Susan, Ranger Brycen, Ranger Jasmine, and many more end one of the series of tours at the Lincoln Home:

- Was this room like your family room?
- How was it similar?
- How was it different?
- This video is first in a series.
- Every Saturday we'll add a new one.

If you've amassed questions that you can't answer on the spot, state clearly how the museum will provide answers to those questions. Use the exact same wording if you've already offered this at the beginning of the tour. Here are some suggestions:

- That's a good question that needs a more thorough answer than I can give. Please fill out a question card at the front desk, with your e-mail address, and our staff will get back to you within a few days.
- That's a great question. Use the QR code at the front desk to get a Question Answered form to fill out and e-mail to the museum while you're thinking about it.
- I don't know the answer. Maybe somebody in the group can help. (Honesty is smart. And it's flattering to everybody when the docent asks for help.)

After the tour, jot down notes of what worked, what questions were asked, and what objects or galleries were particularly interesting to members of the group.

Educators might want to keep a list of notes from docents next to the sign-in sheets, or for discussion at their next meeting.

Writers: although you take pride in writing to the clock, it's unproductive to cram your hour so full of presentation that there's no time for conversation. Leave time for a Q-and-A at the end of in-person or virtual programs; note the questions and comments for future guidance. Also, many viewers send links through Chat. At the end of the Zoom meeting, hosts may want to collect and edit these from the generated file and send the list of links to participants.

If you have to end a virtual tour smack on time, give a two-minute warning and a little time for questions before hitting "End Meeting."

NEIGHBORHOOD TOURS

Tours, by definition, make connections as they move around from place to place, showing different variations on a theme. Tours of the museum's surroundings form a different network of connections, expanding to the neighborhoods where people live, places where they work, and the history that all can share. Museums meet new audiences and enjoy the fruits of inclusiveness when they go outside.

Small museums grow larger when they partner with the neighborhood. Seasonal institutions extend their season. City museums acquire some nature.

The Pulitzer Foundation in St. Louis, by design, looks out toward its city. Now it has a park, named Park-Like, that is "a garden for people, plants, and wildlife . . . [where] walking paths and seating provide opportunities for gathering and reflection."

The Shaker Village at Pleasant Hill (Kentucky) schedules several tours to and about its neighbors. Its education component emphasizes how Shakers interacted with their wider community, the "worldly" industries of their town, and the American culture around them. It's an institution conscious of inclusiveness.

Writers at Shaker Village, Pleasant Hill, Kentucky, explain:

Learn about the journey of wool from the field to refined fiber . . . [and] the close connection between the society and the land.

Discover . . . one of the [Shaker] society's most significant contributions—the flat broom . . . the social, agricultural and economic importance of the broom making industry to the community.

Join . . . professional interpreters . . . explore the relationship between Shaker architecture and Shaker theology. Connect past to present . . . tour ongoing preservation projects . . . relate modern architecture to modern values.

Writers: learn about your museum's historic background and physical backdrop, as well as its mission, when setting out to write. Understand its place within the community so you can sincerely welcome diverse audiences to your diverse home. As Tenement Museum says: "Get to know the city by visiting historical sites and learning about the people and neighborhoods that made New York City what it is today."

Another view of museums' expansion is more personal: the perspective of the visitor who receives a "Friendly Hour tour." That is how Mariners' Museum and Park titles its personalized tours for guests, "including those with mobility, cognitive, or physical challenges, who prefer to experience the Museum in a quieter, less crowded environment with reduced sound and lighting."

WRAPPING UP THE TOUR

What was your favorite part of the tour? What memories will you take home with you? Twenty-four hours from now, what will you remember first? Let the visitors summarize the tour for you. It may start a whole new discussion, but if that's where the path leads, the tour was a success.

REFERENCES

"At Home with the Lincolns," Lincoln Home National Historic Site, https://youtu
    .be/zowmjL7zvTg [accessed 11-7-21]

"Current Tours," Visit, Tenement Museum, https://www.tenement.org/building -tours/ [accessed 11-18-21]

"Expand Your Visit," Visit, St. Augustine Lighthouse & Maritime Museum, https:// www.staugustinelighthouse.org/visit/expand-your-visit/ [accessed 10-17-21]

"Foods of the Lower East Side," Explore, Tenement Museum, https://www.tenement .org/watch-past-events/ [accessed 11-6-21]

"Friendly Hours," The Mariners' Museum and Park, https://marinersmuseum.org /friendly-hours/?mc_cid=c9d08a1f9a&mc_eid=f3b56802e0 [accessed 11-21-21]

"Get Wrecked! With Underwater Archaeologists," St. Augustine Lighthouse & Maritime Museum, https://youtu.be/f5OF8THZojw [accessed 11-6-21]

"Lincoln Home Tour," Plan Your Visit, National Park Service, https://www.nps.gov /liho/planyourvisit/lincoln-home-tour.htm [accessed 11-7-21]

"Looking and Reflecting Tour," Programs & Events, Delaware Art Museum, September 19, 2021, https://delart.org/event/looking-and-reflecting-tour/ [11-21-21]

"Member Event—FAQs of Tenement Life," Member Events, Virtual Tour, Visit, Tenement Museum, Nov 18, 2021, https://www.tenement.org/events/member -event-faqs-of-tenement-life/?mc_cid=6f2ac2c026&mc_eid=0521cfbea5 [accessed 10-28-21]

"Mission," Great Basin Museum, https://greatbasinmuseum.com/index.php/mis sion [accessed 10-27-21]

"Neighborhood Walking Tours," Tenement Museum, https://www.tenement.org /visit/neighborhood-walking-tours/?mc_cid=4a1975aee4&mc_eid=0521cfbea5 [accessed 11-11-21]

"Park-Like," Campus, Pulitzer Arts Foundation, https://pulitzerarts.org/location /park-like/ [accessed 11-21-21]

"Shoog McDaniel," Visiting Artist Programs, PAFA, November 10, 2021, https://www .pafa.org/school/student-life/organizations-programs/visiting-artist-program [accessed November 12, 2021]

"Stories of New York," Watch Past Events, Explore, Tenement Museum, https://www .tenement.org/watch-past-events/ [accessed 11-18-21]

"Tours," Learn, Nevada Art Museum, https://www.nevadaart.org/learn/tours/ [accessed 11-10-21]

"Tours," Museum of Contemporary Art Chicago, https://mcachicago.org/Visit/Tours [accessed 11-9-21]

"Tours and Itineraries," Visit, National Postal Museum, Smithsonian, https://postal museum.si.edu/tours-and-itineraries [accessed 11-7-21]

"Virtual: Reclaiming Black Spaces," About, Tenement Museum, https://www.tene ment.org/tour/virtual-reclaiming-black-spaces/ [accessed 10-6-21]

"Virtual Tour of Battleship New Jersey," Battleship New Jersey, https://www.youtube .com/watch?v=kDOFBGIf6Uo [accessed 11-6-21]

"What Animals Can I See During a Visit?" Visit, Milwaukee County Zoo, http:// www.milwaukeezoo.org/visit/animals/visitingtips.php [accessed 11-21-21]

"Wild Connections," Milwaukee County Zoo, http://www.milwaukeezoo.org /news/2021/wildconnections.php [accessed 11-7-21]

CHAPTER 10

Home Page as Entryway

Welcome to the museum. Please come in. Use either front door.

Every visitor enters through one of two doors: the website front door or the actual front door. They all go to the website first, and that's where this chapter goes, too. Here, the entryway is the home page.

Visitors approach museum websites at different stages of the visit-planning process. Some prospective visitors need background about your museum: what it has, what it displays, what it explores through programs. Other visitors have decided to visit and now need details like exhibits currently on view, and dates and times of programs. They all feel expectation—tinged with uncertainty—that greets people at every doorway. Your home page provides reassurance.

Welcome visitors well. This first impression counts. It suggests what lies ahead, puts newcomers at ease, and begins the experience that will hopefully last for years. For most visitors, the first step is a leap of faith.

As Portland (Maine) Art Museum said about its new doorway, after years of planning for it, "This major upgrade will forever change how visitors begin their journey exploring the PMA."

As Milwaukee County Zoo says, just look at these amazing, wonderful photos of all our incredibly interesting animals. Its home page lets pictures do the talking, its virtual entrance a photographic representation of what visitors can experience. Then it gives the details.

Writers: like all good hosts, you don't know the questions and curiosity of your incoming guests. However, you can word the home page welcome so it's an enticing and helpful nudge over the threshold. This chapter now examines museums across the country roll out the virtual carpet for guests.

VIRTUAL FRONT DOOR

Here are the elements, verbal and visual, that a home page should include:

- Visual—select the main image that best communicates the first impression.
- Explanatory narrative elucidating the home page visual.
- Architecture—A building says a lot about what's inside.
- Interior design—especially lobby, provides an actual glimpse of what lies ahead.
- View of the community—local pride.
- Objects and Exhibits—signify your collection strategy and interpretation creativity.
- Person—museums based on a person should introduce that notable right away.
- People—show newcomers the people already visiting the museum. It can be comforting.
- Grounds—the sky, landscapes, flora, and fauna that help define your institution.

At the arguably most comprehensive museum in American, the Metropolitan Museum of Art in New York, the home page shows a series of galleries, filled with paintings, statues, ancient artifacts, and crowds. Eighty blocks downtown at the Tenement Museum of the Lower East Side, a much more focused museum, the home page shows pictures of the museum's story: small tenement rooms where immigrant families lived.

Across the country in Seattle, the Wing Luke Museum of the Asian American Experience home page opens on a Lunar New Year illustration of 2022's Year of the Tiger. Farther across the Pacific Ocean, in Honolulu, Harbor National Memorial Hawaii greets website viewers with a view from the mooring of USS *Arizona*.

Writers: each of these wonderful museums is well worth a visit. You can inform the decision with words that capture the intent of the visuals on the home page.

EXPLANATORY NARRATIVE

Captions and short paragraphs accompany photographs, illustrations, and graphics on a home page. They're concise. They identify the subject of the visual. They summarize, rather than tell a whole story.

This is part of a short introduction to a photo of a nineteenth-century farm building. It's impossible to show 3,000 acres, but words can capsulize the view: "Shaker Village of Pleasant Hill is a landmark destination that shares 3,000 acres of discovery in the spirit of the Kentucky Shakers. Home to the third largest Shaker community in the United States between 1805 and 1910 . . ."

The home page, of the Barnes Museum's botanic garden, shows abundant greenery, but leaves one wondering where it all fits in the renowned Barnes painting collection.

"If Dr. Albert Barnes expressed his passion through art appreciation, his wife Laura expressed hers through the cultivation of beautiful plants and the establishment of the . . . horticulture school that she founded in 1940."

The home page of the Mitchell Prehistoric Indian Village Museum shows the museum and photos of a mud house and skeletons. Interesting, but the headline tells a one-of a-kind story:

"Come Visit the Only Archaeological Site in South Dakota that Is Open to the Public."

Writers: the photos alone would not have told prospective visitors what these museums are, specifically:

- Restored village
- Botanic garden and university horticulture program
- Native American archaeological site

Here's a five-word heading that promises a multitude of narratives: "Welcome to the Wild West" is the heading on the home page of the Buffalo Bill Center of the West, in Cody, Wyoming. There's a loop of photos showing Buffalo Bill, Western scenery, exhibits in the museum, tepees, totems, and bleached skulls. There is no way to condense what else transpires in this five-museum complex. It's a skillful welcome for everyone who approaches.

New Bedford Whaling Museum horizontally scrolls images of whales, water, and ships and for each there's a paragraph of narrative, such as: "An exhibition dedicated to the science and behavior of whales, their cultural impact, the current threats to their survival, and empowering all to support conservation efforts." It neatly explains the exhibits and the vision of the museum.

Seattle's Wing Luke Museum of the Asian-Pacific Experience says the front door is the neighborhood. "When The Wing moved into its current home, it intentionally left out a café, a feature common in most museums. Why? We wanted visitors to eat at nearby restaurants. To support and revitalize the Chinatown-International District, The Wing is intentional in its strategies for neighborhood engagement."

Writers: when you take the space to narrate a longer story, craft one engaging sentence that clearly connects the visual to the museum.

WILKOMMEN, BIENVENUE, BIENVENIDO, ҚОШ КЕЛДІҢІЗ

In 2019 the United States said "welcome" to seventy-nine million visitors from foreign countries. In 2020, there were nineteen million. The simple, one-phrase welcome is an important door opener. With so many different cultures speaking so many languages and dialects, one can only imagine the way they will interpret a home page visual.

Writers can facilitate their translations in these ways:

- Nouns—one of the first things we learn in a new language
- Simple verbs—hold the tenses
- Sentences that describe what is pictured
- Scrupulous attention to the right word—a house is not a home, cabin, or cottage
- Short sentences
- Cautious use of punctuation
- Avoidance of trying to explain the culture

ARCHITECTURE

Considering the many museums that star in American movies, the attraction of architecture becomes apparent. Only in America could a punchy prize fighter run up the steps to a Greek Temple and, far from making an offering to the gods, make the fame of Philadelphia Museum of Art Museum.

Architecture holds the dreams and glory, as well as the exhibits and visitors, of all museums, and good communicators know it.

Harvey B. Gantt Center for African American Arts and Culture talks about how a building communicates in describing a major exhibition of works by architect Phil Freelon:

> The exhibition examines Freelon's work . . . including museums, libraries, cultural centers, and public parks . . . with a focus on projects that foreground African American communities and identities. Freelon often noted that architecture should be more than a container, that it should help tell the story of, and be integral to, the content of these public institutions.

As the Pulitzer Foundation of the Arts says of its renowned architecture: "Presenting contemporary and historic art in dialogue with its celebrated Tadao Ando building, the exhibitions and programs inspire new ideas and perspectives."

Marlon Blackwell, architect for Crystal Bridges Museum of American History in Bentonville, Arkansas, says his discipline is "an extended threshold to the Crystal Bridges Campus."

He was speaking of the new parking garage, and threshold is an apt word. Most visitors to Crystal Bridges drive a fair distance to get there, and the arrival is sweet. When one thinks about it, the car park becomes more significant. So the first threshold is the garage, as it is for many regional museums.

LOBBY

Lobbies create a more formal welcome. It's where visitors see the first details of a visit.

The Crystal Bridges home page shows a large lobby and some people. It looks friendly in uncrowdedness. The page lists the current and coming exhibitions, programs, and events.

The lobby of the Newark Museum of Art first appears on the Plan Your Visit page. Again, it's the place to reconnoiter, and one can see the informative signs above the information counter, get a sense of the place and the other visitors entering. It's welcoming for new visitors to get a preview of their coming experience.

Writers: write captions to lobby photos that supply one more piece of information for wondering visitors. Get the facts and say something like:

- Our lobby Information Desk staff can answer any questions you have.
- Visitors stop at the Front Desk for their free visitor badges.
- Ask at the front desk for information on special exhibitions, talks, and education programs.

"Lobbies for brainstorming" is a provocative idea put forth by architecture reviewer Michael Lewis that includes the scholarly and other levels of curious people who visit museums. In reviewing the newly opened Oklahoma Contemporary Arts Center, designed by Rand Elliott, he sees the real entrance as the lobby where one "steps into a cheerfully welcoming space . . . that offers a range of attractions: a café, a gift shop, and a cozy 'creative lounge' with a full art library so that freshly arrived visitors can immediately start brainstorming."

Don't underestimate the reassurance of a gift shop and café. Shopping is universally familiar. Places to eat, especially for families with children, are essential.

GOOD NEIGHBOR MUSEUM—WINDOW ON THE COMMUNITY

Take another look at the mighty Met. It's massive, stretching for blocks, and it's easy to find. It's also part of an elite Manhattan neighborhood,

Figure 10.1.   For today's generation, the entryway might be the feature image at the top of a museum's home page.
Jupiterimages/ PHOTOS.com via Getty images

near a famous park, and on its front steps one always sees people just sitting and talking, enjoying the comfort of the museum. For a famous place, it sure is neighborly.

The Met home page cuts from one interior shot to another, each a quick view of another part of its collection. There are people in each shot, just a few. The message delivered centers on the splendid collection, one closely enjoyed by real people, not faceless crowds.

The neighborhood of the Tenement Museum is more than miles away. Real tenements resided here, and it's still a commercial place of less-than-grand sidewalks. The home page privileges this environment in photos of the original tenement apartments and the current streets. It takes pride in the neighborhood in which New York immigrants worked and prospered, fire-escape-clad buildings, and all. It's a different story.

Writers: it's your responsibility to bring visitors to the entrance of a museum, because that's where the visit was always meant to start. Too often a website home page plunks a visitor inside a gallery, or in front of an artifact, or—horrors!—faced with a list of facts and details "About" the "Visit." Your words can show visitors the entrance, a more welcoming entry.

Two very different museums take different kinds of pride in their place in the neighborhood. The Kimbell Art Museum in Ft. Worth, Texas, credits a renowned architect as well as his building's contribution to the community. "Now on view in the world-renowned Louis I. Kahn Building, works from our African, Asian, Ancient American, and European collections appear in thoughtful dialogue." The Farm House Museum, "nestled in the center of Iowa State University," shows its 150-year-old house, on a small-town street, and tells how it "functioned as living quarters for various Iowa State deans, professors, farmhands and students . . . shaping a nationally recognized land-grant university."

Both museums are historic, and they rightly say so at the beginning.

A view of the neighborhood through its windows is equally important as museums situate themselves in their communities. Many museums now showcase their vistas as appreciation of being part of the neighborhood.

Writers: if your museum overlooks a scenic element of its geography, put that mention as close to the home page as possible. The New Bedford Whaling Museum says, with Yankee understatement, that it has "breathtaking views of the waterfront and . . . New Bedford Harbor."

It also bears an unbeatable postal address: "18 Johnny Cake Hill." That's worth a page of its own!

PERSON

When you've got a famous name, lucky you. Most of your writing is done for you. Humility works well here because the name tells the story.

America's National Churchill Museum, in Fulton, Missouri, is where Winston Churchill gave his "Iron Curtain Speech." The home page shows clips of the most famous face of World War II, in some of Churchill's finest hours. The museum balances them by showing a photo of the Westminster College Gymnasium; it was the only venue large enough to handle the crowd and the broadcast in which the master phrasemaker coined his immemorial phrase.

Mark Twain House, in Hartford, Connecticut, features a line drawing of the author in its logo in the upper left corner. The camera moves all around the many wings and of the sprawling house. So the virtual visitor sees the famous rumpled visage of Mark Twain, and also his rather unusual house. The headline on the home page reads: "A house with a heart and a soul."

SIGNIFICANT OBJECT OR EXHIBIT

Details signify what a museum is famous for and, importantly, what it stands for. The Guggenheim in New York has its spiraling ramp and galleries

Figure 10.2.   The Lions have welcomed visitors to the Art Institute of Chicago for generations.
Photo Margot Wallace

that make for an eye-stopping exterior; the ramp takes visitors on a defined path as they work their way from top to bottom through an exhibition. The Mark Twain Boyhood Home Museum has a section of Tom Sawyer's white painted picket fence. It recalls Twain's books, of course, and captures familiar experiences. Petersen Automotive Museum roars into view on Wilshire Boulevard in Los Angeles as a multi-story automobile chassis wrapped in whooshing speed lines of stainless steel. The Petersen architecture can be seen a block away. It says "automotive" in all its engineering glory.

It's amazing how many museums are hidden in plain sight. Visitors to a city will often ask directions to the museum, only to learn they're standing in front of it. That's humorous, but interested visitors need cosseting, and a significant feature can help them find the front door.

That significant feature could be a sign or a symbol, large enough to be seen from the sidewalk, or at the sidewalk.

At the front of the small Winnetka Historical Society museum, a traditional house in suburban Chicago, the significant identification is a young trail marker tree, bent from its sapling days in the manner of Illinois Native Americans who used bent trees as signposts through the woods. The museum looks like many houses on its quiet street, and would be easy to miss. The tree identifies not just the location, but the heritage that informs the museum's mission.

Writers: when the exhibitions are visually exciting, turn that advantage into a restatement of your mission. Mission statements sound better when they're illustrated.

Nelson-Atkins in Kansas City (Missouri) exhibits its eighteen-foot-tall Claes Oldenburg and Coosje Van Brugge shuttlecock out on the lawn, in clear view of its original, neoclassical-style building. Although a contemporary wing has been added, nothing says comprehensive museum better than the juxtaposition of sports equipment and pillars—so much so that the shuttlecock is part of the logo. The mission statement begins: "The Nelson-Atkins Museum of Art invites all people to explore the art in its care, and through its broad collection, the depths and complexities of human experiences."

The home page of Mitchell Prehistoric Indian Village Museum, in Mitchell, South Dakota, shows a traditional museum building on its home page, but the heart of the museum is an actual dig, and the headline is what welcomes visitors through the door: "Come visit the only archaeological site in South Dakota that is open to the public."

The statement of mission follows, and one wants to read it:

To promote an understanding of the first people to inhabit in this region by developing, preserving and exhibiting a significant collection and archaeological site; by taking a leadership role in research and scholarship; by engaging and providing access for audiences from all nations; and by delivering innovative programs of benefit to the general public and community.

The Mitchell's page is an invitation to curiosity, accessibility to all nations, and an acknowledgment of forgotten people: let's go in!

PEOPLE

Showing real visitors in a photo on the home page is reassuring. For newcomers, and people intimidated by places far from home, it helps if the first thing they see on the walk to the front-door is people like them. Sometimes too many real people are nightmare-making.

At big, popular destinations, there may be long lines to even reach the entrance. Often, visitors are late for their timed entry. Some hopeful visitors take a chance on the wait list. How a museum manages disappointment and delay is part of the front-door protocol. A little information is welcome.

Many museums post a sign that lets waiters know how long the wait will be; knowledge soothes the restless soul. But why wait until the visitor gets to the real entrance?

At the Pearl Harbor National Memorial in Honolulu, the website shows a Ranger talking to a visitor, and that individual help, especially in a place where thousands congregate, is a wonderful front-door welcome.

The home page makes visiting more welcoming with planning hacks like:

Know Where to Go: Arizona Memorial Place Honolulu, HI 96818. Be sure to use this address. A search for "Pearl Harbor" on Google Maps will take you to the active military base, *not* the Pearl Harbor Visitor Center.

Have a back-up plan. Did you miss your scheduled program time? . . . There are a lot of other opportunities available . . . watch the 23 minute park film on the open air lanai . . . participate in the Pacific Historic Parks managed Audio Tour, or Virtual Reality Center, become a Jr Ranger (sold in the bookstore) . . ."

Recreate Responsibly: Know your limits. . . . Waits for standby space available seating is 1–3 hours long. You must physically be in line and wait your turn, which can be a challenge in the heat and humidity . . .

Be Kind: Let's remember, we are all a community. . . . Be respectful of the resource, fellow visitors, the Volunteers, and Park Rangers assigned to assist you. Pearl Harbor National Memorial tells the story of service and sacrifice. As the final resting place for over 900 sailors and Marines, using your cell phone for talking and texting while onboard the USS *Arizona* Memorial is not appropriate.

Writers: these are words of wisdom for a museum of any size or line length.

SURROUNDINGS AND GROUNDS

New visitors, especially those unfamiliar with museums, language, expectations, and cost, want to know the setting. It's like the first day of school, with so much out there and so few guideposts for the journey. Writers can help write the guide.

Doors are meant to be opened.

New museums and their architects stress the connection between the building and the neighborhood. More precisely, the portal connects the building with people. Queens Museum says it well: "A new ceremonial entry, visible from the adjacent Grand Central Parkway, beckons visitors to the site and serves as a gateway to the entire park beyond."

And if your museum is in an urban, high-rise setting, follow the example of the Museum of Contemporary Art Chicago and show the neighborhood farmers' market. A neighborhood community hosts a farmers' market on the MCA plaza once a week from June through October.

Walking trails, cruising rivers, botanic ponds, historic trees, heritage plants and ocean views: museums with nature as their front door have a distinct language to work with. It's the writer's challenge to use specific terminology correctly and often. Don't say "tree" when your front door is a sugar maple or banyan. Better yet, remind readers if the tree is historic, famous, or as old as the indigenous people on whose land it's rooted. Shaker Village of Pleasant Hill says: "Shaker Village is reconnecting its campus to inspire a new community of adventurers . . . just like Shaker farms were hubs of agricultural ingenuity, The Historic Centre, The Farm and The Preserve are centers of exploration—jumping-off points for trailblazing experiences." When welcoming prospective visitors—of all kinds—via your website, this is a good place to highlight environmental enterprises as has Shaker Village. "Exemplifying the Shaker legacy of concerned care for the land, Shaker Village has converted 1,000 acres of unproductive pasture land to native grasses and wildflowers." Note the connection to Shaker legacy, the mission of the institution that gives visitors another reason to turn a plan into a decision to visit.

E-MAIL WELCOMES

Not all visitors enter in person from the plaza or virtually through the home page. For many, the welcoming takes place via an e-mail, most likely because prospective visitors have already expressed interest in a visit. Call it a prospective welcome.

As Petersen Automotive Museum explains in the small print section at the bottom of all e-mails, the communication is sent "to remain relevant" to its visitors with news and updates.

Writers: that's a thoughtful comment, akin to a welcome. It shows appreciation for the recipient's past involvement.

Try to convert every involvement into a repeat visit. Reach out to attendees at a ticketed event and send an e-mail thank-you note as the Barnes Foundation did: "Thank you for visiting. Come back soon!" The e-mail is headed by a column-wide reproduction of a work from the museum's collection: Paul Cezanne, *A Table Corner*, c. 1895. It's a different level of welcome, a welcome back.

A reopening is time to remind past visitors of why they enjoyed the museum in the past, and how wonderful the experience will be in the future. Jump right in with the next item on the calendar. The Driehaus Museum e-mail announcement said: "We're Reopening. A Visit From Jane Addams, & Pullman Porters." What followed is a warm, welcoming photo of the museum's grand staircase, and all the details visitors expect from an active museum.

SUMMARY

Museums' home page entryways are asked to do a lot. They welcome, yes. They also function rather like the lobby in explaining and smoothing the way at the beginning of a museum visit. Writers: think in triplicate: plan a welcome as would a museum director, a curator, and an educator; then articulate like a writer. Conveying a physical, three-dimensional presence in words on a two-dimensional screen or page is a big endeavor, and a little easier when you remember that virtually every visual needs some words of explanation:

- Captions, wherever the building's photo or an illustration is shown.
- Reference to the grounds, landscaping, garden, a beautiful tree or pond.
- Mention of interior architectural detail. Talk up the effort that made this a habitation rather than a memorial.
- Articles on the building, the main building, conference or auditorium annexes, labs, storage.
- Maps.
- Building's physical location in the broader community.
- Building projects. That includes new research spaces, meeting rooms, air flow, storage, and archive features. New construction demonstrates a welcome in the future.

P.S.

The final word on welcoming visitors comes at the end of the visit: "Thank you for visiting and come back soon." Give this short script to every:

- staffer at the front desk
- volunteer in a gallery
- sales associate at the store
- usher with the bar code counter

Edit the script slightly for your website: "Thanks for visiting our website. We look forward to seeing you."

REFERENCES

"About," Musical Instrument Museum, https://mim.org [accessed 12-29-21]
"America's National Churchill Museum," https://www.nationalchurchillmuseum.org/ [accessed 1-26-22
"The Barnes Arboretum at St. Joseph's University," About Us, St. Joseph's University, https://www.sju.edu/barnesarboretum/about-barnes-arboretum [accessed 12-14-21]
"Chinatown-International District," About, Wing Luke Museum of the Asian Pacific American Experience, http://www.wingluke.org/about-us/ [accessed 1-9-22]
"Collections in Conversation," Kimbell Art Museum, https://kimbellart.org/ [accessed 1-29-22]
"Come Visit the Only Archaeological Site in South Dakota that is Open to the Public," Mitchell Prehistoric Indian Village Museum, https://www.mitchellindianvillage.org/ [accessed 1-24-22]
"Container / Contained: Phil Freelon–Design Strategies for Telling African American Stories," October 29, 2021–January 27, 2022, https://ncartmuseum.org/exhibition/container-contained-phil-freelon-design-strategies-for-telling-african-american-stories/ [accessed 10-7-21]
"Crystal Bridges Announces an Outdoor Play Space and New Parking Deck, Coming Soon," Blog, October 8, 2020, https://crystalbridges.org/blog/crystal-bridges-announces-an-outdoor-play-space-and-new-parking-deck-coming-soon/ [accessed 9-23-21]
"Discovery Starts Here," Shaker Village at Pleasant Hill, https://shakervillageky.org [accessed 1-24-22]
"eMuseum," Petersen Automotive Museum, pam@petersen.org/ [accessed 12-17-21]
"Farmer's Market 2021," Museum of Contemporary Art Chicago, https://mcachicago.org/Calendar/2021/06/Farmers-Market-2021 [accessed 1-9-22]
"Farmhouse Museum," Visit, https://www.museums.iastate.edu/visit/farm-house-museum [accessed 12-28-21]
https://mailchi.mp/ganttcenter/container-contained-opening-celebration-invite?e=b9dc85c20f [accessed 1-24-22]
"Land Conservation," About Us, Shaker Village, https://shakervillageky.org/land-conservation/ [accessed 10-26-21]

Lewis, Michael J. , "Folding Light in Oklahoma City," Art Review, *Wall Street Journal*, January 26, 2022, https://www.wsj.com/articles/oklahoma-city-arts-center
-rand-elliott-jeremiah-davis-anodized-aluminum-fins-11643236527?reflink
=share_mobilewebshare [accessed 1-26-22]

"Mark Twain House," https://marktwainhouse.org [accessed 1-28-22]

"Milwaukee County Zoo, http://www.milwaukeezoo.org [accessed 1-25-22]

"Mitchell Prehistoric Indian Village Museum Video," https://youtu.be/GR8Qpk8
n2Ho [accessed 12-4-21]

Nebehay, Stephanie, "International Tourism Not Seen Rebounding until 2023—UN
Report," Reuters, Business, Reuters, June 30, 2021, https://www.reuters.com/business
/international-tourism-not-seen-rebounding-until-2023-un-report-2021-06-30/

"Nelson-Atkins Museum of Art," https://art.nelson-atkins.org/objects/16574 [accessed 1-28-22]

"New Bedford Whaling Museum," https://www.whalingmuseum.org [accessed
1-27-22]

"Newsletter," February 18, 2021, Driehaus Museum, info@driehausmuseum.org
[accessed 12-27-21]

"Opening the Doors to a More Accessible PMA," https://www.portlandmuseum
.org/magazine/pma-update-2022 [accessed 12-22-21]

"Our Mission," About, Nelson-Atkins Museum of Art, https://nelson-atkins.org
/about/#our-mission [accessed 1-29-22]

"Overview," About, Pulitzer Arts Foundation, https://pulitzerarts.org/about/over
view/ [accessed 1-27-22]

"Peek Inside Some of Our Most Iconic Cars," e-mail, December 17, 2021, Petersen
Automotive Museum, pam@petersen.org/ [accessed 12-17-21]

"Plan like a Park Ranger," Pearl Harbor National Memorial Hawaii, National Park
Service, https://www.nps.gov/perl/planyourvisit/plan-like-a-park-ranger.htm [accessed 12-23-21]

"Plan Your Visit," Newark Museum of Art, https://www.newarkmuseumart.org/visit
[accessed 1-25-22]

"Queens Museum Today," About, Queens Museum, https://queensmuseum.org
/queens-museum-today [accessed 10-1-21]

"The Ringling," https://www.ringling.org [accessed 1-24-22]

"6060 Wilshire Boulevard," Petersen Automotive Museum, February 1, 2021,
https://www.petersen.org/blog/6060-wilshire-blvd/ [accessed 1-28-22]

"Thank You for Visiting," e-mail, August 7, 2021, The Barnes Foundation, http://links
.mail3.spopessentials3.com/servlet/MailView?ms=NDUyMzYwMDUS1&r=MTI
3OTY1MjIwMzQ1NgS2&j=MjA2MTYwMjA5NQS2&mt=2&rj=MjA2MTM5NDY
yMwS2&rt=0 [accessed 12-17-21]

"Three Thousand Acres of Discovery," Explore, Shaker Village of Pleasant Hill,
https://shakervillageky.org [accessed 1-27-22]

"Trail Marker Trees—What's Old Is New," *Gazette*, Winnetka Historical Society,
Spring 2010 (Updated 9-2020), https://www.winnetkahistory.org/gazette/trail
-marker-trees-whats-old-is-new/ [accessed 1-28-22]

"Venue Rentals, About, New Bedford Whaling Museum, https://www.whalingmu
seum.org/about/venue-rentals/ [accessed 1-18-22]

"Welcome," Crystal Bridges Museum of American Art, https://crystalbridges.org
[accessed 1-28-22]

"Welcome to the Wild West!" https://centerofthewest.org [accessed 1-24-22]

CHAPTER 11

Videos

Videos play everywhere, and museum websites, newsletters, and e-mail are livelier for them. Videos are a moving, engaging, people-centered option. They draw viewers in, keep them focused, and give more information per minute than text and pictures can. They don't substitute for photos, maps, or charts, but they often enhance them.

The uses for videos are unlimited, and the structure varies depending on each individual museum's objective. The first rule applies to all museums: know why you want a video in the first place. This chapter surveys the other parts of the framework and how different museums have fleshed them out.

- Who, What, Why—What is the point of this video? Who is the authority? Why does it matter? Or as one college professor says to every brilliant idea: "What's the So What?"
- Motion—the most obvious advantage a video has over text
- The plot, storyline, and theme
- Length
- Objects to be shown
- Close-ups and overheads—all the places a camera can go
- Setting—inside or outside, in the museum or elsewhere
- Presenters
- Actors, historic interpreters
- Demonstration
- Opening frame
- Closed captioning
- Serialization

WHO, WHAT, WHY

Why are we telling this story? We're taking eight-plus minutes. What's the point that carries through from beginning to end?

The Owens Thomas House, in Savannah, houses remarkably intact slave quarters below-stairs and shows a different video each day about enslaved people's lives in antebellum Savannah. The point: enslaved people who worked in city houses lived a different and under-explored life from field slaves on cotton plantations whose stories have been told for centuries; the former also worked an arduous day that required sophisticated skills. And they were on call 24/7.

Battleship New Jersey Museum and Memorial in Camden, New Jersey, wants to tell about the big World War II ship to students, military, veterans, and visitors from all walks—and sails—of life. The virtual tour tells by showing: all the parts of the ship, what they do, and why they matter.

The Metropolitan Museum of Art in New York wants to show a selection of its vast galleries to give an idea of its encyclopedic collection. It also wants to bring people into the picture, to humanize the legend.

St. Augustine Lighthouse & Museum shows a lot of its research, to underscore its ongoing exploration of maritime history and bring to the surface the significance of the seas to civilizations' growth.

The Wing Luke Museum of the Asian American Experience, in Seattle, shows the people whose stories form the mission of the museum. The Tenement Museum in New York shows stories of immigrants through the apartments in the tenement building where they lived.

Vesterheim, the National Norwegian-American Museum & Folk Art School, in Decorah, Iowa, demonstrates the utilitarian products crafted in the manner of early Norse people by featuring artisans working in their work spaces.

These and more museums run videos that preview—only in text, sorry!—on the following pages of this chapter.

MOTION

The most obvious advantage in a video is motion, movement from one scene or object in a museum to another.

Wing Luke Museum of the Asian American Experience communicates the extent of its physical building with a video that pans and moves from lobby to galleries to close-ups of objects.

The Metropolitan Museum of Art utilizes motion to wander through its galleries, survey its exhibits, and move among the spectrum of its visitors. There's immense diversity for this museum to cover, and video's movement helps.

Showing off the Burke Private Events capabilities results in a sweeping video up and down stairs, around corners, into nooks, and outside through windows to show what visitors can experience when they attend an event at the museum. Video's creativity says more about the value of a venue than text ever could.

PLOT, STORY LINE, THEME

Plotting a video and giving it a story line tells those involved where to focus and what to avoid. The triple disasters for a video are being over budget, boring, and useless. A proven way to produce a usable video is to tell a cohesive narrative. Writers: use these phrases as starting points for a plot:

- This story is about . . .
- It follows the museum (or its objects, professionals, galleries, exhibitions, events) through a certain time . . .
- The main characters are . . .
- The story is important to the viewer or listeners because . . .
- The parts of the museum we'll spend extra time with are . . .

The Battleship New Jersey Museum and Memorial has an excellent video that's about a big battleship. A museum this mammoth is too big for a visitor to see on one actual visit, but the video is important to learning the totality of a battleship. The main character in this video is a curator, an expert, who points out, by name, naval objects that will probably be new to most people. The various rooms and guns and navigational tools help visitors understand how sailors lived and worked and their role in a wartime ship.

Another video, a series, comes from the Franklin Institute in Philadelphia, and features an astronomer in dialogue with a social media creator about the sky beyond the museum. The through line is things we don't know about the universe, small but fundamental facts told in short, easily digestible episodes. The video format excels at delivering knowledge a lesson at a time, in this case in a series of episodes.

Canadian War Museum tells its story, by any reckoning a long and, for foreign visitors, little-known one, through a video of Canada's involvement in World War II, in honor of the seventy-fifth anniversary of Victory in Europe. The museum edits together narrated scenes of wartime, and only video can do justice to both a war and a museum. The director of the museum narrates on camera: "now more than ever it's important to reflect on Canada's commitment to that conflict." A reason for the video, a story, an authoritative narrator, and unbeatable action—this is an ideal video for a museum. The narrator ends the video with: "We need also to remember that history does not just exist. It must be nurtured. It must be cultivated. It must be taught. If not it will wither away."

Writers: yours is a significant job at the beginning and end of a video. In the Canadian War Museum video, the narrator establishes the goals of the museum at the beginning, and summarizes them at the end, while the descriptions throughout describe the actions of war that are shown.

At Whitney Plantation, in Wallace, Louisiana, an hour from New Orleans, the mission is unusual: to show the lives of enslaved people who worked inside plantation buildings.

The narrator walks to the door of a shotgun style of building and points to it: "The people who built these houses were African descendants and they were building what they were familiar with." With the point-and-tell advantage of video, an authentic story of enslaved people on Whitney Plantation comes alive. First you see a structure, and then you hear the story behind it. It's not a once-upon-a-time story, but history told as a series of facts, solid facts epitomized by the solid buildings. Writers: this is a good format to follow for telling many stories.

LENGTH

How long should a video be? One hour is too long; yawn! Two minutes is not too short. It's surprising how much can be accomplished in a few minutes. Videos show more than an announcer can say, and that's a plus for learning, prompting the viewer to fill in with their own imagination. Writers: be quiet for a few moments and let the pictures do the talking. There is no rule for a video's running time except this: when you've come to the end of the story, stop talking. It also helps to know how many words constitute one minute. For example, read this paragraph and you'll find it lasts . . . thirty-nine seconds.

Sometimes a museum can sneak in a short video reminder that's more powerful than words. Why say "hurry, exhibition ends soon!" when you can add this message with video: "Here's what you'll miss if you don't!" That's what Blanton Museum of Art, University of Texas, Austin, did with an eight-second video sent in an e-mail reminder of the closing of the Helen Frankenthaler exhibition. No time in this video for more than one close-up of Frankenthaler's works, but one sees enough to be tempted to hurry and see it.

Serialization adds to the length of a video, in a good way. In Vesterheim's "Folk Art in Place" series, each video is about eight minutes, which turns out to be just perfect to listen and watch the blacksmith describe how his forge operates. If the viewer wishes there were more on this or similar subjects, there's the next episode in the series.

OBJECTS

Museums will never adequately define the entirety of their collection. Paintings or fossils, sculpture or period furniture, farm tools or dolphins, stars or sensory gardens: name it. You can name your collection according to your collection philosophy, but only videos can pinpoint individual aspects and place them in context with the whole.

The conservation lab at St. Augustine Lighthouse & Museum invites us into the workspace of a conservationist who shows an artifact from a shipwreck. As he talks about it, the maritime world appears and viewers/listeners understand the scope of this lighthouse and museum. "Our divers first saw this . . . on the surface of the sand . . . in 2010 . . . when they returned a year later it had almost completely corroded." Objects and the people who work with them both have a story and video tells it vividly.

Another object, also maritime but much bigger and newer, is the conning tower of a flagship. A curator at Battleship New Jersey, in Camden, New Jersey, walks us through the ship on a video tour and explains: "When you add three hundred tons of armor for the third level of the tower for the admiral, you have to lose that weight and lose two guns." He puts the parts of the battleship in perspective with the whole ship and with history. That's what museums do, and videos, as they investigate the metal pathway through the ship to indicate the broader picture.

CLOSE-UPS

When the camera moves close up on an object, it focuses the eye and positions viewers to think about what's being seen. It fosters learning, rather than teaching.

At the saddle shop of the Buffalo Bill Center of the West, a video opens on an intricate embossed design being polished. Only later does the voice-over narrator reveal that it's a saddle. The image makes one wonder and the sound makes one watch and listen as the narrator says: "Let's listen to some of the intricacies of building these beautiful leatherworks."

Buffalo Bill Center of the West collects and interprets many objects within its five-museum complex; like all museums, it can display only a small fraction. Videos expose many more to view, with the added advantage of a presenter to provide a one-on-one tour.

Vesterheim Museum of the Norwegian Experience casts local artisans to explain Norwegian crafted works. Each video is about eight minutes, which turns out to be perfect to hear, for example, a blacksmith at a forge show a trident spear with a close-up look at the three tines. The blacksmith at Goose Prairie Forge also tells the history of the object: "Based on one found in the

Figure 11.1. **Videos can be found wherever there's writing: website, blogs, e-newsletters, gallery labels, and virtual classes. Anything can be screened with a scan code.**
hobo_018/ E+ via Getty Images

northern part of Norway from the Viking Age and it was used to spear eels
. . . probably small fish and eels formed a good portion of the diet." Then
the blacksmith moves to an easel with a drawing of how a point is forged:
"and then I'm going to . . . [get] a short but sharp point on the end and then
I'm going to double it back." Even before the video moves over to the anvil
to show how this tool is forged, the two close looks at those barbed points
and the audio description of eels on the end of them provides an image of
the Norwegian experience that mere text under a photo could never achieve.

Another episode in "Folk Art in Place" features a wood carver in his
shop, an accomplished artisan who carves wood decorations and paints
the incised parts. The detail of the workmanship and tools, not to mention
the finished work, are more beautiful when seen extremely close up. The
advantage of an on-screen presenter, who speaks with pride of knowledge,
gives voice to the use of what he's crafting: "Pigment with powdered tree
bark . . . hundreds of years ago . . . utilitarian uses . . . spoons, cups, bowls .
. . the people were very poor and they didn't have a lot of stuff and this way
they could decorate their objects and make them look nice."

Milwaukee County Zoo videos appear throughout its newsletters and
website. The animals fascinate, of course, and the zoo knows when to let its
fur, fin, and feather collection speak for itself. A three-minute video shows
a great ape connoisseur picking up a scrap of straw, tasting it, and flinging

it away dismissively. Then the picky eater picks up another tidbit, fingers it around and around, and daintily nibbles at it. You can see adroitness. You watch a gorilla's alertness as it shifts its gaze through the corners of its eyes.

Writers: when you have great video, you don't have to say much except, "What are you learning here about gorillas?" And then sit back with satisfaction because you can expect an answer.

OVERHEAD SHOTS

At the opposite end of the spectrum from close-up is the overhead shot. The first zeroes in on a detail. The overhead sweeps the viewer in to await the details.

In movies, on all formats, the overhead shots of cities, towns, and landscapes signal inside information to come; overheads are almost mysterious, certainly very promising.

The video on the home page of the Mark Twain House & Museum in Hartford, Connecticut, hovers over the many-gabled rooftop of a dark and endlessly large house. It implies many stories inside. The text says: "A House with a Heart and a Soul."

A more urban example of the overhead establishing shot stretches the suspense longer, moving above and around many towering buildings, looking down on a network of city streets. The viewer understands that momentous things will happen at ground level. Finally the viewer sees, at ground level, above a modern building entrance: "Rhode Island School of Design." If the viewer is looking for design colleges, this is the only headline needed. RISD, in Providence, Rhode Island, is well known.

Writers: if you don't have a drum roll to introduce your museum, start by describing what's included in the wide swath of an overhead. Or any long shot, for that matter. The impressiveness of the camera work also encompasses the museum. Some impressive starting words:

Inside these walls are . . .
At the end of the driveway lies . . .
In Providence there's a special place where . . .

DEMONSTRATION

Close-ups are integral to demonstrations of museum conservation. At the Conservation Lab at the Smithsonian American Art Museum you can see what the conservator working on a nineteenth-century painting means when she says: "and that would account for the buckling of the paint layer;

the cracking is profound and you can see the burlap fabric that it's printed on is deteriorated, fraying."

The words are as precise as the tools and procedures. These are details the viewer in the gallery would never see. Writers: that's a point worth making.

Detail by detail, demonstrations show you the parts and how they interact. The demonstration format is rather talky. The person showing you details of how something works is a conversational person.

St. Augustine Lighthouse & Museum presents a series of videos on the museum's ongoing conservation of shipwreck treasures and exhibition preparation. Behind the scenes, activities of widely different departments focus on what only a video can uncover. "And then we started the process of removing the all the unwanted material . . . the accretion of sand and shells and sediment that's hardened over hundreds of years . . . and I used an aircraft's pneumatic chisel that shaped like a pencil." The viewer sees corroded surfaces of nested copper cauldrons and they also hear what conservators think about their work: "[It's] meaningful for me because it's something that would have been used every day."

Conservation is not restricted to large museums. All museums support the tenets of conserving; visitors are interested in the science involved in art and history. When you invest in videos of your conservation efforts, the benefit is not just the end result; the process is preserved, too. All museums have processes that are worth documenting.

SETTING

At Whitney Plantation, the enslaved peoples' quarters tell the story. They are small; the enslaved people lived indoors, but meanly. Their "homes" are connected, side by side, with a long porch extending from end to end. The guide points out that it allowed for stepping out one's door and congregating with the others. It was their social life. The setting could never be captured in a photo and text.

The setting for the Franklin Institute series looks like a lab with the night sky visible through a large window. This is where scientists work to discover the many pieces of information that this video series wants young scientists to know about. The video cuts away to scenes of the sky, and close-ups of a few maps and charts, and the total effect is scientific. Just the message the museum wants to convey, and video pictures it. Older amateur astronomers will enjoy it, too. It's that informative.

Vesterheim Museum of the Norwegian Experience invites viewers into artisans' studios and workplaces as part of its Folk Art in Place series. The goal is to explain Norwegian crafted works, tools of all kinds, and decorative objects that comprise a part of the Norwegian-American experience. Video shows the tools on the wall and tabletop. The story is a serialized one, with each episode focusing on a different craft. Cumulatively, it shows the physical breadth of the museum, as well as the variety of exhibits.

The extent of a museum's "setting" varies greatly; it could be a center-city street, a small-town landmark, an out-of-town destination, a multi-building campus, or a space inside another cultural institution. Visitors will want to know, especially if accessibility and/or transportation is a factor. The Visit page video on the website of Hancock Shaker Village in Pittsfield, Massachusetts, gives a visual synopsis of the museum.

Number of buildings on the museum grounds
Distances between buildings
Surfaces of walkways and pathways
Costumed interpreters
Photos, drawings, and diagrams
Voice-over narration for background information on museum history

If your museum is far enough from town for visitors to consider it a side trip, these details make the journey less intimidating.

Writers: notice your visitors, but then imagine others who might not be visiting. Part of the responsibility for accessibility is thinking beyond the obvious to the many challenges of people you don't yet know, which includes their workday schedules and budget, as well as other physical realities. Include in the video narration script information like:

- How long it takes to get here
- What kind of transportation is needed to get here
- Our beautiful grounds are all paved and fully accessible
- There are five buildings in our restored village, each accessible by smooth gravel paths
- All guided tours last 45 minutes
- There are stairs, escalators, and elevators between all our floors
- Benches for viewing our artwork are in every gallery
- There are beverage stands at several points throughout the garden

SETS

To show special events—like the performances during Dia de Los Muertos Celebration at Nelson-Atkins Museum in Kansas City, Missouri—sets might need to be designed as settings for the spectacle. It's video for entertainment and where performers, music, costumes, are staged.

Other settings, usually interior, are too small to allow cameras and lighting. Or they have equipment that are fragile or off limits. If that's your museum's situation, re-create a small section of the actual setting to suggest the whole. In these cases, the camera will focus on the presenters and the objects.

PRESENTERS

The main characters in Franklin Institute's astronomy video series are an astronomy professor and a social media creator, each of whom understands their particular audiences. They make a good team, expanding the range of experiences and knowledge. One talks science as an achievable calling; the other represents the world young adults are familiar with. These real people deliver a message before they say a word. It's a video! Different people, of different ages and backgrounds, can see that the video is meant to speak to them.

"Behind the Scenes" at the Conservation Lab of St. Augustine Lighthouse & Maritime Museum stars real conservators talking about their job, a series of researchers showing what ongoing work has scooped up from the ocean floor. Video adds a lot of meaning to the stated purpose of describing the conservation of one object:

- View of an actual lab—looks user-friendly, not intimidating
- A real person, in t-shirt and jeans
- Listening to an expert talking about the history of an object found in a shipwreck conveys a lot of information. Hearing is how many people learn best. And as noted earlier in the chapter, a few seconds of talk says a lot.

Buffalo Bill Center of the West, before it gets to the details of a Western saddle, leads off with a single presenter. He has the manner of an authentic Westerner and he talks like an approachable expert. Museums that want to talk at any length about their objects need presenters who people want to listen to.

Writers: here are some thoughts about selecting a presenter:

- Invite guest speakers for brief interviews.
- Convince a staffer to show and tell their job in the museum.
- Select two people to query each other and share responsibility for the eight minutes they're on camera.

Let each presenter talk with their hands; that is, extend their arms to show a range of pieces, or point to a detail of what they're talking about. Only a video can do that! Presenters who point to an object will have an easier time speaking with precision and expert knowledge. They start their talk with a pointed finger and:

"this 19th century . . ."
"this utensil was probably used for . . ."
"look at how solid this . . ."

Or

"listen to how solid this sounds . . ."

Two people in a video work together and move the talk along. If one fumbles a thought, the other can clarify. The camera can move from one speaker to another, or to a map or object, to change the visual pace.

ACTORS

Video allows actors and historic interpreters to play their roles more dramatically.

- The camera can select and edit for the best settings within the museum.
- The costumes can be more elaborate because wardrobe has to fit only for one shoot.
- Multiple takes eliminate un-dramatic lapses.

Nelson-Atkins Museum of Art in Kansas City (Missouri) hired an actor to bring La Catrina, a twentieth-century print icon, to life in a splendid video of the skeletal grande dame with the towering flowered hat; she's a human version of the vanities, death amid beauty, who proceeds through the museum with a slow, regal step.

This was a performance that connected drama with galleries to celebrate Dia de los Muertos. More quotidian scenes are inhabited by costumed interpreters seen walking among the buildings in the Orientation video of Hancock Shaker Village. Actors communicate at a distance; their actions accentuate words.

OPENING FRAME/TITLE CARD

The frame that starts a video is important for five reasons:

- Identifies the museum
- Visually identifies the story to follow

- Provides exact spelling and terminology for viewers who want to follow up with the museum
- Names the title to search for on YouTube
- Reminds viewers of the title listed in the right-hand column of YouTube for future reference

The Wing Luke title card reads: "Step into a Uniquely American Story." The only other visual is the Wing Luke logo, also important for future identification where text might be absent.

Battleship New Jersey Museum says "Battleship New Jersey" in large, headline type, superimposed on a dark and shadowy roiling sea.

Driehaus Museum's virtual lectures lead with an image that will be seen in the lecture. For its talk on Louis Tiffany stained glass objects, a detail is shown. It's beautiful and it identifies not just the subject, but the setting of the museum, which resides in a Belle Époque mansion; beauty is a major part of its identity.

The title frame for the Nelson-Atkins Dia de los Muertos video credits the "México Consulada en Kansas City" as a partner. Connection to the Latino community is an important theme of the museum's celebration.

CLOSED CAPTIONING

You are invited to see the Día de los Muertos altar in Kirkwood Hall at the Nelson-Atkins during museum hours November 1–15, 2021.

Están invitados a ver el altar del Dia de los Muertos en Kirkwood Hall en el Nelson-Atkins durante las horas laborables desde el 1ro de noviembre hasta el 15 de noviembre.

Can you read the second paragraph? A sizable segment of your audience can. Include them by talking their language, where appropriate.

The value of closed captioning extends beyond those with hearing impairment. Think broadly of museum audiences and viewers with issues of:

- English as a second language
- Concentration
- Viewing in groups, as a family or work group
- Classroom settings
- Conference settings
- Unequal microphone quality
- Acoustics in any given museum space
- Re-posting videos

Closed captioning enhances all the benefits of a video with the tried and true advantage of printed text.

SERIALIZATION

Many videos are episodic. They occur with regularity and this builds viewership for a museum website, or attention for its e-mails. Even a series of two or three allows more objects or exhibits or expertise to be shared. And if you've found a good presenter, keep that person working. Start each video episode with a sequential comment: "This week we're visiting . . ."

Wrap each segment with a thanks and a preview: "Thanks for watching,, next week we'll take a stroll through the butterfly garden."

"Behind the Scenes" at the Conservation Lab of St. Augustine Lighthouse & Maritime Museum is a slow-paced, congenial way to learn about maritime research. It lends itself to several episodes because undersea work covers many years and many different people. It's not a one-off tale. Visually the episodes end with:

- Outside view of the white clapboard lab buildings—more than one conservation going on here!
- Picture-in-picture of another artifact conservation project coming next
- Invitation from the researcher to come back again

Writers: note the conversational tone of voice when real people are inviting viewers to come back to the museum: "This will be on display a little later when we reopen . . . you come back next year . . . stop by any time to ask us questions . . . and remember to love your lighthouse."

As after any talk or lecture, the speaker ends with a summation. The guide of an architectural tour ends the walk with: "The burying ground here at Hancock is a single monument that represents all the hundreds of Shakers who have been buried here over the years and that seems like a nice metaphor for Shaker life, suppression of individual ego and identity to a common communal experience."

Writers: it's always a good idea to wrap up a communication with a specific idea that relates to the museum. Writing a video, remember that it will end, and look for an image that serves as a summation with your words. A title frame with the logo of the museum serves as well. And if you're stuck for words to end your story, this is universal:

Thank you.

REFERENCES

"About the Nation's Oldest Port® National Heritage Area," Explore & Learn, St. Augustine Lighthouse & Maritime Museum, https://youtu.be/Pjs-dxu4f04 [accessed 9-19-21]

"American Artifacts: Whitney Plantation Slavery Museum," American History TV, C-Span, October 5, 2015, https://www.c-span.org/video/? [accessed 1-3-22]

"Behind the Scenes: Artifacts in the Conservation Lab," St. Augustine Lighthouse & Maritime Museum, https://www.youtube.com/watch?app=desktop&v=xQgZnPC cVwo&feature=youtu.be [accessed 2-5-22]

"Conservation of William H. Johnson's Paintings," Paintings Conservation Lab, Conservation Center, demo American Art Museum, https://americanart.si.edu /art/conservation/center/paintings_lab [accessed 2-4-22]

"Dia de los Muertos Video/Video del Dia de los Muertos," Nelson Atkins Museum of Art, https://nelson-atkins.org/nelson-atkins-at-home/virtual-dia-de-los -muertos-2021/?utm_source=website&tum_medium=homepage-square&tum_cam paign=dia-de-los-muertos-2021&utm_content=virtual-exhibition [accessed 2-4-22]

"Explore Printmaking Around Austin," Blanton Museum of Art, The University of Texas at Austin, e-mail, February 2, 2022, https://mailchi.mp/blantonmuseum /august20-181397?e=1cc1747e31 [accessed 2-3-22]

"Extra Credit: Finding a Stargazing Spot," The Franklin Institute 2022, https:// beyond.fi.edu/videos/?utm_medium=email&utm_source=marketing&utm_cam paign=Beyond%20FI%20Reminder%201.28.22 [accessed 1-29-22]

"Folk Art in Place: Episode 2," YouTube, Vesterheim, https://youtu.be/MHGt95W8waA [accessed 2-5-22]

"Folk Art In Place: Episode 5, How To—Kolrosing," YouTube, Vesterheim Museum of the Norwegian Experience, https://www.youtube.com/watch?v=dOplC9Sj6Ds [accessed 2-4-22]

"House and History," Owens-Thomas House & Slave Quarters, Telfair Museums, https://www.telfair.org/visit/owens-thomas/ [accessed 1-16-22]

"A House with a Heart and a Soul," https://marktwainhouse.org/ [accessed 2-1-22]

"How Are Fleet Flagships Different?" Battleship New Jersey, https://www.youtube .com/watch?v=TOrnsQM4bqU [accessed 1-31-22]

"Milwaukee County Zoo Welcomes New Gorilla Troop," Milwaukee County Zoo, https://youtu.be/XtRuo4TSBEE [accessed 2-2-22]

"Mission Accomplished: Discovering a Revolutionary War Shipwreck Video," https://www.staugustinelighthouse.org/2020/04/09/mission-accomplished-dis covering-a-revolutionary-war-shipwreck-video/ [accessed 2-6-22]

"National Churchill Museum," America's National Churchill Museum, https:// youtu.be/kDOFBGIf6Uo [accessed 12-27-21]

"Orientation Video," Hancock Shaker Village, https://hancockshakervillage.org /visit/orientation-video/ [accessed 2-5-22]

"A Practical Guide to the Cosmos with Derrick Pitts and Kalpana Pots," The Franklin Institute, https://youtu.be/PPqwAK14vys [accessed 2-6-22]

"RISD Museum," https://risdmuseum.org/ [accessed 1-21-22]

"The Scout Saddle Shop at the Buffalo Bill Center of the West, https://youtu.be /DoEUaKcR3fU [accessed 2-4-22]

"Shaker Architectural Tour," Hancock Shaker Village, YouTube, https://www.you tube.com/watch?v=dC4H5Bxp27c [accessed 2-7-22]

"Step into a Uniquely American Story," https://www.youtube.com/watch?v=GKzY coAKAFo [accessed 2-4-22]

"Surrealism Beyond Borders, Met Exhibitions," Metropolitan Museum of Art, https://youtu.be/CBLMibOwqdw [accessed 12-27-21]

"Telling Our Story: Canada and the 75th Anniversary of Victory in Europe," Canadian War Museum, https://youtu.be/_fV9IaGm9xQ [accessed 2-5-22]

"Virtual Tour," Elevate Your Event, Private Events, Burke Museum, https://www.burkemuseum.org/private-events [accessed 1-14-22]

"Virtual Tour of Battleship New Jersey," Battleship New Jersey Museum and Memorial, https://youtu.be/kDOFBGIf6Uo [accessed 12-27-21]

"Virtual Tour of Eternal Light," Driehaus Museum, April 10, 2021, https://driehausmuseum.org/programs/detail/watch-virtual-tour-of-eternal-light-the-sacred-stained-glass-window-of-louis-comfort-tiffany [accessed 2-5-22]

"Welcome to the 11th annual Día de los Muertos celebration!/¡Bienvenidos al 11vo aniversario del Dia de Los Muertos!" https://nelson-atkins.org/nelson-atkins-at-home/virtual-dia-de-los-muertos-2021/?utm_source=website&utm_medium=homepage-square&utm_campaign=dia-de-los-muertos-2021&utm_content=virtual-exhibition [accessed 1-31-22]

"What Is Vesterheim?" About, https://vesterheim.org/about/ [accessed 1-31-22]

CHAPTER 12

E-mail Newsletters

E-mail delivers the goods. It announces your exhibitions, programs, and news. It carries fuller information for engaging a wide range of readers. It allows you to say exactly what you want your audiences to hear. E-mail can be delivered any day of your choosing, at any time. The overwhelming advantage of e-mail is control, and it's the only form of communication that gives you that power.

You can imagine the recipients you want to reach because they have already opted to join or remain on your mailing list. So you can control your messages. Because you control the timing, you can send follow-up reminders. Because you control the subject line, you can make subsequent changes so as to reach your audiences in different ways. The usefulness of e-mail is boundless: 306.4 billion were estimated to have been sent in 2021, and that number is projected to keep on rising.

With its global audience—global in geography, demographics, and interests—e-mail demands that you employ arresting images, intriguing stories, activities that are described to capture their value, and an ongoing respect for knowledge and satisfaction.

This chapter covers both e-mail and newsletters because they've become so intertwined. Despite the other uses for e-mail and many delivery systems for newsletters, this particular team is unbeatable for the sustainability and success of museums. Wherever "newsletter" is used, delivery by e-mail is assumed. It's the writer's job to convey news and announcements in ways their many audiences will understand and continue to read.

SEVEN PARTS OF AN E-MAIL NEWSLETTER

The seven parts of a newsletter combine to make them unequaled at getting out information to the widest, and most interested, audience.

1. Date
2. To:
3. From:
4. Subject Line
5. Images and Captions
6. Message
7. Links

PARTS OF A NEWSLETTER: DATE

Timing is everything with news, and with e-mail a museum's announcements, upcoming programs, ongoing activities, objects and artifacts of current significance, and timely research can be mailed at the appropriate date. That means that information is received when audiences are most pre-disposed to listening. Save-the-date announcements can be sent six weeks prior. Reminders can be sent twenty-four hours ahead. Follow-up thank-you notes and satisfaction surveys can be sent the next day.

Scheduling a newsletter offers another way to focus on different audiences because you can time the e-mail for specific hours of the day. Different audiences read their e-mail at specific times. Educators, for instance, might like early morning e-mails. Caregivers of small children might like nap time. College students work at night. If you have a truly global audience, be cognizant of different global time zones. For viewers in India, 4 a.m. is just fine. While digital timing is not the writer's job, writers must be aware of time and culture differences. There's no big advantage to "Good morning!" if it's afternoon in Warsaw.

A schedule indicates continuity and loyalty to its audiences. It subtly encourages readers to return. It's sticky. There are several ways for an institution to say we'll stay in touch regularly.

- Look for Smith-Jones Museum News every week
- Look for more news in the next edition of Museum News
- Battleship New Jersey August 2021 E-Newsletter

A subcategory of the date is the time. Readers of regular briefings and daily or weekly updates know what time to check their inbox.

PARTS OF A NEWSLETTER: TO

Audiences amount to more than you think; there are so many of them, plus so many you haven't thought of. People sign up from many different prompts: your website, social media, store orders, QR codes, front desk and store signage, and in-museum kiosks. If they attend a program, they know you but you don't know them, yet their digital addresses appear on their event registration. If they're a new donor, that gets an exclamation point, and speed entry onto e-mail lists!

One particularly galling example of people you should know but don't: the companion of the person who got the e-mail newsletter and planned the visit. The Friend Who Came Along is the friend who found the time, made the trip, walked all around, saw many new things, maybe stopped in the store or café, and told her friends about it later. This Friend came, saw, and engaged. Yet The Friend is not on your mailing list. The friend who came with a friend is part of many unknown audiences.

While e-mail newsletters can develop the newest of visitors into support-ers, it's productive to focus on the person who planned the visit. There are dozens of audiences they could be part of, and each will respond to parts of your newsletter. Get to know and understand their motivations. Some of those audiences are:

- Local
- Tourist
- Fan of a museum's genre
- Expert or expert-amateur in museum's genre
- Caregiver of children
- Member of club or affiliation
- Educator who returns on their own time
- Newly retired person
- Teenager who wants a quiet space
- College student with a project
- People anywhere in the world who like virtual lectures
- People who received a gift membership
- Museum lovers for whom English is a second language
- Shy people
- Attendee at a program or event
- People at work—remember, e-mail is constantly in front of people at work

This partial list suggests the types of person and motivations that comprise the big, unwieldy body called your market. A more complete description can be found in chapter 1, "Audiences."

PARTS OF AN E-MAIL: FROM

One's name poses more problems than one might think. Some institutions have more than one name, with the parent organization sometimes taking precedence. This happens at academic museums with very important university parents. Many museums shorten their legal names to something immediately familiar. Many museums have merged or changed their names. No writer can affect the name, but it behooves them to upgrade the interest level of the subject line to irresistible. Also, clicking on the left-hand column immediately triggers the opening of the right-hand screen; the ownership of the newsletter must be immediately apparent.

"Smith-Jones Museum Newsletter"
"QNews from Queens Museum"
"eNews from Johnny Cake Hill," the newsletter of New Bedford Whaling
    Museum

Deciding on the From line matters; that's the museum the recipient signed up for, the institution worthwhile enough to add to the quantity of e-mails in their inbox.

PARTS OF AN E-MAIL: SUBJECT LINE

Please take the following quiz:

From the following list of actual e-mail Subject lines, select the ones with subjects you instantly understand. Note: The capitalizations are the museums'.

- "Check on our upcoming schedule of YouTube events"
- "Teachers: It's Time to Play."
- "Harvest Time in the Garden"
- "Join us for a tour of re:collections"
- "This Week at the [name of museum]: Fall Preview and More"
- "Reminder: Creature Feature and August Adventures Day"
- "Thank you for your order (#1234567)"
- "QMail from the Queens Museum"
- "Backyard Scientist Backpacks & other summer activities, conserving rough-nosed horned lizards, and more"

Remember that the From line has already identified your museum. The Subject line, which really does have enough space, allows a description of the news and announcements to come when you click on the message.

Writing a Subject line

Writing a subject line resembles writing a headline or title, and that's an art in itself. The writer must encapsulate the entire message that follows and acknowledge that different audiences respond to different words. The rule of three applies: write three different subject lines, lean back, and then pick the best. It usually isn't the first.

First try: Our Lecture of the Month for April features all the other people who lived in our historic house.

Second effort: Meet the grandfather who built the house, the house-keeper, and the oldest son who lived at the Thomas Smith House.

Third iteration: Journey back to April 1850 and a typical day at Thomas Smith house.

Writers might try varying the subject line by eye-view. Subject lines will start with:

"Child's-eye view of . . ."
"Arborist-eye view of . . ."
"Costume designers pick their favorite Impressionist paintings"

Nevada Art Museum offers this teaser in the Subject line: "Look Who Is Talking About Land Art." As a Subject line, it has it all—teaser question, interesting topic "land art," gossip. Open the e-mail and a colorful sculpture photo greets you.

Tenement Museum's wide and growing catalog of digital tours run the danger of seeming too similar, especially since they're communicated in frequent e-mails. This Subject changes often to keep curiosity fresh: "Secrets from the Tenement Museum."

Newberry Library, Chicago, proclaims its newsletter status and then dares to claims news that is 100 years old. "E-News: Where Chicagoans Drank During Prohibition."

Tip for Writers

Don't waste the valuable real estate of a subject line to say "New This Week" when that space could say: "New Science Talk This Week."

PARTS OF E-MAIL: IMAGES AND CAPTIONS

Many e-mail newsletters start with a splashy full-screen, beautiful photo. It's arresting, and it functions as an informative message if coupled with a caption.

"The spacious Smith-Jones Wing opens today."
"Olmec vessel, one of the many treasures in our Americas galleries . . ."
"Author Stephen Chen's kitchen, where he prepares the recipes collected from the world's cuisines. Click here to attend his lecture . . ."

With a glamorous building or sweeping new wing, captured with an architecture-enhancing photo, it's tempting to omit any caption. Writer, don't fall into that trap. Name the museum, its design and architect, and its relevance to visitor experience.

When a "view in browser" link converts a news announcement column into a full-screen newsletter, a big change occurs. This highly evolved communication, while retaining all the parts of its ancestor e-mail, now is clothed in colorful adornments like photos. The images could be artifacts and objects, book-signing authors, at-work conservators, or a starlit terrace. Every museum has an array of beautiful photos to choose from and the real problem is writing tell-the-tale stories to accompany them.

America's National Winston Churchill Museum in Fulton, Missouri, opens its e-mail to videos featuring the famous man whom fortune has rendered endlessly photogenic. Writers have it easy with Sir Winston, but even less renowned images can acquire great captions with concise explanations of their newsworthiness. A simple trick is to start the caption with three little words: "This photo shows . . ." Photos are powerful, and words are still necessary.

"Winston and Clementine, 1929"
"Waving to the Crowd in Sheffield"
"Churchill Reviews Troops in Italy, 1945"

The Tenement Museum newsletter is a brand builder telling the stories of the families at the heart of the museum. One front-page image shows a banner-wide photo of an early-twentieth-century street scene. The page-wide photo changes all the time, like life on the lower east side. The captions to these photos are sometimes long and detailed, necessary to completing the fascination of the photos.

This kitchen cabinet (right) in 97 Orchard Street was originally built in the 1930s by Adolfo Baldizzi, a skilled cabinet maker who struggled to find work during the Great Depression . . . our newest digital exhibit . . . shows how we invited experts to help us carefully move and preserve the cabinet, and what was discovered hidden behind it.

Figures 12.1–12.3. E-newsletters arrive in mailboxes exactly on time, perfect for announcing seasonal events, ticketed speaker events, and classes.

Sandra Lund / iStock via Getty images

Tips for Writers

Tip #1: Use visuals, the bigger the better. This letter is about news, and photos or illustrations lend immediacy. Select the visual first and write the caption to complement it.

Tip #2: If images are hard to find, grab a shot from a video, copyright permitting. Screenshots command attention when standing still, as well as when they're moving. Less clarity is expected here, and sharp captions come to the rescue. For "local farmer demonstrates tractor," substitute "local farmer stops for a lunch break. In 1920 plowing was an all-day excursion."

Tip #3: Long captions are desirable. Readers are drawn to photos and like to read longer, informative text that relate to them.

Tip #4: Understand and internalize your museum's brand identity. That helps keep the tone of voice on key. Every paragraph in the Tenement Museum's written material relates to a story of the people who emigrated, raised families, worked, and prospered from their American beginnings on Orchard Street. Stories of the residents, not the tenement apartments themselves, are the heart of the museum.

Tip #5: If the photo is one of several in the newsletter, two short paragraphs are fine. Keep it as short as possible because the link at the bottom of the announcement will tell the rest.

STRUCTURE

Museums are busy places, in person and virtually, and their newsletters are accordingly very full: announcements of upcoming events, programs, exhibitions, acquisitions, virtual programs, and more. Sometimes ongoing columns appear and they add continuity. Bios of staffers' projects add dimension to long-term activities such as research projects and conservation. If you have an archive of newsletters with volumes and numbers, your history becomes manifest. Because your newsletter arrives at readers' addresses with regularity, and offers readers a full slate of events likely to interest almost everyone at some time or other, structure is essential. Here's a suggested outline:

- Name and logo of museum
- Five to seven announcements
- Titles of each announcement
- Short paragraph for each announcement, describing the event, program, speaker, exhibit, item
- Day, date, time, length (if applicable)
- Cost (if applicable)

- Curiosity paragraph to introduce future or seasonal events or longer-term projects
- Credit to partners or sponsors, if any
- Links

If the newsletter is opened in the browser, announcements become articles and, including the link to "read more," can be longer and deeper.

New Bedford Whaling structures neatly and the events shine through. "Creature Features" are announced with "Shark Week," "Seal Week," "Horseshoe Crab Week," "August Adventures Day," and "Hands-on Activities at the Museum on Wednesdays."

The well-organized screen includes credit to an activity sponsor, a reminder to donate, and total focus on the specific audience interested in filling the long vacation days of August.

SCHEDULES FOR EVERYONE

When museums develop a series of programs, the goal is serial attendees, continuity, and engagement. The reader's goal is scheduling. E-mail newsletter recipients are asked to block off time on their already full calendars, and that's a complex scheduling job. Make the commitment easier by clearly listing the dates and days of the week.

Pennsylvania Academy of Fine Arts, in one mailing listed Special Tours, Pre-College Portfolio Classes, and Artist Survival Strategies, speaking to several audiences within PAFA's sphere. And it also encouraged readers to check back regularly for "new experiences and highlights."

When asking readers to schedule an event well into the future, remember to name the event:

Parents, August Vacation Fun is coming up
Get ready for September Annual Bulb sale
May House Walk Just Around the Corner

Since e-mail lets you time the message to the week, take advantage of that timing. If there's a May House Walk in the offing, announce it in April. "Just around the corner: May House Walk."

REMINDER ANNOUNCEMENTS

Once you've announced an upcoming event, send regular reminders. You've planned long and hard for it, and so have those who plan to attend. Make sure they remember. One event reminder—for a speaker or author signing—might include the presenter's bio. They expect, or hope for, the publicity.

Follow-up announcements are also called thank-you notes. They are scheduled as rigorously as the event itself. The people who attended are an invaluable audience that took the time, spent the money, and really enjoyed being in the actual or virtual museum. Thank them very much. It's also an opportunity to remind them of the next program coming up. And, by the way, a brief survey questionnaire can be added.

NEWSLETTERS TO BRIDGE THE GAP

This is a big topic. Your gaps might be seasonal, and visitors will lose track of you between seasons. Some gaps can't be easily explained, and it's a truism of marketing that customers sometimes just go away. Audiences that have not been included will drop out easily. Museums and programs that were difficult to access will be cast aside. Lack of diversity on just one visit might make visitors, in-person or virtual, hesitant to return.

Newsletters, because of their regularity, can keep all audiences in the loop. Appeal to the amorphous diaspora with several tactics:

- Write regularly.
- Write subject lines to appeal to many different audiences.
- Show photographs of diversity.
- Develop programs that, by their name, will be recognized in the subject line as inclusive.
- Offer events that are free and easy to access.
- Schedule events at times that aren't "white collar times," but rather are accessible to all working adults.
- Introduce, in the newsletter, program leaders or moderators who represent diverse backgrounds.

GAP ACTIVITIES

Chautauqua Institution, Chautauqua, New York, is a summer gathering of wide-ranging lectures, classes, and cultural events, offered over nine weeks in summer. Each week Chautauqua focuses on a topic, and each week *Literary Arts News* arrives in recipients' mailboxes with a reading list for adults and children. The listed books help put the summer ideas in tangible form to absorb at home. The books will last beyond the summer and keep the Chautauqua enthusiasm alive for the other forty-three weeks of the year.

Any museum with seasonality could launch similar projects, in any format, on any platform, or for any budget. At-your-leisure lists of books or videos reinforce an institution's mission. This ongoing reading and viewing remind newcomers and members that they're part of your community and a greater community of shared interests.

- Indoor reading from the botanic garden
- Movies about the Great Migration historic battleground
- Use the opportunity to honor members of your broader community
- Native American Stories
- Books to read for Latin Heritage Month
- Book suggestions from the library
- Ten local houses of worship recommend these books

Speaking of the community, it often falls to the writer to remember these community helpers:

- Special thanks to our partner . . .
- Special funding for this event courtesy of . . . [with logo and logo line]
- This monthly lecture event is free
- All our monthly lectures are closed-captioned/signed
- Our museum is completely accessible and compliant with ADA standards
- Contact us if you need special accommodation

SUM UP AND LOOK AHEAD

E-mail occupies a large part of many people's day. It reaches more people than social media. It skews older than social media. It carries your name into the daily lives of more people than you'll ever imagine. You control its content, delivery schedule, recipients, and image. As museums adapt, it's a digital rocket to new territory. For writers, it's a prized platform. Newsletters are as old as free speech and as current as hashtags. They contain limitless ideas, diverse voices, depth of research, and a museum's identity. Together, they give writers plenty to say, and that bounty makes writing easier.

REFERENCES

"Books to Read for Latinx Heritage Month," *The ReadDown*, Penguin Random House, https://www.penguinrandomhouse.com/the-read-down/hispanic-heritage-month [accessed 8-13-21]

Chautauqua Literary Arts: Week Seven 2021," Literary Arts News, Chautauqua Institution, https://mailchi.mp/chq/chautauqua-literary-arts-week-seven-2021?e =717627d0fc [accessed 8-29-21]

"E-News: Where Chicagoans Drank During Prohibition," e-mail, The Newberry Library, Aug 26, 2021, https://mailchi.mp/newberry.org/where-chicagoans -drank-prohibition?e=47a7eb5d7f [accessed 8-27-21]

https://mailchi.mp/chq/chautauqua-literary-arts-week-eight-2021?e=717627d0fc

https://mailchi.mp/nevadaart/fallclasses?e=db5836b8f1

https://view.enews.chicagobotanic.org/?qs=4850e2b6cf9ab339dfc86b79f93aac 0c50c2624386a5c7310a0e16d926f764146a10dd1982720d4e90e2cb5d4614fc7b 91665c14cd6fdf0c7220dc3a5854610d9aabfaf0d95cd70132662f5598b5da3e

https://www.nationalchurchillmuseum.org/ [accessed 8-29-21]

"Native American Stories: Examination of How Native American Stories Are More Than Mere Words," American Indian Heritage Foundation, http://indians.org /articles/native-american-stories.html [accessed 8-13-21]

"PAFA From Home," https://www.pafa.org/museum/education/resources [accessed 8-29-21]

"Reminder: Creature Features and August Adventures Day," eNews from Johnny Cake Hill, New Bedford Whaling Museum, August 2021, https://myemail.con stantcontact.com/Reminder—Creature-Feature-and-August-Adventures-day.html ?soid=1128002165729&aid

"Secrets from the Tenement Museum," Experience Tenement Museum: Upcoming Events, *Member News*, Tenement Museum, https://mailchi.mp/tenement.org/ex perience-the-tenementmuseum-991996?e=0521cfbea5 [accessed 8-29-21]

"Upcoming Events," Experiencing the Tenement Museum, Members News, The Tenement Museum, August 2021, https://mailchi.mp/tenement.org/experience -the-tenementmuseum-991996?e=0521cfbea5 [accessed 8-29-21]

CHAPTER 13

Blogs

Blogs have blossomed into a magnificent asset for museums. What began as a web page for updates—of programs, events, projects, ideas—became a strategic tool for success. Blogs maintain interest, build familiarity and loyalty, reach new audiences, expand inclusiveness of existing audiences, attract membership, inform supporters and collaborators, give voice to scholars and experimenters. Let's start writing!

Blogs are based on these tenets that help writers get organized:

Focus on a theme—they're based on one topic or thesis.
Research—they use multiple sources of information, writings, or interviews, often with citations, although that's not necessary.
Length—about 500–2,000 words. Shorter and they're just a blog post, a blurb or overview. Any longer and it's a chapter for a book.
Author or authorial voice—not all blogs are signed, but they should be. They represent the concept and development of one voice, or a team of like minds.
Serial—individual blogs might reoccur several times on a museum site. More likely, the blog itself will be a weekly or monthly feature.
Name—blogs gain credence when they are unique to the museum and its mission; when stuck, call it Our Museum Blog.
Theme, originality—think of an edited column or article, whose idea has been green-lit by a superior or board.

FOCUS

Whatever the theme of your museum's blog—and more about that later—narrow it to a single-minded topic. Blogs capture interest by being

171

singularly interesting, one-of-a-kind sources of a certain kind of information. Blogs lend continuity to a museum's universe, which is by definition evolving. Readers can depend on a blog as a consistent resource. Visitors allocate time to a specific blog for a reason—don't waste their time on an inconvenient surprise.

Themes range from an intern's summer job helping the gardeners rake the lily pond to historic research. Stretch your blog ideas as far as they will go, and then pull back to achievable topics. The idea is to capture some new people from the wide world of diverse audiences; since you don't know who they are, any blog idea could be a great one. Many kinds of subjects could bring people of all backgrounds together. All parents want to know more about children. All home cooks like vegetable gardens. Movie fans like film discussion groups. Teenagers like science projects. Who knows? Cast your net wide.

To adapt an idea from another cultural institution, consider New York's Metropolitan Opera cookbook, recipes of the great operas. Recipes of Main Street, campfire cooks, Science Snacks. Serve up a recipe every month. If blog topics are a stretch, write a credentials paragraph about the blogger that squarely connects them to your museum's mission.

After you find a theme for your blog—or blogs—give it, or them, a name, and a place on the website that's easy to find for repeat visits.

LENGTH

Don't confuse blogs with blog posts. The latter are short blurbs or squibs, choose your scrunched-up term, that are meant to announce, not to tell.

Blogs are long enough to be fully informative, thoughtful, and worthy to be read at any time. They've been seen as short as 500 words and as long as 2,000, though 500–800 is usual; that's the length of a newspaper column. Just the appearance of length gives gravitas, and that's because it allows for an introduction or lead paragraph, explication, a few details, some informed quotes, and a summary. Concise, to the point, full of the facts that make reading interesting, not a bit of filler.

NAME AND LOCATION

You name your galleries, often after donors. You name your events and education programs. Names convey uniqueness. When you name something, you show you love them. Call your blog the Smith Museum Blog, which carries the museum's name, and then think about a name that relates to the content or purpose of the blog. The Artifact Blog. Science Research Blog. Children's Hour Blog. Capital Campaign Blog.

Blogs are just one of several written formats your museum utilizes: Newsletters, Program Descriptions, Educator Handouts, Fundraising Materials, Print Magazines. They're capitalized here—your computer knowingly calls it Title Case—to show how a proper name can stand out amid generic offerings.

How to find a name? Group idea sessions are always good, especially when group discussion has waned a bit. Here are some idea starters:

Your location, geography
Town's nickname or slogan
Most popular exhibit
Founder's business
Town industry
Name of museum's garden, main portal, or oldest tree
Architectural style of your building
Words that refer to your kind of museum—art genre, science discipline, era of history
Words that relate to your collection

Some museums put the Blog tab on the home page. That lends importance, and so do other places on your website. If your blog resides in the About menu, it might imply a series of blogs about the museum's history. Visitors who see the blog in the Education menu will expect teaching programs, exercises, or developments, for children and adults.

Writers might write: The February Gardeners at our museum are busy with . . ."

AUTHOR OR AUTHORIAL VOICE

Many blogs are authored by contributors to local publications, community experts, and museum staff members from unexpected departments—why not ask the registrar, as well as curators, educators, and interns. They speak with enthusiasm because this is recess for them; they get to use new words and develop new thoughts; this expansion of voices will resonate with audiences you never thought of.

When you assign a staffer as your blogger, name them and show their photo. It's a good credential, and you also send a message about inclusiveness. Use their photo, if you can, and by all means make it flattering. It shows your diversity. When blogs indicate their author's staff job, they tie the blog more tightly to the museum. Using a staffer makes the blog both informal and uniquely informed. Stating the staff person's title helps validate their knowledge and, if writing outside their field, their enthusiasm. You can imagine a title for them.

Curator Mary Thomas: Book Reviewer
Intern Jenny Smith, Local Historian
Senior Scientist Liz Jones focuses her research on northwest river ecology and has published three monographs on water plants. She contributes the February Recipe . . .

SERIAL WRITING

Blogs come with an expectation of regularity, a set schedule of articles. Strategically, this encourages repeat visits to the website, and a buildup of familiarity and loyalty. It's the 1,001 nights concept—don't let them lose interest in you. When you refresh your blog weekly, or monthly, you increase the chances of matching up with new and diverse audiences.

Write about the schedule that readers can expect. Say things like:

"Next month we'll visit the restoration lab."
"Stay tuned for our weekly web cam update."
"Our Louisiana Artists series is part of the Smith Museum Blog's about American artists in our collection and that of other museums around the country."

Blogs give virtual visitors content filling the gaps between in-person visits. This is important for zoos and botanic gardens and other museums with seasonal openings. Blogs can expand the content of virtual programs, and complement them with written and visual stories. The Driehaus Museum, in Chicago, offers a screenful of choices from Tiffany goblets to Victorian parlor games, complete with excellent photography. They're well researched, which makes writing about them easier. They're factual, not adjectival.

"Victorian Parlor Games & Puzzles for a Pandemic," April 28, 2020.
"A Tale of Today: Up From the Ashes—Pullman Porters and the Great Migration," February 18, 2021.

Note the dates. These are just blogs out of a dozen on one page, and the serial nature, the continuity, sends a strong message of continuity and commitment—a museum one can rely on for continuing information.

PROPRIETARY NAME

The Smith Museum Blog is a tolerably good name because it names the museum. Bedtime Buckaroos from the National Cowboy Museum is better because it's relevant to the museum, and distinctive; not many others museums could use it.

THEME

Once you know the guidelines for a blog, you can attack the challenge of its theme. Many a theme has proven unsustainable because it didn't fit into a regular schedule, or was too scholarly, or lacked enough substance for 800 words a week. Sometimes themes are off strategy—they imperfectly represent your brand or its goals. Some fit hand-in-glove with your goals, and these should be ranked before the final cut. The available writers matter, too, of course. Who will write your blog and which theme suits them? An

Figure 13.1. Wallpaper, French, ca. 1805. This image is from the website of RISD Museum, Providence, Rhode Island, which states that "The images on this website can enable discovery and collaboration and support new scholarship, and we encourage their use. This object is in the public domain [Collective Commons]. The museum considers its collection as living documents that can be augmented." Writers: when adding images to website articles or blogs, add information on use, creator, materials, and trends and styles of the period.
Courtesy of the RISD Museum, Providence, Rhode Island

unspoken rule among professional writers: don't write about anything you don't know.

How to find a theme? There are many places to start, from strategic to creative, helpful to inspiring, mission based to horizon broadening. If an institution has access to wonderful photographs, build a theme from visual cues. Think of your audience's interests—all of your audiences and all of their interests! Read the blogs of other institutions, everywhere. Don't stop at the accustomed borders.

BLOGS AS LEAD GENERATORS

Blogs can be used by museum marketers for all the reasons a business uses them; museums call it finding new audiences. Museums, like companies, want current or prospective customers to search for them, to use an online search for information on their specific interest. Consumers of things know how to search for sneakers or coffee makers, and businesses are brilliant at writing copy with key words that shoppers type in the Search box. Museum writers can be equally clever, and blogs are one place to seed key words. The lessons from corporate bloggers are worth noting:

Choose words for distinctiveness.
Use words relevant to your specific museum, its collection, and its exhibits.
Use synonyms, never the same word twice.
Try bold, unexpected words that attract readers, as well as search engines.
Add subheads to longer blogs and write them with distinctive words, as well.

Don't bore the robot. Blogs work in your favor with viewers who use search engines because of their length; there's plenty of space to use key words, all perfectly natural in the context of an informative article. But keep length in check, count your words, and edit for 500–800 words in length. This is long enough to use all the synonyms search engines might look for, not so many as to annoy the robot. Search engine algorithms are trained to ignore text that is too packed with search words. Human readers, of course, get bored by unnecessary repetition, too.

Find a detail:

"Today the baby ferret wasn't interested his breakfast. I think he prefers . . ."

"One of my favorite objects in the side parlor are the picture frames. Each one is a work of art . . . ."

"Look at this bonsai! Did you know they have curators? This one was acquired for our collection to . . ."

"Today I'm going to show you some sixteenth-century helmets. Their stories are quite different from the archaic helmets I wrote about last month . . ."

Explain the visual:

"This is called a Tall clock because of this . . ."

Tell why you're intrigued:

"I love the way animals have different moods."

Relate today's blog to a previous one:

"Last week this was just a bud . . . look at [tbd name of rose] today."

Relate today's blog to a future one:

"Next week I'll be working with the gardener at the lily pond. Stay tuned."

Quote a visitor to the exhibit:

"You'd be amazed the questions kids ask. One woman was looking at a statue that stood about seven feet high, and her grandson said: 'the guy who made this, how did the he get up to the head?'"

Share a Reaction

"Hello, gallery guard here again, back with my personal, guard's-view critique of our museum's wonderful objects. This week I'll tell you what I like about . . ."

BLOGS FOR EDUCATORS

Here's an opportunity to reach out to your community for its advice. Collaboration with teachers, principals, boards of education, and interest groups will give you plenty of ideas and support for future projects.

Education, especially from the viewpoint of educators, is too broad for one blog. Your audiences might be thinking of grammar school, or ten-year-olds, but educators are thinking of lesson plans, formats, standards, and next month's meeting agenda. Getting together is a must. By the way, collaborators are also museum visitors, members, supporters, and volunteers.

BLOGS FOR CHILDREN

Bedtime Buckaroos comes with nary a yawn from the Cowboy Museum. Bedtime stories are for kids, a diverse audience that embraces the parents and caregivers who read to them—for years. As with any blog, consistency is key. The magic of this one is "bedtime." Its consistency is based not on the consistency of the writer, or the dateline, but the schedule of the household.

A video children's story has its singular charms and cautions, and be cautious particularly about the words that accompanies the visuals. They must tell a story, but the plot shouldn't run away from the visuals.

Video games, based on objects in your collection, also fulfill the blog requirements of interest and consistency, and many gamers are looking into it.

Any game that can be printed at home reaches multiple audiences in addition to the child and the printer-outer. They lie around for a while. So make the headline or title short and 48-point type.

BLOGS FOR SCHOLARS

If you've seen a Call for Papers, a conference paper proposal, or any kind of proposal that hopes for an acceptance, you know the organization fixation of academics. Respect their lifelong habits when you plan a blog.

It will have a title, a hypothesis, a singularity, and lots of citations. The blog will be long, well down the spectrum toward 2,000 words. It demands a writer who is either an academic, or a person with top interviewing skills. Different authors are fine.

Readers of scholarly blogs are like the scholars who write them: they come in all types and ages, and their common quest is knowledge, and lots of it. They like details, techniques, news, equipment, dates, sizes, names, failures as well as successes. They want you to take them places they haven't been, or to a place they want to remember better.

Science, arts, history, architecture, the environment, cultures, railroads, space, and more are some of the topics scholars study. Scholarship and its accompanying research is a big tent, inclusive, diverse, equitable, and accessible. Blogs by and for scholars will reach many audiences with an uncountable variety of interests. And, of course, scholars also come in all ages and cultures of origin, worldwide.

A reminder: scholars are curious people; they create. Give them that expectation.

Computer History Museum exemplifies the unsuspected reach of scholarly blogs with its CHM Blog, Mining for More than Data, the gist of which is real gist—minerals and labor that go into making robots. Data may exist in a cloud of input and algorithms; the robots are made of real stuff like lithium. The results of data mining are also quite real: schools to teach it, governments to regulate and legislate it, criminal justice systems to solve and salvage. Writers of CHM's blogs are curators, journalists, and scholars who write articles like they conduct research: finding a thesis that offers new perspectives.

Scholarly blogs zero in; think of the mechanisms in an airplane; they also expand out, like the aviation industry's role in global economics. To condense scholarly blogs into writerly information, look at these parts of a good blog for scholars:

Title: The teaser, suggests the content, a glimpse with wit.

Subhead: States the thesis, the new perspective.

Opening paragraph: Outlines the scope of the article; 100 words should do it.

Paragraph headers: Every three or four paragraphs, employ two to four words to state key points.

Wrap-up paragraph: Summarize any solution, one that actually happened or is hoped for in the future.

Tone of voice: This is a blog on a website, accessible to everyone, including people for whom English is a second language. Keep it light. It might help to write the summary first, which will be conversational and maybe even humble. Imagine you're in a Zoom meeting with your cousins, peers who understand you, even if they're not scholars. Tell them about the idea you had for a blog.

Blogs offer graduate students the opportunity to research thesis material, and the blog written by Fahim Rahim shows that kind of scholarship. It has a thesis—the relationship of artifacts to the ecology and landscape of eighteenth- and nineteenth-century Boston, cited and referenced primary and secondary sources, digital touches (blogs are digital, after all), readability, visuals, and links to its subhead material. Rahim is an MA student in Boston and a spring 2021 intern of Paul Revere House.

BLOGS FOR INTERNS

Win, win, win: assign interns to write blogs.

College students have impressive talent than extends well beyond their major area. They're still exploring options and they bring curiosity, diligence, and ability to the task of writing.

In an article for Buffalo Bill Center of the West blogs, an intern applies the journalistic approach to 800-word articles about citizen science research into to the local ecosystems, in this case collecting data on the seasonal blooming of plants, over a long period of time.

The museum gets a blog writer and a new category of people familiar with and favorable to its mission. The intern gets a job and a résumé item.

The task of writing this blog becomes easier because of the subject matter and the placement. It deals with a scientific project, and good interviewing skill can elicit the researcher's terminology. Because the researcher is talking to a non-scientist, they'll make every effort to speak in lay language.

BLOGS WITH A MISSION

Some blogs report news, like a new exhibition. Some are ongoing updates, like the conservation of an artwork. Some report interesting research projects. Almost any item important enough to be mentioned on your home page would benefit from a blog to branch it out. For a mission, when a mission statement doesn't do justice to your objectives, blogs bring breath and life. Several singular characteristics of blogs will help promote your mission and the blog becomes an ambassador.

Take the example of The Quilt Spot, blog of the National Quilt Museum in Paducah, Kentucky.

The title: it highlights a goal—it might be just one of your goals—of your museum.

Regularity: repetition builds visits to your website, allows you to repeatedly bring examples of your mission to your loyal followers.

Longer articles: a little lengthier than a post, a blog's length allows for stories that enrich a museum's objectives and show the mission's relevance.

Different authors: they speak with different voices, each reflective of the writer's age, background, personal interests, and perspectives on your museum's goals. Imagine the range of different audience their voices will reach.

Creativity: bloggers are storytellers without portfolio. They observe well, see unexpected happenings, have an insight to share. They sell your mission.

Whitney Plantation Museum, in Wallace, Louisiana, is "the only museum in Louisiana with an exclusive focus on the lives of enslaved people." On its home page is a tab called "history" that offers a good example of what a blog could look like. There are four topics to choose from—Slavery, Plantation Owners, Buildings and Memorials, and Additional Resources:

Outbound links—each with a photo. Each features a 1,000-word, deeply researched article about its subject. Each of these sections is expandable, especially the section on Additional Resources, which lists outside articles, podcasts, books, and videos. For a writer, the format is a simple outline for other articles. Some museums' staffing can't accommodate regular blogs, and this format is expandable at any time.

Florida Museum of Natural History publishes a blog of about 500 words, complemented with a dozen photographs about scientific challenges and how ingenuity addresses them. The blog's mission is celebrating science, inviting all audiences to share in the fascination of discovery and ingenuity. As the introductory paragraph says, "we think science is pretty cool."

Subtly included in every blog is a list of resources, partners in the particular research reported in the blog, and other blogs and articles. Despite its brevity, the Florida Museum blog covers a lot of territory with verbal and visual cues for readers of diverse backgrounds, interests, and levels of science literacy.

The Driehaus Museum blog connects its mission in the description of one of its blog series:

> As a part of the Driehaus Museum's ongoing mission to expand upon the shaping of Chicago during the Gilded Age through our *A Tale of Today: Up From the Ashes* series, this Black History Month we look to the Great Migration, the Chicago Defender, the Pullman porters, and the roots of Chicago's Black working class.

Schedule your blog, even if it's one a month. Repetition enhances any message, and blogs carry some of your most important messages. They reinforce your brand's reputation and mission. They reach out to your loyal audiences. They help explain individual objects and programs. They include writers, often interns, who become ambassadors themselves.

Long form journalism is known for research, explanations of events that no one has explained before, spotlighting an important topic, and exposés in the best sense of the word—insider information.

Creativity drives blogs. The format invites trial and experimentation. The National Quilt Museum, in Paducah, Kentucky, is a paragon of blogging. Its blog, named the Quilters Spot, is featured with visuals on the home page. And the blog's ongoing feature is the Block of the Month, with background on the block's design and heritage, a free downloadable pattern, and instructions for the novice who just has gotten more fascinated by the whole topic. Bios of each block's creator honor the artists, whom quilters recognize as art form innovators. The artist talks about the idea and process of the specific block and its quilt's place in the world of quilt design. There's also a mission behind sharing quilt patterns:

Welcome to The National Quilt Museum's Block of the Month Club!

Through the Block of the Month Club, The National Quilt Museum aims to challenge quilters to experiment with new techniques and styles while having fun connecting with quilters from all over the world, and learning more about the museum in the process!

BLOGS FOR REPEAT VISITS

As a lure for return visits to your website, blogs deliver. They're sticky. If the subject has an intriguing theme, and each episode regularly contributes to that theme, the writing becomes easier.

Writers are helped in their job when the blog subject has a rich theme—one with the prospect of lots of material. If your staff and interns have a regular chore—feeding the animals, programming a lecture series, guiding a tour—consider it as blog material. If you work with community partners on events, blog about preparing for them. If a staffer has an interesting hobby that's relevant to museum-going—rock climbing, sampler stitching, traditional recipes—write about them. Keep the blog to one day's work at a time. One rock wall, one community meeting, one sampler. The 500–800-word length, while not mandatory, is long enough to be informative, short enough to encourage revisits.

A good blog theme will come with good visuals. Consider the photo possibilities when you choose a subject. Shots from a smartphone camera are excellent, especially if the writer can overcome amateur shyness and move in for close-ups.

Some days, the writing may sound like a journal and the images might be imperfect; that's fine. The theme and its regularity are key. Of course, some budgets allow for magazine-quality articles, photographs, and illustrations. The rules of brevity, interesting facts, and diversity of subject matter apply to everyone; money never papered over a sloppy idea.

ANCILLARY THEMES

Some themes might seem more of a sidebar than part of your museum mission, but could be quite important to your audiences. Remember they are a varied and constantly changing group. Children become teenagers. Newcomers become Local Audience or, better, Members. Family Events become Adult Events. Working people retire. And Inclusiveness includes not just the people you don't know, but those "*unknown* unknowns, the ones we don't know we don't know." Defense Secretary Donald Rumsfeld's quote nails the challenge of inclusiveness.

BLOGS FOR FUNDRAISING

This is the kind of constantly updated and detailed information sometimes seen in member or donor newsletters, or in the annual report. Updates on a fire-walled website reassure donors of an institution's stability and transparency, and blogs are built upon adherence to constancy. Space in a blog allows for stories about your inclusiveness, which donors need to know. Blogs give photography its due, and good photographs are key to many capital campaigns.

Blogs are creative and unique. Remember, many institutions are competing for the same donor dollar, and you need to demonstrate your particular need for and application of their funds.

The content of the blog is essential, as is its regularity and manifestation of progress.

BLOGS FOR UNDERREPRESENTED AUDIENCES

According to *The Inclusive Historian's Handbook*, historic houses face challenges with the many audiences who believe they have nothing in common with the people who gave life to these homes. Many house museums have changed their structures, emphases, exhibitions, and stories to relate realistically to the world today. Big job! What can a museum writer do? Write a blog.

For house museums whose grandeur seems out of touch, write about:

Immigrants who settled in the area and their challenges
Craft skills used in the industries in town
Children in the community and their schools and education
Minorities and fringe groups of the time
Laws and social strictures of the time and place

For other types of museums, write about:

Museum's plans for inclusiveness
How handicapped people have been served by the science of a science
 museum
How handicaps and physical challenges have been met historically

Tips for the Blogs Already in Progress or Planned:

Use quotes from people in underrepresented groups, not from a curator or educator who possibly comes from the majority.

Write about challenges and solutions, always a smart blog format. Don't sugarcoat some simple project; it's degrading. Show the ingenuity of the group that worked on the project.

Write captions to blog photos that highlight the challenge/solution; don't just name the participants. The former says smart and museum-quality, the latter says also-ran.

Use photos that aren't posed, that show an organic gathering of many kinds of people working on the project. It must look like the real-world museum project it is, not some make-work exercise. Include age ranges in the photo if you can. Older people look different, conveying diversity without screaming it.

Must the blog author also be a member of the minority group? Not necessarily. The idea is empathy, not sympathy. The goal is to include, not single out. The ideal is a team of equals, not a committee of the underrepresented.

WHO ELSE LIVED HERE

For every person of fame or privilege whose name is on a historic house, there's a community surrounding them. The Paul Revere House, Boston, gifts its readers with an exceptional blog, The Revere Express, which puts one famous white man in context with a broader community, including its enslaved people.

The Revere Express blog of July 24, 2021, expands a comment in Revere's written account of his ride to a well-researched article on slavery in Massachusetts in the pre- and post-colonial eras.

IN PRAISE OF BLOGS

Blogs are a writer's dream and a museum credential. They zero in on a subject unique to the museum, demonstrating scholarship and creative investigation. Highly readable, they draw in readers, new and old, and keep them coming back. They give museum staffers an outlet for their curiosity, and that gift gives everyone pleasure. Many museums award Blog a heading on the navigation bar, right up top, and it deserves pride of place.

REFERENCES

Driehaus Museum, February 18, 2021 https://driehausmuseum.org/blog/view/pull man-porters [accessed 8-15-21]
https://driehausmuseum.org/blog

https://nationalcowboymuseum.org/blog/bedtime-buckaroos-dream-carver]
https://quiltmuseum.org/BlockOfTheMonth/ [accessed 2-15-22]
https://quiltmuseum.org/the-quilters-spot/botm/botm-round2-starting-soon
https://quiltmuseum.org/wp-content/uploads/2021/07/augustbotm2021-final.pdf
https://www.clariantcreative.com/blog/how-long-should-a-blog-post-be?
https://www.facebook.com/groups/NQMBlockoftheMonth/ [accessed 2-15-22]
https://www.paulreverehouse.org/the-revere-express/
https://www.whitneyplantation.org/history
Krueger, Radha, "Beer for Butterflies," #MuseumLife, Florida Museum Blog, Gaines-ville: Florida Museum, August 6, 2021, https://www.floridamuseum.ufl.edu/exhib its/butterfly-rainforest/
McKibben, Ryan, "A Tale of Today: Up from the Ashes—Pullman Porters and the Great Migration," February 18, 2021, Blog, Driehaus, https://driehausmuseum .org/blog/view/pullman-porters [accessed 1-9-22]
"#MuseumLife," Florida Museum Blog, Florida Museum of Natural History, Uni-versity of Florida, https://www.floridamuseum.ufl.edu/museum-blog/ [accessed 6-15-22]
Parson, Emily, "Mining is More Than Data," *CHM Blog*, Computer History Museum, June15, 2021, https://computerhistory.org/blog/mining-more-than-data/
Rahim, Fahim, "Whose Common: 1750–1850," The Revere Express, Paul Revere House, May 21, 2021, https://www.paulreverehouse.org/whose-common-1750-1850/
Rodwin, Nina, "Mark Hung in Chains: Slavery & Paul Revere's Midnight Ride," The Revere Express, Paul Revere House, July 24, 2021, https://www.paulreverehouse .org/mark-hung-in-chains-slavery-paul-reveres-midnight-ride/
Serre, Brennen, "Wildflower Watch," August 3, 2021, Buffalo Bill Center of the West, https://centerofthewest.org/2021/08/03/wildflower-watch/
Turino, Kenneth C., Zannieri, Nina, "Historic House Museums," The Inclusive His-torian's Handbook, April 12, 2019, https://inclusivehistorian.com/?s=+historic +house+challenges [accessed 6-21-22]
Zack, Dan, "'Nothing Ever Ends': Sorting through Rumsfeld's Knowns and Unknowns," *Washington Post*, July 1, 2021, https://www.washingtonpost.com /lifestyle/style/rumsfeld-dead-words-known-unknowns/

CHAPTER 14

Print Material

Print or digital? That's like asking, in-person or virtual. Print is always an option, and a good one. This chapter peruses foldout mailers, brochures, maps, and enveloped invitations and letters; they all share the goal of determined reading. Print pieces unfold; their pages turn; their photos, illustrations, and diagrams have captions; and they demand being read with some concentration. On the following pages are guidelines for writing real pages.

ADVANTAGE OF PRINT PIECES—THE BEAUTIFUL SPREADSHEETS

Before starting any proposed project, back up one step and ask, "Why?" Why print and not a web page? Why an expensive magazine and not an online, illustrated blog? Why a printed invitation and not an e-mail announcement to be copied and pasted into a calendar? Why a map at the information desk and not at a kiosk?

Print pieces can be spread out with everything seen in one sweeping glance:

- Exhibitions—with dates
- Objects—relevant to exhibition or current talk, or just interesting
- Speaker—with date, day of week, time
- Classes—with teacher bio, cost, learning outcomes
- Performances—descriptions with relevance to museum
- Membership—integral to sustainability and repeat visitorship

ALL IN ONE SPACE

Print pieces are geographic, available inside the museum where visitors have already entered or sent to a targeted zip code.

Print pieces are inclusive; there's space in that unfolded brochure or mailing for translations into a second language and photographs, which demonstrate diversity better than words. Queens Museum does a good job of translating everything on its website into Spanish, and that can be adapted to print.

Print pieces introduce new issues, ones that might not be found on a website, such as land acknowledgment statements. The Art Institute of Chicago puts its statement in its self-guided gallery tour brochure.

Print pieces expand on topics, such as bios of diverse speakers or class instructors, or close-ups of a science exhibit, without "clicking here." Field Museum does that well. All in one space.

Here are some other examples of print's value:

- Staying power—they lay around, stay around, get handed around—Chautauqua Institution's calendar
- Seasonality—they can be timed for the season, and sent to the right zip code. Chicago Botanic Garden's February Orchid Show (inside!)
- Readability, thanks to larger type, bigger images, and larger layout—any museum with older visitors or visitors who speak English as a second language
- Envelope—personalized letters and inserts can be sent in an envelope—one of several printed pieces utilized by Driehaus Museum
- Flat pieces of paper can be circled, checked, annotated—Alliance Française class list
- Useful for self-guided tours—the Art Institute brochure

FOLDOUT BROCHURES

The dimensions of a typical foldout brochure or mailer vary widely from 8 ½ × 11 to 9 × 24, depending on size of budget and printer recommendation. On the panels of a mailer there's space to explain coming exhibitions, show photographs of exhibits, catalog the month's classes, feature a speaker, announce special workshops, expand on the content of talks, and direct readers through a museum's rooms and galleries. For new visitors or prospects, a brochure will introduce them to lesser-known places like labs, makerspaces, outbuildings, gardens, and walking trails.

Chicago Botanic Garden shows a map of its grounds with suggested walks and their length:

- Fitness Walk 1.8 miles
- Bridges to Wellness 1.74 miles
- Zen Walk 1.2 miles
- Prairie Views 1.76 miles
- Harvest Hike 1.65 miles

It also shows landmarks along the way:

- Nature Play Garden
- Zigzag Bridge
- Fruit and Vegetable Garden

To optimize the capaciousness of a foldout brochure, plan to include at least six subjects—dozens of subjects for a 22" foldout—for the reader to peruse.

Writers: The word "peruse" is important, and some of its synonyms are "scrutinize," "study," "research," and other verbs that indicate absorbing a lot of the museum's information. The following are the some of the reasons to ask targeted readers—those in your geographic area—to read carefully.

NEW EXHIBITIONS

The Field, in Chicago, deployed a fold-out mailer to announce its new exhibition, "The Machine Inside: Biomechanics, October 22, 2021–January 9, 2022." The Field puts on big shows, with state-of-the-art exhibits for visitors with high-level curiosity. Field visitors have learned to expect hands-on, deep-involvement learning. Biomechanics? It takes some explaining and a printed piece is made to be perused.

Figure 14.1. Imagine the people who lived in this historic house, their food, books, family life, and visitors. With printed pieces, there's space to populate each room with stories and additional photographs. Let's go inside and look around.

YinYang/ iStock via Gettyimages

The 11" × 15" foldout mailer staked out a large territory, big enough to also:

- Give details of biomechanics
- Show some hands-on displays
- Illustrate the displays with photos
- List membership benefits
- Describe photographically three other gallery exhibitions

And there were two panels devoted to membership benefits and the price list. This geographically defined mailer was also sent to people living in the metro area apt to visit the Field.

The Art Institute of Chicago used a fold-out brochure as a Visitor Guide to its newest exhibition, "Thinking of You. I Mean Me. I Mean You." The fold-out, which has the wingspread of three feet, also contains floor plans for four levels and countless galleries. One panel shows sturdy visitors to the encyclopedic art museum "What to See in an Hour" in a four-row photo display of captioned photos. Here's how it reads: "Short on time? Here's a must-see guide to the Art Institute. If you entered at Michigan Avenue, start at the top [of the four rows]. If you entered through the Modern Wing, go in reverse order."

Each of the twelve stamp-sized photos carries a caption like this one:

Face Mask (Ngady Mwaash)
Gallery 137, first level.

FAMILIARIZATION FOR NEWCOMERS

Permanent exhibitions are comprehensive and daunting for newcomers. At the Illinois Holocaust Museum, the Karkomi Holocaust Exhibition encompasses a fifteen-plus year history of Jewish life in Germany, and it summarizes that period in an 11 × 22, eight-panel Self-Guided Tour brochure. You can see why the spread of a printed piece is necessary for even a summarization of an exhibition.

The following brochure text condenses multiple didactic panels in a series of large galleries:

1. "Introductory Film—Local Survivors Reflect
2. Jewish Life Before World War II
3. Germany: A Fragile Democracy
4. Jewish Community Responds to Nazism 1933–38

. . .

7. Germany Invades and Occupies Europe
. . .
10. The 'Final Solution' Begins
. . .
15. Railcar
. . .
17. Jewish Armed Resistance
. . .
20. Death Marches
21. Liberation
. . .
28. American Awakening/Freedom of Speech"

Writers: When long lists are called for, concise text must follow. That means about sixty words per paragraph.

CLASSES FOR EVERYONE

Fold-out mailers give distinct space for all levels of classes. A class schedule is useless if the grade or experience level is unclear. Writers, like educators, must apply terms like "level 1," "intermediate," "Part II," "techniques specifically for dim lighting," and "required text." Creative class titles are effective only when the learning level is indicated. Then come the class descriptions.

Here's how Alliance Française de Chicago, a cultural institution with the imprimatur of the French Embassy in the United States, names and describes its classes in its 8½ × 22 foldout brochures:

- Symposium on the Arts of France
- The French Table
- Touring French Wines: The Art of Blind Tasting
- Chic and You: The Film Series
- La Littérature de la Sérénité
- Media library
- Cooking classes
- Café-Conversation groups
- Film Club

With a fold-out mailer, there is space for class descriptions like this:

Symposium on the Arts of France—Our museum-quality series returns with a stellar cast of speakers to tell us about life in the French garden, formal or informal! A fundraiser for our educational and cultural programs. In English. Online AND on-site.

Advanced Beginners—Le I-Can-Do-A-Lot—You've got the basics covered and can hold a simple conversation. Build on your vocabulary.

Corporate Classes—Expand Your Employees' Horizon—Whether you work with a French company, travel often, or want to offer a new perk to your employees.

And in another mailer, the classes were laid out a little differently, reaching different audiences with headings like:

- Private Classes
- Preschool
- Chez Kids Academy—"Immerse your child in an enjoyable, rich and varied French language and cultural program!"

Cultural institutions, often housed in multiplex arts buildings, have assumed many of the qualities, and quality, of museums. To compete, they need to explain themselves, and the spaciousness and individuality of a fold-out mailer defines their goals elegantly.

As museums and cultural institutions welcome more diverse audiences, space will be needed for translations.

Writers: when writing about classes, which usually carry a fee and the weight of gravitas, use professional terms and state all the rigorous requirements. Never speak down; always write up. Remember the intelligence level to which you want learners to aspire, and bring out your best vocabulary. Work with the Education Department on terminology and reading level. Sometimes that rigor looks like this: "Alliance Française de Chicago offers a variety of language certification exams . . . DAEFLE, DELF/DALF, TAPIF Evaluations, TEC, TCF, and private language exams."

GALLERY PLAN

Gallery plans are well-served by websites and on-site signage, but printed plans offer the added advantage of availability on the spot. And their size helps encompass the scope of the museum. At the Chicago Botanic Gardens, in suburban Glencoe, Illinois, the galleries are Gardens, Aquatic Garden, and Enabling, English Walled and Japanese Gardens. There are Meadows and Prairie, Plant Science Center, and Islands. They're all beautiful to look at, and their beautiful names beckon across the 17 × 30-inch page. Plans of course also show restrooms, dining, first aid, and Wi-Fi access.

Then there's the de rigueur membership panel. When visitors see the expanse of what they're getting from a museum, the pitch for members makes sense. As the Garden puts it: "Become a member and take advantage of all that the Garden has to offer."

LAND ACKNOWLEDGMENT

In a fold-out brochure, gallery guide, or map, there's also space for space itself—the land on which the museum stands. It is no small matter.

Museums that have started discussions of land acknowledgment statements consider it a process, involving all aspects of the museum and representatives of Indigenous Peoples councils. Many museums are already displaying a land acknowledgment on all published materials; it is considered Indigenous protocol. On a print piece, where information can be seen in one glance, it looks intrinsic to the museum, as it is.

Here's one definition of a land acknowledgment statement, from Northwestern University:

> A Land Acknowledgment is a formal statement that recognizes and respects Indigenous Peoples as traditional stewards of this land and the enduring relationship that exists between Indigenous Peoples and their traditional territories.

The wording used by Art Institute of Chicago in an exhibition brochure is:

> The Art Institute of Chicago is located on the traditional homelands of the Council of the Three Fires: the Ojibwa, Ozawa, and Potawatomi Nations. Many other tribes such as the Miami, Ho-Chunk, Menominee, Sac, and Fox also called this area home. Today, one if the largest urban American Indian communities in the United States resides in Chicago.

LETTER IN AN ENVELOPE

This artifact of an earlier era is still functional. And it serves several important purposes:

- Membership invitation—personalizes the request to purchase membership
- Membership thank you—repeats list, and encourages use, of benefits
- Invitation to a higher-priced ticketed event—personal touch eases the sale
- Invitation to a free event—adds importance to what could seem a free-for-all
- Container for inserts—a museum can send a targeted, personal message in an e-mail, but only an envelope holds stuff.

Here's what unfolds on the table when one opens a membership letter from Driehaus Museum:

- Two complimentary admission tickets for friends
- Member card with bar code and expiration date
- Coupon for free gift from the store
- Printed list of membership benefits at different levels

Letters on letterhead stationery have an advantage and disadvantage. On the minus side, a businesslike, formal appearance and four paragraphs of text.

On the plus side, a written document states in writing the tax deductibility of a membership or donation.

Wording that would be excessive in another format, imbues a letter with the look and feel of the museum. The Driehaus Museum, which is housed in the 1890 Belle Époque Nickerson Mansion uses "historic," "beautiful art and design," beautiful museum store," "opulent interiors," "mansion," "brilliant," "cultural enjoyment." They make a business letter gracious.

The date at the top and signature at the bottom show accountability. For membership, event tickets, or donations at a high level, this is a look big-check signers are accustomed to.

CALENDARS—MONTHLY, QUARTERLY, OR SEASONAL

Take a look at your museum's Visitor To Do List. If there are more than twenty items on it, they'd look better in a foldout print piece with a grid calendar.

The print calendar is a quick read and a visual scheduler. As everyone's work-life balance shifts, seeing a month-at-a-glance calendar organizes their options.

A 9 × 24-inch fold-out shows a whole month or season of activities in one space. It's easy for the reader to highlight or circle activities and plot how they fit the household's schedule. These printed pieces are large enough to intersperse illustrations and photos to register activities visibly. They let the reader pore over a printed page to get the details.

THE NEW MULTIPLEX

Cultural institutions have become a Swiss Army knife of learning experiences; cutting-edge only begins to define their activities, which borrow so much from museums.

Chautauqua Institution in upstate New York is a cultural institution unique for its bounteous diversity of cultural offerings in one place: a leafy, lakeside, spread-out village of hundreds of buildings. There's a museum, and also theater, music school and practice rooms, theater school, art gallery, literary group hall, small class rooms, waterfront, gym, assembly hall, denominational houses, miles of pedestrian walks, and, at the hub:

The Amp, a 2,000-seat newly renovated amphitheatre hosting over sixty-three days the great names in arts, culture, economics, government, education, diplomacy, religion, sports, entertainment and . . . you get the picture.

Actually, one needs a calendar to get the picture of this nine-week immersion course.

The 23 × 18 foldout brochure shows every speaker, performance, and lecture for all sixty-three days. On the flip side of this piece are photos and descriptions of concerts, dining, day trips, stores, and recreation.

Scale this down for your museum. Chautauqua provides a clear example of how to graphically explain what today's museums, in their fullness, accomplish. In each square of a calendar, along with the activity, there is enough space for a writer to mention:

Collecting. Add to an exhibition or exhibit calendar entry, a short description of the museum's collection where appropriate.

Preserving. Writers can widen museum audiences by describing the science and learning behind an object or exhibit included in a talk.

Displaying. Writers might point out the relationship between exhibits on a museum tour.

Interpreting. Make some calendar squares a little larger to add context with a photo or map.

Nourishing. Leave a space in the calendar for writers to remind visitors how much more they can see when they stop for a café break.

Merchandising. The store isn't consumerist, it's memory-making. On a day without a calendar event, why not extol the learning available in the museum store's books, educational games, stationery with reproductions of exhibits, and all souvenirs that bring back memories of the visit.

Acculturating. Writers: there's space in a printed piece to add a few simple words like "your whole family," "later hours," "ASL signers available," and "all videos are closed captioned," to your text. Make room for text translations, land acknowledgment statements, and photographs that visually demonstrate diversity. All this in a calendar? Yes, because this is one print piece that stays around for a long time.

Reaching out. Where appropriate on a calendar, for example a special event, write about facilities rentals for meetings, parties, and conferences. They broaden the definition of a museum's goals, and widen the reach of museums. A writer's goal will be to replace words like "gala" with more inclusive terms such as get-togethers and award ceremonies. Remember the obvious words like accessible.

SCHEDULE A WEEKEND

Some museums and institutions, like Chautauqua, and also Baseball Hall of Fame Museum in iconic Cooperstown, New York, and Shaker Village in Harrodsburg, Kentucky, strategically promote their hometowns. Destination museums are proud of their heritage and place in the community. Inn rooms and historic recipes are requisite to community awareness. All museums add hospitality to their schedule when they include their hometown credentials.

Writers: use terms like "rooted in the community," "partnering in the spring house walk," "visit our neighbor museums while you're in town," "if you're doing research here, if you're bringing the whole family, if you're new to the area, be sure to visit . . ." Writing about a community is good museology.

SUMMARY

Sometimes, nothing equals a printout. Mariners' Museum and Park, Newport News, Virginia, redefines a printed piece, on the education page of its website, as an educational exercise; it can be printed out from a home or school computer, and then folded up to "Create an Astrolabe." Folded paper endures.

As museums spread out over eras, galleries, and acres, and visitors spread out to get a better look, museum writers have a clear edict: Give them some space! Give audiences old, new, and prospective a generous amount of paper. Print that paper with information, photos, charts, and maps, that can be unfolded on a flat surface, looked down at, and read. Use the large sheet to include more audiences, provide more details, and give more reasons to visit. Writers: print pieces need you.

REFERENCES

"Calendar of Events," Chautauqua Institution, Chautauqua, New York, 2021 Season, June 26–August 29, 2021, brochure

"Karkomi Holocaust Exhibition," Illinois Holocaust Museum, brochure

"Land Acknowledgment," Native American and Indigenous Initiatives, Northwestern University, 2021, https://www.northwestern.edu/native-american-and-indigenous-peoples/about/Land%20Acknowledgement.html [accessed 10-19-21]

"Les Lumieres," Alliance Française de Chicago, Cultural Season 2021–22, brochure

"The Machine Inside: Biomechanics," Field Museum, September 3, 2021–January 9, 2022, mailer

"Map," Chicago Botanic Garden, 2021

"Membership Program Thank You Letter," Driehaus Museum, August 20, 2021, letterhead letter

"Plan a Getaway," Stay, Shaker Village, https://shakervillageky.org/the-inn/ [accessed 10-2-21]

"Printable Activities," Resources, Mariners' Museum and Park, https://exploration .marinersmuseum.org/resources/ [accessed 8-26-21]

"School Programs 2021–22," Alliance Française de Chicago, brochure

"Space Rentals," Visit, Harvey B. Gantt Cultural Center, https://www.ganttcenter.org /visit-the-gantt/space-rentals/ [accessed 11-1-21]

"Thinking of You. I Mean Me. I Mean You." Visitor Guide, Art Institute of Chicago, September 19, 2021–January 14, 2022, brochure

"Thinking of You. I Mean Me. I Mean You," mailer, Art Institute Chicago, Fall 2021

"Walks," Chicago Botanic Garden, Fall/Winter 2021–2022, brochure

CHAPTER 15

Seasonality, Holidays, and Remembrances

Exploit the seasons for all they're worth because they're worth a lot. They change the pace, force you to be relevant, appeal to many different audiences. And there are so many seasons beyond the big four. Summer, fall, winter, and spring each have holidays, festivals, named months, and locally significant days.

SEASONAL WRITING ADDS MORE THAN A MONTH

When museums add a season—think Anchorage Museum of Art's "Summer Fest" which starts in July—they get a season paired to their situation. This is what else gets added:

- New and expanded audiences
- Repetition
- Community and civic pride
- Continuity
- Urgency
- Cultural Heritage
- Remembrances
- Data

When seasonality is expanded or repositioned on the calendar pages, other opportunities open to reinforce awareness of the museum and its relevance in the life of today's audiences. New programs encourage new language, the words new audiences really speak.

This chapter will suggest sound marketing reasons to rewrite the calendar with new seasons, holidays, and celebrations. It will borrow, gratefully, examples of calendar-expanding projects from other museums.

Writers: here's help for the scourge of overused words. The bounty of seasonality enhances your communications with its own terms and phrases to supplant the clichés of the usual calendar items. The language of other cultures' holidays and seasons is vivid, impressive, and not overused.

NEW AND EXPANDED AUDIENCES

When you expand a holiday to a season, you expand audiences. Different people see your museum in a different light. Shaker Village of Pleasant Hill, Kentucky, borrows terminology from Halloween and applies it to the trail-walking, scenery-watching season, speaking to adults with

Howl at the Moon Trail Hike
Spirit Stroll
Boo Cruise on the Kentucky River

Any museum can adapt a holiday into a seasonal experience for other groups. In and around Pleasant Hill, Halloween occupies several weeks on

Figure 15.1.   Seasons add reasons to visit a museum, and they're universal.
shironosov/ iStock viaa Getty Images

the calendar for adults, adults without children, outdoorsy types, romantics, leaf-watchers, and people of all ages.

There's another audience to attract with an expanded approach: people who can't visit a museum in person. During Black History Month, Driehaus Museum in Chicago features a well-researched blog article that surveys: "The Great Migration, the Chicago Defender, the Pullman porters and the roots of Chicago's Black working class . . ."

In "A Tale of Today: Up From the Ashes—Pullman Porters and the Great Migration," the Driehaus continues a series of articles on events that informed the Gilded Age, the period in which the museum's building, a merchant's mansion, was lived in.

It honors Black History Month by showing its relevance to local history, and it welcomes prospective visitors by showing them another way to access the museum.

Here's another group that won't access some outdoor museums: people who hike, bike, or stroll down the lane. Winter could be a very off season for villages like Shaker Village of Pleasant Valley, Kentucky. However, when the leaves start to turn, it turns toward indoor activities like meetings. It promotes its hotel with authentically restored Shaker-style rooms, and meeting rooms with up-to-date facilities. A decades-long history of restaurant and catering comes to the fore with this reminder of its scenic outdoors: "seed-to-table" menus.

The new audiences who come inside include residents of the community, businesses in the community, donors, and out-of-town attendees at conferences. They all have friends and families who might be interested in the museum. And once inside, they themselves might see something worth coming back for.

Because Black History Month is well established as a staging area for programs, museums have four weeks in which to explore new audience enrichment projects. Gantt Center for African-American Arts + Culture explored a concept to reach an underserved market: Black art collectors. "The Collectors Roundtable includes a diverse group of Black Americans who discuss their collections, inspirations for acquiring works, and advice for aspiring collectors." It positions the virtual roundtable as homage to the Black South and its arts and culture—and so much more. It recognizes a special interest group, it gives art lovers a new outlet for their interests, and it is open to all ages. What a wise realization that habits of culture start young.

The young are also targeted at New Bedford Whaling Museum, which created February Vacation Week from February 21 to 25 in 2022, as a good time to: "explore themes of conservation throughout the Museum." By setting aside a discrete block of time, the museum focuses on young people plus those who are interested in conservation. The latter is a new audience any museum might consider as it also encompasses scholars and donors.

And then, a museum can call winter for what it is, cold and snowy winter, and turn reality into a lot of fun. Crystal Bridges Museum of American Art announces boldly on its website: "The 2021–22 Winter Guide to Crystal Bridges: The museum is the perfect place to come in from the cold and warm up with art, music, coffee, shopping, and much more. Use this guide to plan your winter trip to Crystal Bridges and learn what to expect during the season."

It expands its audience into procrastinators, children with cold-averse parents, and all those people who have gotten accustomed to sitting out winter. Don't rule out any audience!

Writers: inclusion includes groups that haven't been categorized yet. Part of the writer's job is to find a phrase or two to include these segments of your market.

REPETITION

Once is not enough.

Return visits throughout the year are hampered by the repetition-averse. Museums must promote each new exhibition, bolstered by a new acquisition or a new program. Seasonality helps because museums change with the seasons. Classes change, tours change, and special events change.

One visit per season to a museum would be wonderful. However, seasons last a full three calendar months—why not fill the calendar with a little more? At botanic gardens, the changes happen all the time and some promote the changes that natures bestows.

Longwood Gardens, Kennett Square, Pennsylvania, encourages two fall visits with its changing colors of fall photography classes.

At Chicago Botanic Garden, winter is guaranteed cold season. Temperatures vary, but February is a good bet for indoor preferences. So the Garden's annual winter orchid show brings garden lovers into a hothouse favorite and a selling point of carefree wildness. Not your typical valentine, and that's a February message writers should heed. "February is for orchid lovers: The Orchid Show: Untamed, February 12–March 27, celebrates the irrepressible spirit of wild orchids."

Locust Grove welcomes the New Year with a preview of coming months: "Although it seems quiet (and snowy) at Locust Grove, behind the scenes we're . . . getting ready to relaunch familiar programs and introduce new programs in 2022. . . . When you walk to the historic house, you'll be walking on a completely new path."

A preview and a promise: that's a forward-looking way to keep your mailing list involved through the slower months of winter.

DAILY GREETINGS OF THE ARTISTS

Many museums participate in posting tweets on artists' birthdays. It's a cheerful, pictorial reminder of the museum, daily throughout the years. For museums, it shows more of its collection that the galleries could. And, of course, it reaches the broad and deep social media audience that has expressed a like, love, or follow for museums.

Jacob Lawrence was born September 7, 1917 #onthisday. In "School Room," Lawrence's vibrant, deceptively simple style is evidence of his belief that "When the subject is strong, simplicity is the only way to treat it."

Nelson-Atkins Museum, Kansas City, Missouri, returns almost every day on Twitter to greet you with happy birthday messages to artists in its collection. A work by Jacob Lawrence, Yasuo Kuniyoshi, Jacques Lipchitz, Gustave Caillebotte, brightens any day, and if it's their birthday, viewers happily applaud. Celebrating a seasonal event is a gimmick and a good one; it showcases a museum's collection, teaches about an artist, and conveys continuity. You can count on these birthday presents from Nelson-Atkins.

Writers: maybe you can write promising words like "First" before your museum's seasonal event. Or, "we hope this will be the first of many seasonal events." Make a season stand for something specific to your institution and community.

Peabody-Essex Museum, in its website calendar of Indigenous Day Events, says: "Take part in honoring these communities, their elders past and present, as well as future generations, through our first Indigenous Peoples' Day celebration."

COMMUNITY AND CIVIC PRIDE

Racine Art Museum honors the community of food and brews, entertainment, and togetherness, as well as artists, with its Annual Art Benefit, a street fair with a purpose.

Word on the Street: SAVOR 2021. The museum tells its current audiences: "Party with RAM while giving back to the community by supporting the arts!" Support of one's community includes its cultural institutions, and all parties are boosted by their partnerships.

Seasonal events in small communities boost more than civic pride. They bring in residents and tourists alike for visits, lectures, and workshops throughout the year.

The National Churchill Museum in Fulton, Missouri, hosts an event on March 5 every year, commemorating Winston Churchill's "Iron Curtain" speech there, at Westminster College, in 1946. It brings in scholars and other luminaries whose gravitas establish its bona fides.

Its lecture series annually hosts diplomats, university presidents, ambassadors, authors, and U.S. presidents as speakers. It offers customized tours for educators, clubs, church groups, retirement communities, performance groups, and bus tours, the kind of visitorship smaller cities and towns crave.

Writing for these events is made easier by the boldface names involved, from Winston Churchill on down. Names are another form of strong nouns that are basic to good writing. If you don't have famous speakers, give the talk a strong name.

Historic Houses look like houses, and that misrepresents them. Visitors, as well as donors and members, may not realize that house museums collect, research, archive, and interpret artifacts and eras. Sending a holiday greeting offers a new way to present the collection. Driehaus Museum, in its Thanksgiving e-greeting card, featured a poster from its collection that swirled with Art Deco Thanksgiving festivity. Do all mailing list recipients of the Driehaus know about such Belle Epoque objects? Now they do. It's in the caption citing the source of the image.

Writers: use famous names connected to your museum to remind targeted audiences of your museum's involvement in their community.

There are four important names at Oshkosh (Wisconsin) Public Museum: *White Christmas*, the movie; Rosemary Clooney the movie star; U.S. military veterans; and local charity Operation Waverly. The museum gets snow and Christmas like all its neighbors, and it gets something else in "White Christmas: The Exhibition," courtesy of the Rosemary Clooney House in Augusta, Kentucky. Not relying on this gift to fill the community stocking, it joins in Operation Waverly in collecting donations to assist homeless veterans. "As a component of the *White Christmas* exhibition, we will be offering 'Operation Waverly' to assist homeless veterans in our community."

The power of small museums and other cultural institutions is multiplied when they team up during a season that's universally known for goodwill.

Harry S. Truman has been sending Labor Day and Rosh Hashanah greetings for years since his death, courtesy of the Truman Library Institute and Twitter.

HAPPY LABOR DAY! Today we celebrate American workers and the U.S. President who prized their contributions to our nation's strength, prosperity and well-being. #LaborDay #FairDeal #HarryTruman

It was accompanied by a photo of President Truman giving a Labor Day Address in Detroit, 1948.

CONTINUITY

Continued interest is always a goal for a museum, especially with local people who are already familiar with it. How to keep them coming back is an ongoing deliberation that Tenement Museum digs into its archives to answer. There's always another story of the immigrant families that lived in the tenement building on the Lower East Side. In October 2021, that story was the Clairvoyant Housewives of the Lower East Side. With a slight connection to the witching month, and a magnetic connection to women who work (in the home or elsewhere) in general, it keeps the stories of the museum—its mission—always in view.

The month of October is seasonal for everyone, but only a natural science museum can claim Fossil Month. The Burke in Seattle eschews autumn leaves for one of the important parts of its collection and rightly celebrates fossils: "Celebrate the 12th anniversary of National Fossil Day with the Burke's Fossil Costume Contest!" To transform a museum-owned event into a participatory one for visitors, the Burke continues:

> Your costume can depict a living version or fossilized form of an ancient plant or animal.
> Include the following info with each entry:
> What's your fossil? Include the name of the fossil you chose.
> Share what you learned! Feature a fact about the fossil that you learned during your research.

Creativity is requested, and also a bit of commitment completing an application.

Writers: everyone loves the idea of a contest, and the idea blossoms when they actually sit down to consider entering. Make it easy for them.

The Wing Luke Museum of the Asian Pacific American Experience doesn't get complacent about obvious calendar events. For Lunar New Year it puts a large orange symbol of the Year of the Tiger on its home page under the heading Upcoming. It lists some of the events. It treats this regular occurrence as fresh and new. And for many audiences to the website, it will be new. It's a lesson for all museums. "Join us as we take our Lunar New Year Fair outside! Explore the Chong Wa Playfield for an afternoon of fun with the Wing Luke Museum. Enjoy Lunar New Year-themed storytimes, interactive Lion Dance Talks, take-and-go craft activities, and connecting with community organizations."

Writers: if your museum is fortunate in having a connection to an annual calendar event, give it a heroic introduction. There will always be newcomers to your community, with different interests and museum expectations who will enjoy hearing about it. As for traditional audiences, there's great benefit in generational continuity. The halo effect extends across the museum to the community and beyond.

Museums are arts institutions, and when they partner with other art forms, like drama, it's a match made in, let's say Merchant's House, in New York. The museum and Summoners Ensemble Theatre got together in the

Figure 15.2.   Catrina, iconic symbol of Dia de los Muertos, leads the day of remembrance in communities throughout the Americas.
loeskieboom / iStock via Getty images

stately double parlor of the Greek Revival 1832 landmark mansion, for a December-long engagement of *A Christmas Carol.*

The timing is seasonal, plus. Charles Dickens knows no season. However:

> In December 1867, Charles Dickens arrived in New York City for a month of sold-out performances of . . . *A Christmas Carol.* Join Mr. Dickens, portrayed by John Kevin Jones, as he tells his timeless Christmas tale . . . surrounded by 19th century holiday decorations . . . and richly appointed period furnishings. . . . Strictly limited engagement! December 1 to December 31.

A traditional holiday season, turned into the month of December and a partnership with other fine artists. It's a different way to look at the calendar, at the Merchant's House Museum, and the community that was and is New York.

Writers: wherever you can give credit to a museum partner, whether it's Charles Dickens or a local theater company, do so generously. While expanding the boundaries of the calendar, it's opening the boundaries of your audience to other arts patrons.

Racine Art Museum also recognizes artists a little farther than its usual purview by coordinating its 2022 exhibitions with the entire year: "The International Year of Glass 2022." Here's how it words its focus-and-leverage strategy:

believing that the last few decades have been a historically significant time for artistic advancement, RAM has concentrated on the achievements of glass in the U.S. and abroad to capture a clear picture of the movement's growth. . . . While pleased to highlight the work of glass artists at any time, RAM is especially proud to do so in 2022 as part of this initiative.

Events such as International Year of Glass are products of broad scope and large budget organization whose visibility enlarge small city museums admirably.

Writers: give a lot of credit. It's a given that museums of any size owe a lot to partners with a greater name recognition and more resources. The other side of the partnership owes museums a lot in gained credibility and community respect. In your writing, give equal credit to both the big name and yours.

URGENCY

Museums belong to the Large Purchase category. People don't purchase a museum visit—and its attendant cost of time, transportation, thought, and effort—every day. For many, even tourists, it's a visit that can be put off for tomorrow. A sense of urgency puts museums in the today category, and seasonal events can be written as urgent. Here are some seasonal events that urge visiting now:

"Heirloom peonies for sale for a limited time! Divisions of our heirloom peonies are on sale while supplies last!"

At Locust Grove Estate, in Poughkeepsie, New York, peonies have bloomed since the 1890s. There's a story involved:

They were planted for Martha Young. Martha's daughter—Annette Young— eventually opened the gardens to the public . . . [and these] perennial divisions will give you a chance to enjoy a little bit of our garden in yours for years to come.

Ready to plant now for blooms in the spring.

First come/first served—we're sorry but we can't reserve or ship peonies.

Now, a typical calendar event in upstate New York becomes a gardener's race. It's local, targeted to a swath of audience that plants perennials, and it's an event that must be attended immediately.

After New Year's Day, a familiar reminder comes from Alliance Française de Chicago in the form of a New Year's Resolution, appropriating a popular worldwide event in the first weeks of January:

Our French Classes Start Today.

What a better way to start 2022 than by learning *le français* at the place for all things French in Chicago? . . . It's not too late.

Battleship New Jersey offers a seasonal event that's so enticing one might wish its Native American Heritage Day event lasted longer than the weekend of November 27, 2022: "Guests can learn about some of the Native Americans that have fought in the military: the Code Talkers. Learn how to send secret messages by learning the real Navajo words used during World War II and beyond."

Writers: you can avoid cliché writing by using specific examples of celebration events that honor accomplishments, not myths. Native American Heritage Month celebrates a large part of American communities, people we should know today.

CULTURAL HERITAGE

America is a country of many cultures, all part of our heritage. Not all people's holidays appear on calendars, but that is changing. In 2021, legislation was signed into law establishing June 19 as Juneteenth National Independence Day. In Birmingham, Alabama, cradle of the Civil Rights Movement and home to Birmingham Civil Rights Institute, the day has long been a: "festival of heritage and culture celebrating the emancipation of enslaved people in America." The whole community is involved, with local organizations organizing genealogy workshops, health information tents, entertainment, food, and togetherness.

Inevitably, increasingly, seasonality and holidays will be inclusive and diverse. Take for example, Diwali, observed on the Hindu calendar in October or November, in 2022 on October 24. Hindus around the world celebrate Diwali, or Deepavali—a festival of lights and fireworks "that unites people . . . a time when people embrace one another with joy and laughter." And it stretches back more than 2,500 years. In India, the five-day celebration traditionally marks the biggest holiday of the year.

Writers: when researching holidays of cultures with which you're unfamiliar, include sources from other countries. They describe holidays in different ways than Americans do. It's the difference between including other cultures, and being inclusive.

From Worcester, Massachusetts, the world looks very close when, each fall, it schedules a day of events to celebrate Diwali, India's most popular holiday. Worcester Art Museum schedule of events is written with proper nouns to honor the culture with its own language. Here's a sampling of the day's activities:

- Story time with author Geeta Pherwani, *Reena and the Diwali Star*
- Diwali lamp lighting

- Special docent tour: *Honoring Lakshmi: Lotus, Mudras, and other symbols in Hindu and Buddhist Art*
- *Mithai*, Sweets making demonstration—Kalakand recipe
- Mandala Art activity
- Rangoli Sand Art
- Learn more about India and the India Society of Worcester
- 11:30 a.m.–3:00 p.m., Museum Café, traditional Indian cuisine available for purchase

The Asian culture is part of American communities throughout the United States. According to the *Wall Street Journal*, the Asian population in the U.S. is 20 million or 6 percent and growing, with bigger increases in the Midwest and northern plains. Of note to small museums, smaller communities are actively promoting immigration to its industries, and industries like towns with arts opportunities for incoming employees and their families.

Around Thanksgiving, a traditional programming time, museums are now acknowledging the roots of harvest thanks and remembering indigenous peoples.

Peabody-Essex Museum, in Salem, Massachusetts, offered a lineup of events for Indigenous Peoples Day, October 12, 2021, that is noteworthy for its wording: "Join us in acknowledging Indigenous people from the many nations who have lived on and moved through this place . . . and those who still live and work in this region. . . . Sing along with Miss Bethany, then enjoy a reading of *We Are Water Protectors* by author Carole Lindstrom (Anishinabe/Metis), who is tribally enrolled with the Turtle Mountain Band of Ojibwe."

Writers: the protocols for writing about indigenous people are still being written, and they include:

- Identification of tribal affiliations in two different ways
- Reminder that indigenous peoples aren't just historic figures, but your neighbors.

REMEMBRANCES

The traditional holiday season starts on December 7, the anniversary of the attack on Pearl Harbor in Hawaii, in 1941. A distant time, perhaps; a worthy memory absolutely. It's not just American history, but a trope embedded in American culture.

Baseball Hall of Famer Bob Feller served aboard the USS *Alabama*, and on December 7, 2021, the eightieth anniversary, Baseball Hall of Fame Museum, Cooperstown, New York, remembered Pearl Harbor Day with virtual and in-person events. Tribute was paid to baseball players who served, and the community of American veterans was honored. In seasons that are loaded year-round with calendar items, museums stand out when they circle remembrance dates.

Here's another December event that redefines the season: Luminaria Nights at Longwood Gardens in Kennett Square, Pennsylvania. "Join us for a display of reflection and remembrance . . . as thousands of luminaria light the way against the backdrop of our moonlit winter garden and within the warmth of our Conservatory. . . . We invite you to light your own luminaria in hope, in remembrance, or in tribute."

Luminarias appear in many neighborhoods, from San Antonio, Texas, where they've been part of a city tradition for forty years, to Walla Walla, Washington. The lights that started in Mexico centuries ago are very much a part of America's cultural heritage, and, not incidentally, they glow in Canada and Europe, too.

DATA

Any time a museum adds an event, there's an opportunity to collect new data. Viewers ask for more information, tickets, or—hopefully—the newsletter.

Much credit goes to Petersen Automotive Museum for loading its calendar with wonderful seasonal events and, at the same time, sources of data from its auto-enchanted followers.

An important date on the calendar of aficionados of any category is the annual get-together. Museums with a similar focus can coattail on the event as does the Petersen Automotive Museum with a book published to coincide with the world-famous Grand National Roadster show. The writer captures the excitement of the show and connects it to the museum:

[Own] your own copy of *Deuce!: 1932 Ford Hot Rods* only found at the Petersen Store. If you weren't able to make it to the now longest-running indoor car show in the world, you can get lost in pages of cultural history, technical specifications, and an aesthete's sensibility to narrate the story of hot rodding's evolution from lawless to legitimate.

Like all the text on the Petersen website and in e-mail announcements, the museum ties the details of autos together with their history and their artistry. Good writing underscores the scholarship and design expertise of the museum.

Then there's the Super Bowl.

For Super Bowl LVI in Los Angeles, Petersen partnered with some powerful organizations in "Taste of the NFL/Party with a Purpose."

Marketers have long been grateful for the commercial possibilities in the roman numeral party season between New Year's and summer. Petersen supplied some horsepower for that holiday bandwagon in 2022 by hosting "Taste of the NFL/Party with a Purpose," along with the NFL and GEN-YOUth to support food security.

In addition to its own mailing list, Petersen now has interested clicks from local food retailers, a respected philanthropy, and football fans.

Just when football ends, Petersen celebrates Presidents' Day with a special tour of cars in its vault. In an e-mail with the Subject "Hoods Up for Presidents' Day!" the museum invites readers to make good use of the February 17–22 long weekend and spend ninety minutes on a tour of the museum's vault, specially opened for the event.

More data rolls in, probably from visitors with children or out-of-town friends who like autos.

Fundraising, in all its iterations, is another tool for gathering data. Chapter 17 on fundraising explores the customary uses of donations, and the unexpected consequences need a little attention. When a donor completes a purchase of donation, a lot of new data is made available.

After the Super Bowl, the next big calendar event is Valentine's Day, and Milwaukee County Zoo enlists its denizens to help lovers send greetings to people and donations to the zoo. The data collected includes names, addresses, and types of people who send valentines, and zip codes outside the usual Milwaukee marketing area. These are a few of the possible cards to choose from, and that choice suggests which animals are popular.

- "Giraffes—Let our herd tell your loved one they are head and shoulders above the rest.
- Gorilla—Tell your valentine that you are wild about them from our gorilla troop.
- Opossum—Have Pendleton the opossum tell your special person how much you like hanging out with them."

The Martin House Museum, Rochester, New York, tells e-mail readers: "Be Our Valentine: Your purchase supports our mission. And we LOVE that."

Mailed gifts collect data on ages of interest to its mailing list, prices viewers are willing to pay, and which items are popular, as well as postal addresses and zip codes.

REFERENCES

"Biden Signs Bill into Law Making Juneteenth a National Holiday," CNN.com, June 17, 2021, https://www.cnn.com/2021/06/17/politics/biden-juneteenth-bill-signing/index.html [accessed 2-9-22]

"Boo Cruise," Events, Shaker Village of Pleasant Hill, October 30, 2021, https://shakervillageky.org/events/boo-cruise-4/ [accessed 11-19-21]

"Capturing Fleeting Fall in Our Gardens: Continuing Education, Classes and Workshops," Longwood Gardens, https://longwoodgardens.org/events-perfor mances/events/capturing-fleeting-fall-our-gardens?utm_source=newsletter&utm _medium=email&utm_content=Fleeting%20Fall&utm_campaign=Fall%20 CE%20Push%20-%20Conditional [accessed 9-24-21]

"The Chap-Book, Thanksgiving No," e-mail, November 25, 2021, The Richard H. Driehaus Museum [received 11-25-21]

"A Christmas Carol 2021," Merchant House Museum, December 1-31, 2021, https://merchantshouse.org/christmascarol/[accessed 11-20-21]

"Deuce! Celebrate the Grand Nationals," e-mail, February 5, 2022, Petersen Automotive Museum Store, info@petersen.org [accessed 2-5-22]

"Fall Community Day 2021: Diwali," November 7, 2021, Worcester Art Museum, https://www.worcesterart.org/events/community-day-fall/ [accessed 2-5-22]

"February Is for Orchid Lovers," e-mail to list, Chicago Botanic Garden, February 9, 2022, enews@enews.chicagobotanic.org [accessed 2-9-22]

Frank Lloyd Wright, Architect, https://mailchi.mp/3adf6dabcbbd/spreadlove?e =11b4d28fb7 [accessed 2-7-22]

"February Vacation Monday, February 21st–Friday, February 25th," February News & Updates, e-mail February 9, 2022, New Bedford Whaling Museum, ecincotta@whalingmuseum.org [accessed 2-9-22]

"June 19 in the Birmingham Civil Rights District!" Events, Birmingham Civil Rights Institute, June 2021, https://www.bcri.org/bcrievents/juneteenthcelebration/ [accessed 2-9-22]

"Happy Rosh Hashanah!" @TrumanLibInst, Twitter.com, Truman Library Institute, https://www.trumanlibraryinstitute.org/ [accessed 9-8-21].

"Homage to the Black South: Art and Culture Appreciation Series—Black Art Collectors Roundtable," e-mail to mailing list, February 9, 2022, Harvey B. Gantt Center for African-American Arts + Culture, harvey@ganttcenter.org [accessed 2-9-22]

"Hoods Up for Presidents' Day!" e-mail from Petersen Automotive Museum, February 7, 2022, Petersen Automotive Museum, pam@petersen.org [accessed 2-8-22]

https://merchantshouse.org/calendar/ [accessed 11-20-21]

https://www.burkemuseum.org/calendar/fossil-costume-contest [accessed 10-14-21]

https://www.burkemuseum.org/calendar/fossil-month-activities?utm _source=newsletter&utm_medium=email&utm_content=Learn%20more&utm _campaign=education-enews-oct-2021 [accessed 10-14-21]

https://www.history.com/news/the-ancient-origins-of-indias-biggest-holiday

https://www.nationalchurchillmuseum.org/john-findley-green-lecture-series.html

https://www.stltoday.com/travel/virtual-celebrations-help-fulton-mo -mark-75th-anniversary-of-churchill-speech/article_3de77c06-744b-5d55-a864 -3a6dc5a72859.html

https://www.wsj.com/articles/where-is-america-diversifying-the-fastest-small-mid western-towns-11628860161?st=jrvef5ddidmzz5d&reflink=article_copyURL_share

"Indigenous Peoples' Day," Events, Peabody Essex Museum, October 9, 2021, https://www.pem.org/events/indigenous-peoples-day [accessed 10-9-21]

"Locust Grove," Calendar, https://www.lgny.org/gardens [accessed 2-28-22]

"Luminaria Nights," e-mail, Longwood Gardens, February 9, 2022, e-mail, enews@ longwoodgardens.org [accessed 2-9-22]

"Luminarias," Holiday Traditions, About ABQ, Visit Albuquerque, https://www.visit albuquerque.org/about-abq/culture-heritage/holiday-traditions/ [accessed 2-9-22]

"Meetings + Retreats," Gather, Shaker Village of Pleasant Hill, https://shakervillage ky.org/meetings [accessed 2-9-22]

"Native American Heritage Month Programs," November 27, 2021, Battleship New Jersey, https://www.battleshipnewjersey.org/event/native-american-heritage -month-programs/ [accessed 11-5-21]

#onthisday, Nelson-Atkins Museum of Art, @Nelson_Atkins [accessed 2-2-22]

"Our French Classes Start Today," e-mail February 7, 2022, Alliance Française de Chicago, info@af-chicago.org [accessed 2-7-22]

"Pearl Harbor Remembrance Day," December 7, 2021, Virtual Voices of the Game, e-newsletter, Baseball Hall of Fame Museum, https://baseballhall.org/events /pearl-harbor-remembrance-day?date=0 [accessed 11-19-21]

"Recommended, International Year of Glass 2022," Racine Art Museum, https:// myemail.constantcontact.com/Three-New-Exhibitions-Open-Next-Week.html ?soid=1101481332095&aid=YXVUhNHbiKk [accessed 2-2-22]

"Spread Love with a Gift from the Martin House, Martin House Frank Lloyd Wright Architect, https://mailchi.mp/3adf6dabcbbd/spreadlove?e=11b4d28fb7 [accessed 6-15-22]

"A Tale of Today: Up From the Ashes—Pullman Porters and the Great Migration," Blog, Driehaus Museum, February 18, 2021, https://driehausmuseum.org/blog [accessed 2-9-22]

"Taste of the NFL: Party with a Purpose," Super Bowl LVI Los Angeles, January– February, 2022, https://www.nfl.com/super-bowl/event-info/event-overview/ [accessed 1-31-22]

@TrumanLibInst. Twitter.com, Truman Library Institute, https://www.truman libraryinstitute.org/ [accessed 9-8-21].

"The 2021–22 Winter Guide to Crystal Bridges," Welcome, Crystal Bridges Museum of American Art, https://crystalbridges.org/blog/the-2021-winter-guide-to-crystal -bridges/ [accessed 2-10-22]

"Upcoming," Wing Luke Museum of the Asian Pacific American Experience, January 29, 2022, http://www.wingluke.org/single-exhibit/?mep_event=4790 [accessed 1-20-22]

"Virtual Tenement Talk: Clairvoyant Housewives of the Lower East Side," Member News, Tenement Museum, October 7, 2021, https://mailchi.mp/tenement.org /experience-the-tenementmuseum-992200?e=0521cfbea5 [accessed 10-7-21]

"When Is Diwali in 2022," Information, News, India Today, December 17, 2021, https://www.indiatoday.in/information/story/when-is-diwali-2022-date-time -history-and-significance-1888890-2021-12-17 [accessed 2-9-22]

"White Christmas the Exhibition," Oshkosh Public Museum, http://www.osh koshmuseum.org/oshkoshpublicmuseum/ [accessed 1-31-22]

"Will Zoo Be Mine?" Events, Milwaukee Zoo, February 2022, http://www.milwau keezoo.org/events/virtualvalentines.php [accessed 2-2-22]

"Word on the Street: SAVOR 2021," September 25, 2021, Racine Art Museum, https://www.ramart.org/savour-2021/ [accessed 1-2-22]

CHAPTER 16

Storytelling

Stories abound in museums. One reads them in mission statements and hears them at donor events. They're told in children's story hours and read in Letters from the Director. Stories endure because they bespeak heritage. They relate the museum's history and its trajectory to the present. Stories capture individual museums' distinctive personalities and animate their collections.

Universal and timeless, stories appeal to diverse audiences of all backgrounds and experiences because they've been told for millennia. It's not just cultural, but also biological. Researchers have found that our brains are wired to acquire and access information in the form of stories. When readers read a story, they can also see it. In this research blog, they follow the progress of a teacher's experiment, exploring whether youngsters can learn photography in a virtual class: "For nearly a decade, I've been teaching kids the basics of photography, venturing outdoors with them and [exploring] . . . nature through a camera lens. I never imagined that one day I'd be teaching nature photography to . . . a computer filled with curious faces."

Readers of stories want to know how the tale ends—if, for example, the virtual photography class was successful. Spoiler alert—it was. More about teacher Kristen Grace, and her story, later.

Significantly for museums looking to reach new audiences, people take the time to read or listen to a well-told story about what a museum does and why. They can visualize it through stories.

Stories aren't so long that they can't be used as wall panel text or part of an e-newsletter announcement. Of course, they're great for children's story hour!

This chapter shows how a museum of any size or genre can utilize storytelling. Writers: gather around and hear eight ways a story might sound.

WHY STORIES WORK SO HARD

Stories work in museum writing for these important reasons. Stories are:

- Conversational
- Narrated
- Problem-solution formatted
- Serial
- Likable
- Positive
- Peopled
- Moral

START A CONVERSATION

When people talk about their own experiences, or those of another person, their voice gets personal. If you, as a writer, are preparing a presentation or a letter, pretend you're having a conversation with a person in front of you, actually or virtually. When you're conversational, facts sound truer. Listeners know what your aim is, and they're willing to follow you to the end. Natasha Egan, Director of the Museum of Contemporary Photography at Columbia College Chicago, wrote:

> Dear Friends,
> It is hard to believe that it is already a new year! Reflecting on 2021, I want to thank all of you for joining us . . .
> Our team has been continuing the . . . work of centering racial equity within our institution . . . I am proud of the strides the MoCP has been making in the realm of justice but recognize that there is still a great deal of work to be done.

Everyone who has been to a talk or lecture knows that the speaker starts with a bit of conversation:

> "How many historians are in the audience?"
> "Hello. I see there are viewers from all over the country. I'm in my lab in . . ."

NARRATION AND NARRATORS

Stories told about distant events in distant places are told by narrators. Narrators earn that title by being the friendly, omniscient voice. Narrators are well-versed in the subject. They take obvious pleasure in its nuances and anecdotal details. Narrators display a gravitas that supersedes mere knowledge and inspires trust. Narrators understand the whole story and their narrations have an arc that:

- starts with a situation or project
- demonstrates empathy for that point in time
- takes steps to facilitate the project
- moves the story ahead with care and vision
- ends up with productive results
- gives the listener a takeaway

Whitney Plantation Museum, in Wallace, Louisiana, the only museum exclusively devoted to the lives of enslaved people in America, starts the tour at the plantation church because, as the tour guide says: "This is the place where we can actually see their [enslaved people's] names."

Then, because the guide is a knowing narrator, the narration continues with her talking about the surprising sight of Muslim names at the church: "Many slaves were captured in East Africa which was a crossroads for trade with the Arab world."

This narration starts intriguingly, with the enslaved people's names. The viewer is ready to walk along with the narrator as the video tours the museum's grounds and completes the story.

Another platform for narrated stories is a blog. Researchers often write blogs to tell—and hopefully work toward publication of—stories about scientific research. The research is impressive and, because even science stories are beguiling, they're followed to the summary at the end.

The narrator of the blog of the Natural History Museum of Utah, at the University of Utah in Salt Lake City, brings other people into the narration at the start. The details of the science are less daunting because the story arc involves real people. Here are some examples of great science short stories, starting with scientists tossing us an intriguing bit of information:

"Science never sleeps. Every day, scientists from a litany of different disciplines and backgrounds are asking questions, recording data, testing hypotheses . . ."

"Paleontologists are discovering dinosaurs at an astonishing rate, with a new species being announced about every two weeks. One of the latest—and strangest—is a dinosaur named *Stegouros elengassen* from Chile."

"Planetary scientists have been fascinated with the differences between Earth and our closest planetary neighbor, Mars. . . . This year, scientists discovered an important way Mars deviates from what we see here on Earth . . ."

Dear reader, don't you wonder how the story ends?

PROBLEM-SOLUTION CASE STUDY

Stories, from fairy tales to cable detective shows, subsist on problems and solutions. The structure is irresistible: thrill at the problems and find satisfaction at their solution.

Case studies are also problem-solution stories. They were born in science research and flourished in medicine as techniques for gathering information about a problem and assembling that data into possible solutions. Case studies start at the beginning, progress, experience a few mishaps and adventures, and end with an answer—very much like stories. Blogs can be erudite, witty or literary; blog writers can tell a good story.

Problem-solution stories, in science, art, or history include:

- observant people
- discovery of something perplexing
- curiosity and exploration
- knowledgeable conjectures
- ingenious solutions to the problematical discovery

Here's how Florida Museum of Natural History, an institution with a formidable research department, used the story-telling approach to continue telling its audiences—scientists, educators, parents—about that children's photography project that started at the beginning of the chapter and continues here: "This is how I found myself talking to a computer filled with curious faces about how magical it is to encounter the outdoors with a camera—all from the confines of four walls with no bugs and no dirt. How was this going to work?"

Figure 16.1. "Narcissa Thorne . . . employed techniques of stage design . . . for instance, the chairs around the kitchen table face outward, and the . . . furniture . . . [is] arranged to . . . allow . . . viewers to see each element . . . also encouraging them to imagine scenes playing out within the space."
Art Institute of Chicago. A17: Pennsylvania Kitchen, 1752

Step by step, the educator takes readers through the case history of her problem-solution experience:

- locked-down youngsters
- videoconferencing
- technical details of lenses
- appreciation of nature
- pedagogy of observation, exploration, analysis, and teamwork

SERIALIZATION

The story format is so effective, each tale can stand alone. However, writers may find that one story begets another. Episodic blogs, videos, and lecture series are valuable to museums because they keep readers and visitors coming back. When a series tires out, writers can start a new series. The number of episodes per series varies: four for a lecture series, six for a research blog, unlimited for a series of demonstrations or artifact-based stories.

Vesterheim, the National Norwegian-American Museum and Folk Art School, Decorah, Iowa, has assembled dozens of videos—and counting—that show the Norwegian-American experience; they are manuals for storytellers. Chapter 11, "Videos," describes the visual aspects of the series.

Serialized stories demonstrate continuity. If told, they have the same tone of voice, be it folksy, serious, or sincere. If watched, the series' sets bear a similarity. There's comfortable familiarity in hearing the same voice and seeing the same surroundings. Familiarity is another advantage of stories. Listeners and readers settle back and absorb them.

Writers: to preserve continuity of a serialized story, make sure that from episode to episode:

- The theme stays the same.
- Settings resemble each other.
- Narrators maintain the same tone of voice—serious, folksy, sincere.
- Number of people in the cast of characters—either in print or on a screen—stays the same.
- Layout of the printed page stays the same. Consistency on a website will keep its wildly proliferating pages in check. The Driehaus Museum blog adds new stories regularly, and their dignified organization on the Web page assures the reader that each one is part of the series.

LIKABILITY

Likability is an underappreciated advantage of stories. They feature relatable characters, follow plots and back-stories that enliven museum objects, and end well by fulfilling the quest. Of course audiences like them.

Don't let likability dissipate in a welter of information:

- For every fact, give a real-life explanation. The Bronze Age wasn't just 2,000 years ago; it was when halberds were used for weapons in Ireland. And there are skull scars to provide evidence.
- Mention a personage—contemporary, fictional, or historic—where appropriate to illustrate a detail.
- Have the narrator show a photograph or chart to illustrate the story— it's honest to admit the storyteller doesn't know everything.
- Ask listeners and readers to return for the next installment—this suggests that the storyteller is having a good time with the audience.

Many museums ask children in classes to tell their own stories; it helps newcomers from diverse audiences feel more comfortable in a new place. The magic is that all ages and backgrounds can tell a story about themselves, and everyone in the room will like it.

The likability factor serves speakers well when they have to give a serious report. They can make their case plus soften some hard truths when a story accompanies the slides. Stories help explain a report and keep the ensuing discussions collegial and productive.

It will aid speakers immensely if they rehearse their presentation out loud. It is a performance. Hear how it sounds. If presented virtually, speakers might check their camera as well as the microphone.

Writers and speakers, learn how you sound and see how you look.

Figure 16.2.   Rhode Island Parlor, c. 1820. This parlor scene is another of the miniature rooms designed by Narcissa Thorne, exhibited at the Art Institute of Chicago. One wonders, or imagines, who visited here and who in the household they visited. So begins a story.
Art Institute of Chicago. A11: Rhode Island Parlor, c. 1820

ORAL HISTORY

Ordinary people become accomplished writers when you ask them to tell their stories. They relish the details of their life and speak in nouns. They're visual treasure troves and provide museums and historical societies with objects like "snow apples" to be preserved, if only in the reader's imagination. Listen to Hattie Whitcomb of Bethlehem, New Hampshire, recalling her childhood.

> I was born at home in a small farmhouse in Bethlehem, NH, about two miles from the village. There weren't any nearby hospitals in those days.
> One of my brothers named me Hattie Evaline Whitcombe but my father didn't like the name. He wanted me named Winona, but he always called me baby. My father had a small farm. He kept three horses and usually five cows. He had a pair of oxen to do the heavy work.

Oral histories are artifacts to be collected; they are also interpretations. Recording the reminiscences of many different people provides a diversity of background, age, and geography that needs to be preserved in usage, not just an archive. Broad inclusiveness makes interpretation more objective, less personal. Diverse stories can be compared and contrasted, analyzed and contextualized.

Writers can catalyze memories into stories with a prompting script:

- Talk about where you were born.
- Who were your parents, their history?
- Were you close to your siblings?
- Where did you go on family trips?
- Talk about growing up in a small city.
- What about living in a big city. What was the best thing? The worst?
- Your neighbors—any interesting characters upstairs, downstairs, next door, down the block?

Writers: help your amateur oral historians visualize their memories.

- Describe your first house, home, apartment.
- Thinking about your school, do you see your teacher, classmates, classroom?
- What did you wear?
- What was your favorite food, toy, game?
- Your parents— do you have a favorite photo of them?
- Holidays: how did they look in your home, your neighborhood?

Your script can move through time as quickly or slowly as you think your storyteller wants:

- What was the weather like growing up?
- How did you meet your spouse?
- Thinking about your first job—how old were you?

Hattie Whitcomb recounts,

In my childhood, the children didn't call their parents mom and dad the way they do today, it was always Mama and Papa. I loved my Papa very much so when he came in one day and asked me to help him, I was delighted. He had some hay ready to load on to a cart and a storm was coming up. He wanted to get the hay in before it got wet. As I was the only one of the children at home at that particular time, he asked me if I could drive the team so he could pitch on the hay. I was only about eight years old and I was thrilled to have a part in such a responsible job.

Figure 16.3.   The entrance hall of this old Tennessee house holds many stories. Where do the doors lead? Did anyone slide down the banister? What was Tennessee like back then?
Art Institute of Chicago. A31: Tennessee Entrance Hall, 1835

Be attuned to when it's time for a more external line of questions.

Food and mealtimes play a large role in history. Talk about time in your youth, or any time in your life.

Technology! At one time, it was escalators in the department store. Or the newest combine, or car with a tape deck, or lightweight tablet. Your insights on technology in one's life.

Important events in history. Attitudes in your town or city. Who was considered heroic.

For example, Battleship New Jersey has been interviewing U.S. servicemen for their stories. The simple staging has an off-camera interviewer and a full screen shot of the service member answering the interviewer's questions. Aldo's Saggese talks about his time in occupied Japan:

> I had a better feeling for Asia. That was something as a kid growing up in Philadelphia hardly anybody thought about Asia but I had an affinity for, I could detect in Asia a beauty to the country even though there were [*sic*] a lot of destruction, but even the small homes had gardens and I thought what a difference from what we thought we would find in Japan.

MAKING STORIES RELEVANT

Old as the story tradition is, new stories help museums open their doors wider, to newer groups of people. Tenement Museum joins a nationwide program, Your Story, Our Story, to document the stories of immigrants who, far from historical, are very much part of the present.

Here's a young Turkish woman:

> My mother makes manti at every family event, a traditional Turkish dish that melted into the diverse culture of Uzbekistan. . . . My mother immigrated to America from Uzbekistan in the 1990s. . . . As my family sticks close to each other to get through, I am feeling closer to my culture than ever before.

From Billy Quock, recording his story for Your Story, Our Story, at Wing Luke Museum for the Asian Pacific American Experience:

> My father, Yoen Quock, was born in Taishan, Guangdong, China in 1916. Because of poor economic conditions and clouds of World War II forming near and in China in the 1930s, he made the bold decision to emigrate to the United States. . . . His first glimpse of and first "home" in America was the United States Immigration and Naturalization Service (INS) Building in Seattle. The Chinese Exclusion Act mandated that all immigrants from China be detained, investigated, and approved for entry. After multiple interviews with immigration officials, over two months, he was admitted to the United States in March, 1938.

PEOPLED

Stories read easily because they follow the antics of people. The National Baseball Hall of Fame Museum lavishes its websites with stories about the wondrous happenings that befall players, coaches, umpires, and fans. If the story is about Mike Schmidt's borrowed bat or Cy Young's used razor blade, the writers add a few supporting stars to entrance the reader for a few more minutes online.

> It's not unusual for games to be delayed, postponed or rescheduled in the early days of a baseball season, when the spring weather is fickle and brings snow, hail, rain and/or sunshine in a matter of hours . . . but it had before never wreaked havoc like it did on Oct. 27, 2008 . . . Rays' clubhouse manager Chris Westmoreland knew his team needed to be prepared . . . recalled Shane Victorino, the Phillies' center fielder . . . "I looked at my arms and it was starting to, like, freeze on my arms."

At Driehaus Museum, its blog brims with stories about people whose experiences relate to the museum's place in turn-of-the-century Chicago.

> As a part of the Driehaus Museum's ongoing mission to expand upon the shaping of Chicago during the Gilded Age . . . we look to the Great Migration, the *Chicago Defender*, the Pullman porters, and the roots of Chicago's Black working class . . . Nate Young reveals aspects of the Great Migration . . . Young's great-grandfather . . .

Writers: a storyteller can transform a photograph from 1900 into a tale of the people who interacted with them. Imagine the adaptations:

- wall panel
- blog
- outline for a talk
- social media posts

THE END

Stories have an ending and that's satisfying. It lets the speaker button up a scripted tour, a blog, or a talk. It makes the museum sound buttoned up.

National Baseball Hall of Fame Museum ran a year-long series of stories on Roberto Clemente during the fifty-year anniversary of his legendary play in the 1971 World Series. The series concluded with this comment from a longtime sportswriter:

People who were around, at the time of his death, recall it the way we here in the mainland would recall, say, when President John Kennedy was assassinated or when the space shuttle [*Challenger*] blew up. You remember; it becomes a touchstone event in your life.

Writers: try ending a talk using the word "story":

"Thank you listening to this story about Florentine artists."
"Thank you. The story of our solar system continues."
"Thank you for coming to our first talk about our city's Gilded Age stories."

MORAL

Traditional tales, often called sagas or legends, bring out the moral in storytellers. Writers couldn't make it through their first quill without having an end point in sight. To that end, they give their stories a moral. It's a good lesson for museum writing.

Just look at any tweet, blog, wall panel, or speaker event and there's probably a suggestion that the writer has a point to make. A good concluding sentence should deliver a summation, a reason for being written. Writers: read your final paragraph when you finish the first draft. If your piece doesn't summarize a succinct point of view, rewrite!

The ending to a story should:

- Summarize
- Reprise the point of view
- Make your point
- Have a subtle moral.

The Tenement Museum is an institution built on the stories of the immigrants who lived there for over a century of New York's boisterous growth and diversifying. Here's how the president reminded readers of the museum's foundation legend along with her message of end-of-year positivism:

> Of course, we all bring our own family memories to the Tenement tours, and I am sure that many of you have family stories of people . . . [who] inspire us to think of ways to move forward, adapt and conceive of new ways of forming community.

And that's the moral to this chapter.

REFERENCES

Allen, Garrett, "#Shortstops: The Muffin Men," National Baseball Hall of Fame Museum, https://baseballhall.org/discover/shortstops/the-muffin-men [accessed 10-25-21]

"American Artifacts: Whitney Plantation Slavery Museum," American History TV, C-Span, October 5, 2015, https://www.c-span.org/video/? [accessed 1-3-22]

Black, Riley, "Blog 2021 12, The Top Science Stories of 2021," posted December 15, 2021

"Blog," Driehaus Museum, https://driehausmuseum.org/blog [accessed 1-4-22]

Breton, Marcos, quoted in Bruce Markusen, "Clemente's Legacy Remains Vibrant Source of Inspiration," Baseball Series, National Baseball Hall of Fame and Museum, https://baseballhall.org/discover/baseball-history/clementes-legacy-remains-vibrant-source-of-inspiration [accessed 12-30-21]

Carter, Matthew, "#Shortstops: ABCs vs. All-Stars," National Baseball Hall of Fame Museum, https://baseballhall.org/discover/shortstops/abcs-vs-all-stars [accessed 10-25-21]

Carter, Matthew, "#Shortstops: Tinker's Tigers," National Baseball Hall of Fame Museum, https://baseballhall.org/discover/shortstops/tinkers-tigers [accessed 1-9-22]

Chibana, Nayomi, "7 Storytelling Techniques Used by the Most Inspiring TED Presenters," July 8, 2015, blog, *Visme*, https://visme.co/blog/7-storytelling-techniques-used-by-the-most-inspiring-ted-presenters [accessed 1-9-22]

Egan, Natasha, "A New Year's Message from Our Executive Director," e-mail, Museum of Contemporary Photography at Columbia College Chicago, January 3, 2022, [accessed 1-6-22]

"Enchanted Adventures: This Is the Rope," Programs & Events, Driehaus Museum, August 12, 2021, https://driehausmuseum.org/programs/detail/enchanted-adventures-story-time-this-is-the-rope [accessed 8-22-21]

"Familie Tid: Scandinavian Storytelling with Rose Arrowsmith!", Vesterheim, https://youtu.be/jHzUyrFLPvY [accessed 11-25-21]

Grace, Kristen, "Kids, Cameras and the Great Outdoors. Virtually." Blog, Florida Museum Blog, September 11, 2020, https://www.floridamuseum.ufl.edu/museum-blog/kids-cameras-and-the-great-outdoors-virtually/ [accessed 12-30-21]

https://nhmu.utah.edu/blog/2021/top-science-stories-2021 [accessed 12-22-21]

https://www.floridamuseum.ufl.edu/science/tag/jaret-daniels/ [accessed 12-23-21]

McKibben, Ryan, "A Tale of Today: Up from the Ashes—Pullman Porters and the Great Migration," February 18, 2021, Blog, Driehaus—https://driehausmuseum.org/blog/view/pullman-porters [accessed 1-9-22]

Minasian, Isabelle, "#Shortstops: Flap Cap," National Baseball Hall of Fame Museum, https://baseballhall.org/discover/shortstops/tampa-bay-rays-2008-world-series-weather-cap [accessed 10-25-21]

"My Mother's Manti Pot," Stories, Tenement Museum, https://yourstory.tenement.org/stories/my-mother-s-manti-pot-my-mother-makes-manti/ [accessed 1-9-22]

Polland, Annie, "Message from the Tenement Museum President," e-mail to mailing list, December 23, 2021

Pownell, Kathryn, "#Shortstops: Walk a Mile in Her Shoes," National Baseball Hall of Fame Museum, https://baseballhall.org/discover/shortstops/walk-a-mile-in-her-shoes [accessed 10-25-21]

Quock, Billy, U.S. Army Portrait, Wing Luke Museum of the Asian Pacific American Experience, https://yourstory.tenement.org/stories/us-army-portrait [accessed 1-10-22]

Roos, Dave, "8 Bronze Age Weapons," History Stories, History, October 29, 2021, https://www.history.com/news/bronze-age-weapons [accessed 1-5-22]

"Saggese, Aldo, 1946–47," Oral History, The Ship, Battleship New Jersey, https://www.battleshipnewjersey.org/the-ship/oral-history/ [accessed 1-9-22]

"Shortstops Series," National Baseball Hall of Fame Museum, https://baseballhall.org/discover-more?category=All&field_related_people_tid=All&field_related_positions_tid=All&field_related_teams_tid=All&field_related_topics_tid=All&field_content_series_tid=828#to-content [accessed 12 3-22]

Taylor, Hattie Whitcomb, "Hattie Whitcomb's Reflections of Life in Bethlehem," February 22, 1898 Timeline, Bethlehem Heritage Society, https://bethlehemheritagenh.org/hattie-whitcombs-reflections-of-life-in-bethlehem/ [accessed 10-25-21]

"256 Stories," #Shortshops, Stories, National Baseball Hall of Fame and museum, https://baseballhall.org/discover-more?page=1&category=All&field_related_people_tid=All&field_related_positions_tid=All&field_related_teams_tid=All&field_related_topics_tid=All&field_content_series_tid=828 [accessed 10-25-21]

"We Want Veterans for Interviews," Oral History, The Ship, Battleship New Jersey, https://www.battleshipnewjersey.org/the-ship/oral-history [accessed 1-7-22]

"Your Story, Our Story: Refugees," Blog, Tenement Museum, September 8, 2021, https://www.tenement.org/blog/your-story-our-story-refugees/?mc_cid=6e852dc6ec&mc_eid=0521cfbea5 [accessed 9-12-21]

CHAPTER 17

Fundraising

Fundraising is a meeting of the minds between the museum and the prospective donor. The museum adheres to a mission as it seeks support for its projects and goals. Prospects have many philanthropies vying for their support and look for a good match. Fundraising is a conversation of talk and listen; even donors of small amounts follow this thought process.

Beware of Fundraiser Tilt, when fundraisers lose their balance and talk more about the museum's needs and less about the donor's. Asking is one-sided. Fundraising includes both sides.

Before you start even a casual conversation, know who is giving you funds: There are several categories, each filled with a wide variety of prospective donors.

- Individuals
- Large donors and supporters
- Local businesses
- Corporations
- Community/Foundations/Trusts

Each Has a Different Goal in Their Philanthropy

Individuals visit often and attend programs and events because you're a reliable provider of intelligent learning. Writers: most of this chapter covers individual donors who contribute to their museum for many different reasons, in amounts of varying sizes. They are an unimaginably diverse group of people. You will be using every kind of media and as many kinds of appeals.

Large donors and supporters understand museums' programming and financial underpinnings. With many requests for support, they put arts and sciences at the top of the list, often for personal as well as public-spirited reasons. Writers: tell large donors that as the museum expands its programs and hours to reach out to all audiences, their support is appreciated more than ever.

Corporate people, officers and others, are interested in brand building, business growth, community presence, and societal obligations. They are particularly interested in issues of diversity and access. For example, the Queens Museum's Business and Legislative Breakfast brings together local business leaders and city and state legislators "to meet, network, and learn firsthand about one of the most important institutions in Queens." Writers: use words like stable, broad-based membership, accountable, supported by our community.

Local businesses benefit from the prestige and the visitors that museums bring to Main Street. They are accustomed to being members of the community that participate and contribute to education and learning. Local businesspeople may also be new in town, wanting to establish themselves. They support all the arts in some way, and are active as volunteers. They encourage membership in museums and employees bringing their families. Writers: use the word "our" as in our city, our neighborhoods, our children's education, our shared goals.

Family foundations believe strongly in generational support of their community. Their families have always given back, honored local accomplishments, and taken pride in civic accomplishment. They think about their families' legacy. Writers: use words like family, inter-generational, community, partners, ingenuity, and legacy.

The person opposite you in the fundraising conversation represents distinct interests that will be part of the discussion. On a screen, in e-mail, on paper, on the phone, it's two individuals talking about their work and their goals. This chapter is structured to prepare you for the range of situations at which thoughts of money changes hands.

Writers: you're not sitting down at the keyboard, you're sitting down to talk, on the page, screen, or face-to-face. The talks could occur at any time, at different intensities. You never know who might want to be included in your journey. Be ready with the right words.

A note about equity, inclusiveness, diversity, and access: Philanthropists are equal opportunity donors; they come from all backgrounds and how much they give will always surprise you.

FUNDRAISERS' TOOLS

Depending on the size and structure of a museum, the person charged with fundraising could be the person assigned to write the appeals. It could be two or more people. Because there are so many ways to raise money, the line blurs and this chapter applies to everyone in the institution.

E-mail or web page, person-to-person or a sign at the ticket counter, the media through which fundraising messages are delivered are key to connecting meaningfully with the person(s) the museum hopes will give it some—large or small—financial support.

Here are some of the dozen kinds of solicitation communiqués:

- Link on home page
  Don't let any visitor get away. These can be a top-line tab or top item on the drop-down menu. It's meant for any visitor to the website, and encourages a different kind of inclusiveness.

- Brochures
  Four-color brochures allow a museum to describe and entire season of events, classes, and exhibitions, with beautiful photos, dates, and locator maps. There's space for a mission statement from the director, or a quote from an artist, historian, researcher, or educator. They're mobile; mail them, place them in the store, hand them out at lectures.

- Website letters from the director
  This frequently appears in the About Us tab. It shouldn't sound like an annual report recap of the year. Specifics and some insider talk are recommended, and a little wit with the wisdom.

- Letters from the director in the member @ magazine
  Same as above, but with more member-appropriate information such as original research projects, corporate collaborations, art on loan to other institutions, member events, and gala success. It's not unheard of to add a personal telephone number or e-mail address.

- Slide presentation
  On a screen in a conference room or a tablet in an office, a slide presentation shows respect for the prospect. It says, you're busy; we've done our homework.

- Across-the-desk presentation to major donors
  This is a personal, nonconfrontational way to discuss support. These talks seem informal, but a formal outline precedes them. A few jotted notes show thought and organization—"we won't waste your time with chitchat"—and each notes represent a rehearsed rationales.

- Printed letters
  They arrive on nice paper, addressed to the correct person with the correct title added. Get the name and title exactly right. Remember middle initials and Jr., Dr., MD, Professor of, Attorney at Law.

If you know the person, keep the letter to one page where each paragraph makes an important point: current goals of museum consonant with its mission; why they mesh with prospect's goals and mission; examples of implementing the goals; problems and obstacles, not restricted to budget, and how they relate to prospect's hurdles; request for a get-together sometime in the near future, a specific date if time is important.

- Letters plus inserts
One way to keep the letter short is to add a standard brochure inserts. Mention it in the P.S.: "I've included our new brochure on the exhibition."

- Social media post
A paragraph or a few words with a fundraising project hashtag will get attention, an early definition of advertising. Social media will raise awareness of the museum, but these are inefficient ways to get leads.

- Hand-written, personalized P.S. on a fundraising mailing
Use real ink. Point out why the person reading it should hand it over to the addressee. "Thanks, as always, for your support."

- Donation at ticket counter
Point of sale is wonderful. Prospects are inside, proving interest in the museum. If their entry is free, few will resent being asked to contribute. "Entry is free for everyone. Your donation will help the Museum keep the doors wide open."

- Donation box at lecture event
These are quiet requests for money. They appeal to many private philanthropists. "Enjoy the show. To support our continuing schedule of events, donate here."

- QR code with "scan here to donate"
Put one next to the donation box and on every other possible surface.

- Person to person
For even the casual, friendship-based appeals, talking points are needed. Whether it's a quick e-mail, phone call, or across-the-desk appointment, some people when asking for money need a script; others can memorize their points. Writing them on paper first is still a smart idea. The goal is learning enough about the other person to have a productive conversation. These opening remarks are basic ice-breakers:

"Hello, Jane. Busy day, I imagine. The last time we talked you were . . ."

"Chris, FYI, attached is an article on what we talked about yesterday."

"Hello, Pat, attached is an invitation to our next exhibition preview party. Hope you can make it."

"Hi, John, just keeping in touch. Perhaps we can talk in the next week or so. How does your month look?"

Remember that when you first contacted the prospect, maybe months ago, you introduced yourself, with your title, role, and intention. The prospect knows you're asking for money and they expect to be reminded.

Use phone calls and e-mails. Don't rely on posts because they don't directly speak to the person you've established a relationship with. Avoid text messages; they're for quick, immediate messages.

Writers: This Tools List is not an exhaustive list, nor is it meant to exhaust you. It should make your job easier. Before you begin the process of asking for money, remember that different kinds of pages send different messages.

FUNDRAISING IS FOREVER

Fundraising missives might shoot straight at a target, but they'll be followed by others for a long time. The reality is, fundraising is long-term. It never slows down. Every member of your staff is a fundraiser.

Here are some long-term phrases to keep at the ready:

"The Museum hopes you enjoyed the tour. Pick up your discount ticket for next month's tour at the lobby counter." (Donations box at the counter.)

"Music under the trees is free to everyone, every Wednesday in summer. If you can support this event with any amount, we can continue this event every year."

"Hello, fellow educator. Thanks for bringing your class to our Museum for Farm Day. We hope your class learned a lot and had fun doing it. Enclosed are some follow-up exercises for them to try at home with their families. There's a discount coupon for family memberships."

Gantt Center for African-American History + Culture complements its traditional donor categories with a visionary category, Initiative for Equity + Innovation. Its web page doesn't mention funds or donations, and the only word suggesting the need for money is "sustainability." The mission instead talks about shared responsibility among the community, major corporations, and educators to "leverage the arts" and "equip the next generation," and "empower" all interested entities to do something. Part of fundraising is raising long-term ideological commitment.

SMALL AND FREQUENT

Keep fundraising small and ask often. Small, regular contributions are just as valuable, and sometimes long-term, as big galas and major drives. They come from people who visit more than once, tell their friends, visit your website, read your newsletters and blogs, shop at your store, stop for a snack, attend a lecture, bring the kids to weekend workshops. That's a lot of occasions to ask for a donation.

- E-mail newsletter: Requests for funds seem logical when they appear at the end of an event announcement.
- Order Here page: Once an e-mail recipient has read about an upcoming event and touched the button for registering and paying, they're ready to listen to a little fundraising. Here are some typical words: "Consider adding a small donation to your ticket order," and "If you enjoyed this virtual talk, help us continue to bring them to you."
- Information kiosk: Connect the appeal to a Q-and-A screen. "Which of these exhibits interested you most? Click on any of the links and we'll send you more information."

REFRAME A DONATION REQUEST TO MEMBERSHIP

A museum can offer membership, with the benefit of discounted admissions, all the time, in many media. And when people renew their memberships, which they do, the donation becomes regular. Here are some membership suggestions:

- To attend the whole series of talks, become a member and save $5 on each.
- If you enjoy our programs, consider buying a year's membership. It helps defray the costs and gives you special member discounts.
- Members can enter the museum an hour early and avoid long lines. Click here to sign up.
- This children's class meets every week from October to May. To get the members' discount for the whole series, click here.

And remember the power of buying someone a gift membership; it's a message that can be communicated on a sign or placard anyplace in the museum:

- "Give the gift of a Tenement Museum membership to those in your life who love learning!"

DONOR IDIOSYNCRASIES

A little reality check belongs here. Donors are individualistic, like all people. Museums with their distinct missions and purposes can use those as advantages in matching up with prospects. Listen to their interests, ask about their day, value their goals, and see how they mesh with yours.

Writers' exercise: jot down one phrase or word that you hear from a prospective donor. Notice one magazine seen in their lobby. Read the comments to their posts. Script a conversation based on observations, rather than generalities. Remember, the museum and the prospect are getting to know each other; then they'll talk business.

DONOR ATTENDANCE RECORD

Take a second look at the attendance record of museum events. Read past the numbers to the names because these are good prospects. Align your donation requests with the events your prospect has already preferred. Your donor request, probably an e-mail, can say:

- We hope you enjoyed our monthly Chamber Music program. Our future musical events include Selections from the Divas, Big Band, and Hip Hop. We hope you'll consider donating to our Music in History initiative.
- Here's your link to the Children's Friday Science/Rocks and Rivers Workshop. Watch for the subject of next week's Workshop. If your child enjoys them, please consider a small donation to the Workshop.
- Thanks for your generous donation. We appreciate your support of our heritage.
- Our seasonal bird-watching walks raise money for wetland preservation and other bird sanctuaries throughout out the Garden. Click here for how to donate.
- Pay what you can to enter. General admission to the museum is free, and your donation adds to the number of weekday hours we can offer.
- I'm sorry I can't attend the Virtual Health in the Arts Gala. I'd like to support the museum with a donation.

These simple additions recognize the donor's interest and remind them of the museum's many ways of furthering them.

THE ASK

As mentioned at the beginning of the chapter, fundraisers can't ask before they listen. However, it's smart to ask why the prospect has selected you above all other contenders for their philanthropy. It may actually clarify the goals of the prospective donor. Here are some techniques for asking:

Connect the request with a specific event or project that needs ongoing support. Use appropriate words for different appeals. For instance, if it's a children's program, talk about the community, equity, and access. If it's for a science lab, use specific terms, costs, and accountability. The Driehaus Museum, a historic house with programming of a scholarly bent, at the end of a newsletter writes a particularly erudite donation appeal. The Chicago museum references Chekhov. Don't shy from erudition: People are always smarter and more generous than one thinks and it's unproductive to second guess who is likely to contribute. Remember the postal worker and librarian in Brooklyn, a quiet couple who went to a lot of exhibition openings; they astounded the art world when the bequeathed the 5,000 works in their collection of modern art to the National Gallery of Art in Washington and galleries in all fifty states.

Figure 17.1.   Local businesses share museums' goals of diversity and a flourishing community. Find out what other interests motivate businesspeople to give time and treasure.
uchar / E+ via Getty Images

WHERE YOU ASK

In another time, when fundraising aimed at high-level pledges, one might politely ask for support at an exhibition, an opening, in someone's office or home. Now there are digital substitutes and besides, there's increased appreciation for the small donor. Large pledges fall victim to falling stock prices and stakeholder backlash. Small donations are consistent. The upshot is all that change brings great opportunity to ask all the people, all the time, wherever you write for them.

Ask in Your Newsletters

At the end, after the announcements: "Your support is appreciated" followed by a "Donate" link.

Ask on Your Website

Your Donation tab is at the top. List the Donate Now link at the top of the drop-down menu. The next five items can relate to estate plans and pledges. Donors giving large funds will look for the necessary information.

Ask on the Counter

This is a transaction location. Money and/or tickets changed hands here. It's logical to set up a sign with a QR code, or even a donation box. "Smith-Jones Museum hopes you enjoyed your visit. A small contribution is appreciated."

Ask in the Store

Other transactions take place here, and they have the added value of an item to take home as a memory. Place the same donation sign here that you printed up for the front desk.

Ask with a Sign at the Ticket-Taker Stand

What better place to ask for a donation than the doorway to an event the visitor has carved out precious time to attend? This is an engaged audience. "Enjoy the show. To support our continuing schedule of events, donate here."

Ask with the "Thank You for Attending Our Program" E-mail

Add "Thank-You Notes" to your list of rules because they must be sent quickly after the event. Attendees deserve appreciation for finding the time (and maybe money) to see your special effort. At that moment, they have gotten to know the museum from another perspective. It's the perfect time for you to suggest a donation or membership.

Ask for Advice

Of course, it's flattering to be asked for advice, so give prospects the opportunity. Writers, try: "Like What We're Doing? Consider making a tax-deductible donation to the Museum. Every gift helps us continue to support the whole community." This is effective in thanking attendees of a workshop or presentation.

Ask for Names of Friends

The staple of job interviews works here, too. Once you've established a relationship with a prospect, including on your website, ask if they have friends who might also be interested in the museum. People asked for large donations will feel comfortable aiding your endeavors. Everybody likes bringing in friends. Writers: This works well under the Support tab of a website. The reader has already clicked enough links to be involved.

Ask for a Volunteer Stint

Give your community the option of donating time instead of money. Each is valuable and many, given a choice, will give money. Many will volunteer. By making sharing a part of the donation process, the prospect feels included.

Ask with Humor

Most people appreciate a sense of humor; it's one hallmark of a good relationship. Plimoth Patuxet Museum gets a little breezy with requests like:

> Put Wind in Her Sails. If you or someone you know can make a donation to the restoration you will be helping to ensure that the ship sails far into the future.

THE LURE OF INTERNSHIPS

Internships captivate donors because they always look for good investments; they like forward thinking and the promise of stability that intern programs promise.

For writers, the appeal to both parties is youth, hard work, and future-thinking. It's the balance that's so important in discussing donations. Use a crisp tone of voice that does not suggest just a feel-good effort. Don't wax eloquent; do talk accountability. State what's given. Address benefits that are monetizable later. Name the expectations for the interns. List the dollar costs where appropriate. As a company financial officer once said: "I've found that when you put '$$' on something, people pay attention." The same applies to any numbers. So here are some suggested words to use, or rephrase, when talking about developing new leaders:

Students must carry 12 paid credit hours
This internship pays $50 a week
Stipends are available
Interns work one-on-one with company managers
Interns will work 25 hours a week

TRANSLATION

For museum communities with large immigrant populations, translating a donation appeal indicates inclusiveness. The museum has removed another hurdle for them and their children. Queens Museum translates donor requests into Spanish on its website, a clear indication that inclusiveness is organic and that equity means everyone is invited to build a better museum. All newcomers want to be a part of their new neighborhood. Writers: on the donation page say, "And when you donate, you'll automatically receive news of upcoming programs for your family." Yes, presence on a mailing list means access. E-mail keeps good museum participants.

501(C)(3)

The U.S. Tax Code is ingrained in every American philanthropist, so put the 501(c)(3) designation on every donation page. Depending on your museum audiences, it might help to explain what this means. The tax advantages that make citizen support of American museums ubiquitous astounds people in other countries: "What! Your government doesn't pay for museums?" The fundraising experience has many angles to explore.

Writers: you will use every media currently available, and stay current with them. You'll learn to talk to audiences who are younger than you, and older, too, so watch your references. You will communicate with people for whom English is a second language, and American is a third. You will talk to people who have families, jobs, obligations, and meetings. In starting the donation process, you'll have only an inkling of what they can and will give, and why. Plan to start each conversation with empathy: "How's your day going?"

REFERENCES

"Business and Legislative Breakfast," Support, Queens Museum, https://queensmu seum.org/support [accessed 9-30-21]

"The Dog Days of Summer Are Over! Celebrate in Person with Our Programming." August 12, 2021, Driehaus Museum, https://driehausmuseum.org/?mc_cid=7f608 1115e&mc_eid=b97d54fadb [accessed 9-30-21]

"Exemption Requirements—501(c)(3) Organizations," Internal Revenue Service, https://www.irs.gov/charities-non-profits/charitable-organizations/exemption-re quirements-501c3-organizations [accessed 10-3-21]

"Gift Membership," Tenement Museum, https://www.tenement.org/membership /gift/ [accessed 9-17-21]

"Initiative for Equity + Innovation," Gantt Center for African-American Arts + Cul ture, https://www.ganttcenter.org/public/assets/IEI-Fact-Sheet-Web.pdf [accessed 9-30-21]

Martin, Douglas, "Herbert Vogel, Fabled Art Collector, Dies at 89," *New York Times*, July 23, 2012, https://www.nytimes.com/2012/07/24/arts/design/herbert -vogel-postal-clerk-and-modern-art-collector-dies-at-89.html [accessed 9-28-21]

"Milwaukee County Zoo Enrichments," Your Friends, Your Lists, https://www.ama zon.com/hz/wishlist/ls/1PW0T3UQE0US0?ref_=wl_fv_le [accessed 9-13-21]

"Primates—Orangutans, Monkeys, Siamang," Your Friends, Your Lists, Milwaukee County Zoo, https://www.amazon.com/hz/wishlist/ls/1863C158SAE82?ref_=wl _fv_le [accessed 9-13-21]

Schaefer Riley, Naomi, "The Woke Threat to Philanthropy: The Weekend Interview with Elise Westhoff," *Wall Street Journal*, July 17–18, 2021, https://www.aei.org /op-eds/the-woke-threat-to-philanthropy/

"Toolkit: Mutual of America Museum Leadership Series," The Association of Midwest Museums, Summer 2021, https://files.constantcontact.com/d87f37a9001/41be0 a94-46f2-449d-8fba-bb8221999594.pdf [accessed 9-14-21]

"A Year of Achievement," Plimoth Patuxet Museums, https://mailchi.mp/plimoth /were-thinking-of-you-269821?e=fbd9846bd4 [accessed 10-3-21]

CHAPTER 18

Research

Research deals with the unknown. It requires curiosity and creativity, two attributes museums honor and strive daily to foster. In the museum world, researchers appear in all levels of expertise, and they search out many kinds of information. Some are the museum curators, some external scholars, and some amateur explorers. Much of the research seen by the public is visitor research, such as visitor surveys, questionnaires, and follow-up e-mails. What flourishes unseen, deep in the drop-down menus of websites, blogs, newsletters, and archived publications, is the large body of scholarly research conducted by historians, scientists, conservators, and curators in dozens of disciplines. This research deserves more sunlight. The former, more familiar research tells a museum how to grow. The latter helps a museum be great, and we'll discuss that first.

Scholarly research, in this chapter, includes both laypeople and academics in its discussion. It embraces museums of all sizes and genres. Small museums plan and produce fascinating research on their areas of interest. Larger museums, with budgets to match, devise long-term, extensive, and expensive explorations. All museums think like visionaries and dig deep for facts as they fulfill their mission to collect, preserve, display, and interpret.

SCHOLARLY RESEARCH

Research ideas proposed and investigated in a scholarly manner deserve credit not only for their intrinsic value but also because researchers wanting to continue their quests need credentials and publication. They need to be cited. Museums must continue to highlight research because without it, interpretation would be impossible, collection would be random, and preservation would be uneven. Displays without the context brought by research would be boring.

The first step is the museums: providing access to research materials. The next step, for writers, is communicating to the world all the succeeding steps: what the researchers have proposed, how they investigate, what they learn, why it matters.

WRITING RESEARCH BLOGS

Several kinds of research projects make good blog material: ongoing projects, periodical reports, and photo documentation. They all move easily into readable form with the simple act of posting the written updates on your website's blog. Blogs are serial; they continue from day to day, or week to week, as does research. Blogs welcome long-form articles, photos, charts, videos, and sound. They're serious. Researchers, if they want to appear in a blog, expect a professional environment. Writers: if you need an interview or quote from a researcher, gravitas all around is the order of the day.

Title your research blog as if it were an article, story, or report. The goal is to entice readership with specifics and novelty:

- Excavation of the Storm Wreck
- Octopodoidea as Predators Near the End of the Mesozoic Marine Revolution
- Realms of Fin and Feet and Wing

The first is from St. Augustine Lighthouse & Maritime Museum, the next two from University of Alabama Museums Collections and Research Department. Both museums enjoy strong research programs.

If each blog is part of a series, it gets a number. Numbers indicate orderliness and progression. Numbering allows reference to past blogs. Numbers signal more to come. Call each blog post an episode, if appropriate.

Start each blog with a recap of the blog's mission. National Cowboy & Western Heritage Museum describes its local history research—which combines video, audio, text, and images—this way: "It's time for Episode 18 of 'Voices from the West,' our blog series featuring audio recordings of historical documents. . . . Our goal is to show that history is . . . about people . . . not just the famous and infamous, but the everyday and ordinary. If you missed previous episodes, you can start here." Short, descriptive title, check. Stated goal, check. Reference to continuity of past and future posts, check. The text here is conversational, not stuffy. And that's appropriate to the website. Researchers are serious, not boring.

Decide how to handle the visuals—as integral, illustrative, or maybe as subjects for a different research project. When writing a caption, short or long, the research guidelines maintain: details, brief review of the aim of research, conciseness, seriousness.

Writers: when selecting a tone or tenor of a blog, written or audio, listen to the researchers, curators, and archivists involved. How they talk and the phrasing they use suggests the tone of voice the writing takes.

NARRATIVE APPROACH

Getty Museum portrays one research project as a story, with photos to illustrate the theme. As with all research papers, these from Getty start with a statement made by a published academician or scholar, and then proposes a new perspective. Here's how Getty writes abut a 2021 research project in its IRIS blog:

> for [Rainer Maria Rilke] . . . what remains of the statue becomes a work of art in its own right. Researchers at the Getty are taking a similar approach when it comes to the study of fragmented objects. "The Fragment" is the 2020–2022 theme for the Getty Scholars Program. . . . Given that fragments are everywhere in the historical record, Getty scholars are looking at a range of objects, from Japanese calligraphy albums to Greek funerary arrangements. . . .
> Why study fragments? For one, because . . .

The elements of a proposal are all there: an existing perspective on a topic, an alternative exploration, the title of the proposed research, representative details of the research, the rationale.

VIDEO BLOGS

Milwaukee County Zoo greets its Twitter followers every day with a close-up of giraffes chewing, rhinos playing roll the watermelon, or a hog turning its back to the camera; it's all part of the daily routine at a zoo. Sheer entertainment? Actually, it's a series of observations that often result in questions, hypotheses, and research. There's a theme, in visuals, to this series of tweets. There's no audio, and seldom any text. One tweet, however, sent out a call for captions. Writers: find out the photographer's goal when they plan visual documentation, and write a research report. It could escalate to a proposal.

Internship programs may need blogs; they usually require a regular log of the students' work, time spent, objectives, and outcomes. Your need for a worker plus their need for documentation of their time and efforts coalesce in a blog. Writers: if you want credit for an internship, document your project with research rhetoric: goal, observations, facts, details, results or conclusions, and implications.

A STRUCTURE FOR RESEARCH WRITING

Website, newsletter, blog, or post, all are spacious enough to include the basic parts of research write-ups.

First, announce that your institution conducts research and transparently communicates its findings to the public.

Then, categorize research projects. Past, Present, Ongoing, and Planned are good categories because they show breadth, depth, durability, and ongoing support from funding organizations. Categories are quick reads, strong signals.

Next, write your research goals. General goals are good, because even if you don't have a current project, you announce your ability and willingness to institute one. Goals will relate to mission and/or collection guidelines, and interpretive programming. Goals prove that adherence to the guiding principles of collecting, preserving, displaying, and interpreting.

Specific goals for individual research projects—past, present, ongoing, and planned—show not only variety and depth, but also curiosity and creativity. Writers: here's an opportunity to loosen up and congratulate researchers for their wide-ranging talent to widen horizons.

RESEARCH PROJECTS ON YOUR WEBSITE

When written up on a website, under the tab Learn or Explore, research projects gain an aura of permanence, a department of the museum, not an activity. On a website's drop-down menus, there's space for archived projects, as well as ongoing ones.

These projects of St. Augustine Lighthouse & Museum record a dazzling variety of research inquiries: "Historical Background: St. Augustine, the American Revolution, and the Loyalist Influx," "Boatbuilding History of St. Augustine," "Lost Ships of St. Augustine," "St. Johns County Submerged Cultural Resources Inventory and Management Plan." The titles envisage the topic. Writers today are encouraged to name their proposals enticingly. Describing a project accurately is essential, and there are always bright synonyms for academic terms. On a website, with its unlimited space, opportunities abound for good writing. Writers: This is your challenge. It's not your job to title a proposal or project, but the narrative that enlightens website viewers is yours to tell.

Here's a research statement of objective, from St. Augustine Lighthouse & Maritime Museum. It starts with the current research goal:

> The current research goal of the St. Augustine Lighthouse Archaeological Maritime Program (LAMP) is to better understand and share the founding story of the oldest port city in the United States . . .

It continues with relevance to a wider audience—

> a story of national and international significance. Above all things, the story of our region is a story about the sea.

Next it puts the research in context:

> Our research aims to shed light on how this colonial conflict led to the founding not only of a city, but of a nation and a global society still in the making . . . and the impacts that our seaside and riverine geography had on our unique culture and heritage.

Then it adds the exclamation point of a detail—

> LAMP focuses its research on the investigation of shipwrecks off the coast of northeast Florida.

RESEARCH RESULTING IN PUBLISHED ARTICLE

The University of Alabama Museums' Department of Research and Collections launched a student and curator project that achieved the pinnacle of research—publication in an academic journal. The story of the project was summarized in *Research News*, on the department's website. While not as academic as the article itself, for which links are provided, the tone honors the scholarly excellence of both the research and ensuing published article.

> "Mosasaur Jaw from the Paleontology Collection Tells Remarkable Story."
> "Main conclusion? Mosasaurs migrated bi-weekly into freshwater."

And,

> "Grooves on the inside of several teeth were made to scrape off enamel for oxygen isotope analyses."

This kind of writing requires careful interviewing and note-taking to transcribe the intent and language of scientists. Listen for the specifics of hypotheses and abstracts and specimen handling, and translate them into lay talk, appreciating that readers are laypeople of graduate-level intelligence.

Writers: include the names of all involved; ask for their spelling and their correct titles. Pay close attention when external professionals are part of the team. Get the name of the publication right. In this case it is "Palaeogeography, Palaeoclimatology, Palaeoecology."

As a research postscript, there's space for Comments at the end of the blog, giving the institution insights into Who is following, Why, and What new information they can add.

VIRTUAL TALKS AND TOURS

The allure of virtual formats for showing off your research is high viewer interest. Where video conferencing was once a necessity, now it is an option, and it appeals greatly to people willing to squeeze in an extra hour of learning. Many virtual tours and talks are scheduled right before dinner, or during the traditional lunch hour. These viewers sacrifice time in a busy day to listen to your museum. Seize the opportunity to brag a little about the research that goes into a talk or tour. The Tenement Museum, whose presentations are based on stories of immigrant families who lived in the actual tenement buildings of the museum, uses the families' belongings, apartment furnishings, and documents to reveal their stories. In a one-hour slide presentation, about five to ten minutes are occupied with explaining how objects reveal stories. In the five tours viewed by the author, the Chat feature was regularly used to ask about that research. Writers: when including research methods in the script, understand that curious audiences enjoy details, facts, techniques, and specialized terminology. Understand this about virtual talk and tour viewers:

- They could be anywhere in the world.
- Their budget can handle the price—often free!—of virtual lectures.
- They're often professionals who are busy during the day and make time for an evening or lunch hour talk.

Even with short research mentions that are incidental to the talk, explain the research goals, stages, expected results, and significance. Talk and tours entertain as well as enlighten, so feel free to highlight surprise findings.

The virtual tours of Tenement Museum exemplify ongoing research and dedication to digging ever deeper for insights.

ARCHIVES

If your archives, or archival materials, are open to scholars, educators, and students conducting their own research, say so loud and clear. If you have, or plan, a research center where graduate students, professors, authors, and amateur historians can conduct research, highlight that. Research happens at all times, to people of all levels of expertise, and it's another area where museums can increase inclusiveness. Articulation of archives belongs on the website, which is spacious enough to describe all the objects, documents, photographs, maps, videos, and publications an institution holds. Regardless of size, however, it's the presence of so much knowledge that matters. Writers: emphasize how your archive represents the mission, collection, and interpretation of your museum.

Here's one way to organize the writing:

- Your collection and acquisition strategy
- Individual artifacts in your collection
- Items particularly applicable for teaching and study
- Photographs, charts, maps, and written documentation
- Oral histories
- Records of museum research projects, biographical material, and exhibitions created by the staff to interpret the collection

"Archive" is a technical term that may confuse or intimidate some of your audiences, just when they've started to show curiosity. Err on the side of over-explanation.

AUDIO IN RESEARCH

Oral histories bring more than humanity to research. When people talk about their own lives, details emerge that no research could ever unearth. Everyone in the business of interpretation understands the value of voices. Underappreciated is the difference between the spoken word and the written word of the same person. Speakers use different words when speaking than when writing; their voices emphasize what's significant in the speaker's culture. The speaker's purpose comes through. Importantly, oral histories convey the background, culture, ethnicity, and individuality of the speaker that a narrator never could.

COLLABORATIONS

One unintended consequence of research projects is collaborations with people drawn to your project.

Collaboration is built in at many stages of scholarly research. Researchers work with university advisers, grantors, partners, teams, interview subjects,

Figure 18.1.   Re-created apartment of Joseph and Bridget Moore, Irish immigrants raising their three children in 97 Orchard Street in 1869, now the Tenement Museum—one of the 150 years of stories told by the objects and documents held in the museum's archives.
Courtesy of Lower East Side Tenement Museum

and academic journals. Undergrads work with classmates, teachers, and a (hopefully) large network of experts and contacts willing to help. Writers: remember to credit all partners and collaborators in a project. It plays an important function in research and can lead to fruitful partnerships for your museum. The Burke Museum spells it out: "Our work is collaborative; we partner with institutions, communities and people around the world to understand our past and create positive change in the future."

CURATORS AND RESEARCH

Curators play multiple roles in the scholarly research behind any exhibition. They select the topic; correspond with contributors, often worldwide; develop a thesis and theme; oversee the title and poster image; contact and persuade the lenders; and persuasively present the bottom line to their own board of trustees. Then there's the hanging or display of the exhibition, labels, panels. Throughout this long and exacting process, they have conducted their own impeccable research. Curators' research directly affects the work of an exhibition's many creators; the public; and the partners of any exhibition. Writers: give curators appropriate credit. Include the details of their role.

New Bedford Whaling Museum starts the well-earned praise of its curators with credit on the Exhibition page for an upcoming show: "This is the first exhibition of Ryder's work since co-curator Elizabeth Broun's 1990 retrospective at the Smithsonian American Art Museum." With one sentence, the curator's credentials lend importance not just to the exhibition, but also to the New Bedford Whaling Museum for mounting it. Another reason to credit curators' research more expansively: credibility and accountability.

RESEARCH GRANTS

Grant writers are experts at persuading funding institutions to support their projects. The guidelines for grant writing are surprisingly simple and devilishly hard to achieve.

State the title, which is the focus of the grant request.

Here's one from the Getty Institute: "The history and legacy of printmaking on the African continent in relation to an understudied body of work from one of America's foremost modern printmakers, Jacob Lawrence."

Be specific so that the title indicates goal, singularity, and level of difficulty that requires upfront monetary outlay.

LITERATURE REVIEW

List other research papers similar to the proposed one. Tell why they led to your proposed project.

Singularity. Explain why your project is different in focus, scope, and perspective. Why you are qualified for this quest.

Opening paragraph. Explain further why your need is special. Try a paraphrased paragraph. If it's too esoteric, add some lay language.

Goal. Write clearly and concisely about what you hope to uncover, reveal, clarify, or debunk. Tell the difficulties impeding others from discovering it.

Cost. Explain how much money you need and itemize it. Be very specific about any sentence that has dollar signs in it.

Summary. Summarize why this project is uncommon, unusual, or previously unimaginable. Ideas that are different are hard to grasp, hard to visualize, and very hard to explain. Writers: start each session at the keypad with this mantra: there's always a better word than my first word. If proposed research is described with words everyone uses, it's too common to deserve a grant.

Grants are good reads. They are unique to a museum's brand, undertaken by experts in the fields your museum covers. They are curious, new, and marvelous. Museums have always demonstrated an open-minded worldview in the paths they take, and it's often led by original research.

TALKING TO THE EVERYDAY RESEARCHERS

Museums attract amateur researchers every day—the people who just like to poke around subjects that pique their curiosity. Curiosity! It needs reinforcement wherever it presents itself, and museums can help. National World War I Museum and Memorial in Kansas City, Missouri, welcomes serious researchers generously.

> The Edward Jones Research Center welcomes all who are interested in learning more about the Great War. From graduate students and professors to authors and family historians, researchers are able to access the Museum and Memorial's 330,000 archival documents and three-dimensional objects . . . it also offers an intimate, ground-level view of the symbolic poppy field.

The institution gives detailed directions so first-timers can find the Research Center. And mentioning the poppy fields gives an appropriate salute to the museum's brand identity.

ENCOURAGE RESEARCH

Scholars, advanced degree candidates, professors hoping for tenure, and professionals who research and publish as a vocation get plenty of encouragement from the academic universe and their own ambitions. Don't forget all the other curious people who visit. Students of all stripes need encouragement to search for information in unexpected places. People looking for information need instructions on where the open doors are. Research buffs are serious people whom museums have the facilities to nurture. The innovative talent that defines researchers imbues a diverse group; the very attributes that produce a good researcher—tenacity and zeal—are those that entice visitors from the fringe to come through your doors.

The following list, a partial one, shows the diversity of researchers:

- Scholars in every field—publication, thesis, CV
- Educators—learning, investigation, analysis
- Students—projects, papers
- Amateur historians, scientists, explorers—inquiry
- Hobbyists—historic references, visual references
- Community decision makers—data, documentation, collaboration
- Tourism departments—history, culture, environment
- Professional speakers—data, local history, references
- Journalists—facts, details, people, oral histories, images
- Government officials—facts, data, government documents such as censuses

- Artists, architects, novelists, playwrights, designers, choreographers, musicians—images, biographical material, recordings, videos, documents specific to individual arts

Writers: learn the basic language of diverse researchers. Look up terms you don't know. The above list suggests key words.

DON'T HIDE SCHOLARLY RESEARCH

Communicate scholarly research as often, and in as many formats, as possible. It's not arcane; it's different. It reaches out to the bright minds everywhere that look for minds to identify with. Its significance extends far beyond your walls and affects people, issues, attitudes, and policies worldwide. The context might be local, but the implications ripple out.

Visitor Research

Who's coming, who's staying, and how come? Basic visitorship information fuels a museum's success and growth. Museums need answers to Who and Why, and they need it updated now. Some say "we did research just a few years ago." Museums know that things have changed. It's in their DNA to adapt.

Visitor research need not be costly. Here are some ways to gather information easily:

- Count the children who visit.
- Count the parents and/or caregivers who visit.
- Count the people who visit alone or with others.
- Note the teenagers who visit or study in your spaces.
- See what exhibits different visitors swerve to.
- Ask the guards for insights—noticing people is their job.

Enlist the services of staffers in the appropriate departments.

- Read and analyze comments on social media and travel apps.
- Tally the ticket receipts of participants in virtual talks, discussion groups, presentations, workshops.
- Convene a webinar, discussion group, or hashtag tell-all.
- Talk to college students—a diverse group with opinions and blatant intelligence.
- Ask purchasers of store items: "Is this a gift?" Surprising information ensues.

- Articulate the kind of data you want. Some are easier to collect than others.
- Critique programs or events

Look further at:

- Verbatim feedback on an exhibition or tour
- Projects developed by other museums and cultural institutions
- Local stories
- Data on out-of-town visitors

Collect data on all areas of the museum:

- Store
- Grounds
- Information desk and guards
- Restrooms, benches, relaxation areas
- Desire for and availability of museum tours
- Physical distances, up and down steps, walkways and paths, ease of door-opening—accessibility is a universal issue
- Special features like the terrace, reading room, meeting rooms, making place

INFORMATION IS EVERYTHING

Learn the importance of "data," which is just another word for information, but one that implies a serious attempt to "let's look at what we have," and then critique and analyze it. Research is useless without analysis, critique, discussion, and next steps. Set aside time, during the workday, to gather a few members of the staff for discussion sessions. Invite people from different areas of the museum. These short gatherings will consist of one agenda item: a look at recent data and asking, "So what?"

Any research, large or small, communicated clearly, can help your audiences understand purpose and advantages of your activities. Transparency, again. The daily bombardment of information alerts everyone to their right to knowledge. It's another kind of accessibility, and one museums rigorously provide.

MUSEUMS' EFFECT ON THEIR COMMUNITIES

Every community critiques and analyzes their cultural institutions. This ad hoc chorus consists of citizens, educators, tourist bureaus, businesses large and small, economic development boards, realtors, elected officials, other cultural institutions, household decision makers, and museums' own staff, volunteers, interns, and suppliers. Show the data you've collected. Others will analyze it differently, or draw separate implications. Others may differ with others' opinions, but everyone respects data. Let your research, scholarly and visitor, show. Research lets everyone look inside your walls.

REFERENCES

"Albert Pynkham Ryder: A Wild Note of Longing," Exhibitions, New Bedford Whaling Museum, https://www.whalingmuseum.org/exhibition/a-wild-note-of-longing/ [accessed 9-3-21]

"The Burke Museum from the Inside-Out," Our Work, About, Burke Museum, https://www.burkemuseum.org/about/our-work/ [accessed 9-4-21]

"Conducting Research at the National WWI Museum and Memorial," Edward Jones Research Center, Explore, The National WWI Museum and Memorial, https://www.theworldwar.org/explore/edward-jones-research-center [accessed 9-3-21]

"Current Projects," Explore and Learn, St. Augustine Lighthouse & Maritime and Museum, https://collections.museums.ua.edu/2021/03/02/octopodoidea-as-predators-near-the-end-of-the-mesozoic-marine-revolution/

Greenwood, Anne, "Realms of Fin and Feet and Wing," Library, Crystal Bridges Museum of American Art, http://finfeetwing.org/

https://salh.wpengine.com/wp-content/uploads/2019/05/Explore-Learn-Research-Archaeology-Project-Archive-Storm.pdf

Lew, Kirsten, "Putting the Pieces Together: Art history is littered with broken objects. How a group of Getty scholars is rethinking the concept of the fragment," Art Stories, Getty Research Center, April 28, 2021, https://blogs.getty.edu/iris/putting-the-pieces-together/ [accessed 8-31-21]

Milwaukee County Zoo @MilwaukeeCoZoo, https://www.staugustinelighthouse.org/explore-learn/research-archaeology/current-projects/ [accessed 8-31-21]

"Mosasaur Jaw from the Paleontology Collection Tells Remarkable Story," Research News, Research & Collections, University of Alabama Museums, July 23, 2021, https://collections.museums.ua.edu/2021/07/23/mosasaur-jaw-from-the-alabama-museum-of-natural-history-collection-tells-remarkable-story/ [accessed 9-1-21]

"Our Collections," About, Tenement Museum https://www.tenement.org/about-us/our-collections/ [accessed 9-4-21]

Sivan, Alexandria, "Innovation in Prints and Drawings Is the Focus of New Getty Grants: Grants made as part of The Paper Project feature diverse and understudied collections," *The Iris*, J. Paul Getty Trust, Los Angeles, July 14, 2021, https://blogs.getty.edu/iris/innovation-in-prints-and-drawings-is-the-focus-of-new-getty-grants/ [accessed 9-4-21]

"Virtual Curator Tour: In Praise of Stuff," Upcoming Events, Experience the Tenement Museum, Member News, August 2021, https://mailchi.mp/tenement.org/experience-the-tenementmuseum-991996?e=0521cfbea5

"Voices from the West—Lula Briscoe Ep. 18," Dickinson Research Center, National Cowboy and Western Heritage Museum, February 18, 2021, https://nationalcowboymuseum.org/blog/voices-from-the-west-lula-briscoe-ep-18/ [accessed 8-25-21]

CHAPTER 19

Volunteers

The wonderful fact about volunteers is: they're already looking for you. In every audience for a virtual class, renewed membership, or tally of receipts from the store, you can see their names—people interested enough to return for more. Maybe they're returning for a change, for more choices. One thing's for sure, there's a new audience in your community that's ready to add their exciting range of talent and energy to your projects.

This chapter will discuss the kind of writing that attracts energetic volunteers, trains them, and retains them.

How to find volunteers? Start where you already have their names:

- ticketed programs and events
- registrations for classes and workshops
- online e-mail announcements where a link has been clicked
- the store

A simple in-store sign with a QR code or on-screen link will work well.

"Want more of the museum? Learn about being a volunteer!"

Writers: you have a powerful ally in the language of diversity; it includes terms like

"cultural insights"
"experience needed from many backgrounds"
"wide range of skills include . . ."

ADVERTISING FOR VOLUNTEERS

The Volunteer page of the website is the most likely place to scout for volunteers. It's easy to find from the home page, since it's usually a top-line tab or drop-down under Support. Writers have a large selection of help words to use:

Support and Get Involved—California African American Museum, Los Angeles
Careers and Volunteer—High Museum of Art in Atlanta
Get Involved and Volunteer—Western Museum of Mining & Industry in Colorado Springs, Colorado
Get Involved and Museum Docents (Volunteer Opportunity)—McFadden-Ward House, Beaumont, Texas

Writers: some other persuasive terms include Learn, Work With, Long-Term, Flexible Hours, and Other Ways to Contribute. What's effective about these terms is their immediate lure. Offer the lure, and then get to the facts. It's professional and you want workers who understand it's their job.

WRITING THE WEBSITE DESCRIPTION

There are as many ways to describe a Volunteer job as there are museums offering them. One rule that applies to all: deliver the details. Writers are at their most ingenious when they deliver the right synonym for a trite euphemism. Details should not bore the reader.

Boring:
Hours are 10 a.m.–Noon, one day a week.

Inviting:
Volunteers work two hours a week and can select either mornings or afternoons, on the weekday of their choice. Saturdays and weeknights are possible.

When mining diverse audiences, remember the new paradigms of new audiences: hybrid jobs, fluctuating schedules, care responsibilities at home, travel challenges. Writers: find the words to emphasize that this museum job offers the flexibility all workers want today. And state the details that show the volunteer–job seeker exactly what is expected.

Here's what Fargo Air Museum needs from volunteers for the full restoration of its BT-13 basic trainer aircraft: "Hard work, time, and dedication from board members, volunteers, engineering students from neighboring colleges and aviation enthusiasts . . . coming together . . ."

Demanding hours, teamwork, specific academic requirements, preferred skills—museum department heads, you might recognize some of these requisite volunteer details. Don't wish for them; ask for them.

Writers: listen to what the bosses really need and write it down.

KNOW YOUR AUDIENCE

Part of the genius of describing a volunteer job is displaying knowledge of your prospective audience. The Fralin Museum of Art at the University of Virginia identifies two groups for its docent program, student docents and community docents, and the difference between the two audiences is clear.

The written description for community docents stresses training and doesn't mince words:

> Community members who are accepted into the program are required to complete the museum's 11-week Docent Training Course . . . learn public speaking skills and techniques for facilitating tours . . . complete a qualifying tour at the end of the course and commit to leading tours at The Fralin for at least two years following its completion.

The student program requires academic rigor, and the written description is appropriately strict: "New docents participate in a semester-long training course in dialogic teaching, public speaking, and education theory. . . . After the training semester, student docents attend weekly education meetings Fridays from 1–2 pm."

Here's what museum department heads want volunteers to know:

- What the job entails
- Rules and regs
- Specific schedules
- Time commitment

At the same time writers are telling volunteers what to expect, they're manifesting the standards of the museum, and that's important when you remember all the other people who read the various pages of your website. Donors, Supporters, and Partners like to know that other people also give— in their own way—to the museum.

DRAWING POWER OF THE COMMUNITY

Contributing to the community is appealing for many would-be volunteers from diverse audiences. Culture groups, neighborhoods, and towns are backstops for many new people looking to participate in their community. Museums should work with those communities in their announcement platforms, but also create their own announcements in e-newsletters, social media, and websites. Museums looking for volunteers reach the audiences in different ways than community posts do: Here's how Shaker Village explains the museum's need for a community project:

> The Preserve at Shaker Village conserves and shares native prairies, woodlands, watersheds, fields, canebrakes and diverse wildlife . . .
>
> Maintaining this trail system is not only important for ensuring a quality visitor experience, but also for protecting a diverse, and sometimes delicate, ecosystem.

Talk about details, the museum goes on to expect this of volunteers: "Volunteers will use hand tools including shovels and loppers, and should wear leather work gloves and sturdy, closed-toe shoes or work boots."

Writers: learn the exact terminology used on the job—such as "ecosystem" and "lopper." It shows the professionalism involved at all levels.

THE DICTIONARY OF JOB DESCRIPTIONS

Application Process. Eligibility. Acknowledgment. Compensation. Candidate Interviews. These words convey a serious volunteer job and pre-screen your applicants. Use them correctly. If the job demands certain skills or experience, don't sugarcoat them. Say straight out that, for instance, the applicants must be graduate students, currently enrolled in an appropriate degree program.

Here's some of the language on the website of the Museum of Musical Instruments in Phoenix:

> Interested candidates should complete the following requirements and submit the requested materials by clicking the link above:
>
> - Cover letter explaining your interest in a MIM internship.
> - Current résumé.
> - International students should provide a copy of their student visa.
> - Interviews for candidates selected as finalists will be scheduled at MIM.

HOW TO INTERVIEW

Writers play a large, though silent, part of the interviewing process; they write the official script for the interview. In a job interview, even one for volunteers, all applicants must be asked the same questions. Interviewers cannot substitute another question, even if the first doesn't elicit a response. They shouldn't prompt a response. Many HR professionals provide the list of questions in advance, and that's something for a nonprofit to consider. If it seems that interviewees need prompting questions, write them into the script for the next round of interviews.

One skilled peer-learning discussion leader uses this phrase when a discussion bogs down: "Let me reframe the question." A version of this works well at an interview's conclusion: "Are there any questions in this interview you'd like rephrased?" Then rephrase them for all interviewees. Incidentally, when you discover questions that aren't well understood, you discover more about your audience.

ASSEMBLING THE LIST OF INTERVIEW QUESTIONS

Interview questions should:

- make interviewees comfortable
- allow them latitude to express themselves
- empower a little boasting
- encourage them to share concerns
- give the interviewer time to state clearly and listen intently

Colleagues at other museums can share interview questions, but all museums have different needs and ways of explaining them.

Writers: in fumbling around for the perfect interview questions, just start pounding them out. Write twenty, cut them down to ten, and then show them around for opinions. Ask for comments, additions, and edits. Rewrite. Here's how the questions might look:

1. Why do you want to volunteer here?
2. What do you know or like about the museum?
3. Where have you worked, at any point of your life, that made you a good worker?
4. Have you walked through the museum recently? What struck you?
5. Have your read through our website? What surprised you?
6. What would you like to know more about?
7. What are you good at? What are you bad at?
8. What was your favorite job? Go back to first grade if you want!
9. Are there any behind-the-scenes areas of the museum that could use your skills?
10. What are your current time commitments?
11. What areas of your life would our volunteer job improve?

12. What would you like to learn? Dream!
13. Talk about any other volunteer jobs or projects you've been proud of.
14. Let's take a ten-minute walk into some parts of the museum [house, exhibition, garden] so you can point out what you like.

The above list shows how the questions look on a printed page. Looks aren't everything. Read them out loud, because that's how they'll sound in an interview.

ZOOM INTERVIEWS

Protocols for virtual interviews, as with any meeting, develop with the situation. A basic rule is professionalism. The museum wants to attract serious volunteers. Some suggestions for people handling the volunteer interview:

- Dress for a business meeting, if only from the waist up.
- Make sure your device, camera, and microphone are good quality.
- For meetings of more than fifteen people, use a screen large enough to accommodate all faces without swiping.
- Use actual backgrounds. In a museum you have some choice of where to sit. No virtual backgrounds. Do not schedule interviews from your home office.
- Adjust the lighting for shadows and glints.
- Check how you look on screen; practice smiling.
- Teaming with a colleague? Coordinate how two people look and sound on camera.

LIST OF VOLUNTEERS AND ASSIGNMENTS

Keep an updated roster of volunteers, their hours, and assignments. It demonstrates volunteer support sought by many stakeholders: fundraisers, grantors, community partners, educators, high level donors and supporters, and accrediting bodies.

Training Process: Stage #1—Selection

The first step in training is winnowing. Ascertain who is willing to go through the training process, or who wants less demanding on-the-job training. Let prospects understand what they're signing up for. Find out if the job descriptions didn't adequately express the museum's needs.

Figure 19.1–19.2. Museum volunteers add their own skills and knowledge to all areas of the museum, from historic wheel-making demonstrations to ecology tours.
urbancow/ E+ via Getty Images

Don't discourage willing people with a different experience than they expected. Don't set anyone up for failure. Do encourage a wide range of volunteer talent and interests by giving all the details possible.

The Metropolitan Museum of Art adds this surprising volunteer job to an otherwise standard paragraph on information desk responsibilities: "[V]olunteers help uncover trends by conducting visitor surveys." The Met continues with the expectations for Guided Tour Volunteers: "Guides select and research artworks from the extensive collection and engage visitors in one-hour conversations offering context and enhancing understanding. Met volunteers lead tours in English or in ten other languages."

No generalities here. Fact-full writing can forestall embarrassment on day one of training if a volunteer prospect discovers the job is more intensive than expected.

The one problem to be avoided is discouragement.

Some museums find other ways to enlist the community of eager volunteers. Queens Museum takes an especially wide-angle view from its position in New York's mostly immigrant and very diverse New York City neighborhood.

> Over the past decade, the Museum has been working to ensure that community residents are involved in the envisioning, production, programming, and maintenance of public spaces and amenities . . . moved beyond the walls of our galleries to address issues . . . from health care . . . to language access . . . and long-term, socially-collaborative art projects.

The Strategic Air Command & Aerospace Museum Boulder, Colorado, tempers the exacting work requirements with desired skills: "You will assist in the areas of science, technology, engineering and math . . . many of the volunteers are retired military or air force. Others bring ability in areas helpful to the restoration process, such as welding."

Working with people is not ignored in the list of job duties. Longwood Gardens points out the requirement this way: "Gardening assistants are assigned to a specific garden area, and work closely with Longwood's gardening staff."

Training Process: Stage #2—Dive Right In

Give the trainees an assignment, a hard one, on day one. A contemporary art museum docent-in-training remembers her first day in the program. The group was plunked in front of a huge Kerry James Marshall painting for two hours and regularly asked: What do you see? What else do you see? Anything else? It was grueling and rigorous to look, analyze, and contextualize. One or two trainees dropped out. Twenty remained for years.

There are many places to publish a written description of the training process: on the volunteer page, in a blog, or as an e-mail attachment to new trainees. Identify a rigorous trainee assignment and describe it in all its painstaking detail. You can always pull back, if requested. It's much harder to add rigor once an assignment has been dumbed down.

Training Process: Stage #3—Small Group Discussions

After a training session, leverage the group dynamic with small group discussions. When trainees talk about what they've learned, they learn better. Ask the group:

- What was difficult.
- What was fun.
- What was surprising.
- What they hated. This is a surprisingly effective topic for generating conversation. It's a little edgy, and that wakes people up at the end of a session. When people dislike something, they get specific. Ask people what they like and the response is cliché-ridden generalities.
- What they worry about. This question quickly dissolves barriers because people with something in common—worries—share.

Read the discussion questions aloud to make sure they sound facilitating, not intimidating. The goal is to encourage talk. Edit the questions as you go for future use. With diverse groups of trainees, it's important to establish comfortable discourse. Groups are inherent to museums. Get volunteers used to them.

Training Process: Stage #4—Next Steps

When each training session starts, whether it's weekly or monthly, it should move at full gear. The leader reviews the outline for the course and the schedule for the day. The participants introduce themselves each time because it's important they can compare notes with each other. Then it's off and running, following the steps in order. At the end of the session, recap what they're learned and list what comes next: day, date, time, length. Throughout the training, next steps help new volunteers:

- Understand the immediate task
- Keep the end goal in sight
- Gain confidence in their role
- Plan their calendar so the museum becomes a part of, but not a burden to, their life

- Provides structure, which lets good volunteers love their jobs
- Encourages them to return for the next session

Retention—Staying in Touch

Once you have found them, never let them go. Keeping good volunteers involved and refreshed is an ongoing job, just as it is in any business. Commitment is important but feeling like a contributor is essential. Continuity demonstrates the museum's expectations of them. High praise, indeed.

- Publish volunteers' schedules two months in advance, at least.
- Give volunteers regular assignments, even if it's only once a month.
- Send e-newsletters.
- Plan annual appreciation events, even small ones. It's a cost of doing business, but it needn't be expensive.
- Ask regularly for suggestions or comments.
- Write a Hack of the Month.

Here's how Harriet Beecher Stowe House, in Cincinnati, handles continuity. One of its standing committees is the Program Committee, which:

- Meets on the second Monday every other month.
- Starts at 5:30 p.m.
- Has the charge to "suggest program ideas and work to secure speakers and other presenters."

The Stowe House assignment is deceptively demanding:

- creative.
- long-term.
- posted on the website—the equivalent of carved in stone.
- team-based—planning programs and signing speakers require working as a team.

There are other requirements a museum can institute to keep its committees vigorous: agendas, meeting notes, and regular reports. Of course, someone must be assigned to read them and comment.

Retention—Reward Creative Thinking

If volunteerism is the new job, and museums are a new kind of workplace, then the people in charge also bear responsibilities. The overseers of volunteers might be museum staffers or senior volunteers, and their roles demand that they encourage the creative thinking of volunteers. This rule for bosses can't be repeated too often: give praise for jobs well done, appreciate what a new volunteer has to learn to earn that praise, work with them on their new ideas, if only to ask for fuller explanations.

Writers: to support volunteers in feeling creatively involved, create a short questionnaire for them to voluntarily complete at the end of their tour:

- Volunteer Name
- Volunteer Assignment
- Date. Day of Week. Hours.
- Please share your observations, good or bad, today:

- Anything out of the ordinary happen today:

- Comments from visitors you think your colleagues would enjoy:

- Did you try something new today? Explain.

Retention—Business Cards and Badges

The expensive part of business cards is the designer who designs them. Printing doesn't cost much and it lets volunteers spread the word to their contacts. If volunteers come from new and diverse audiences, this one act will expand that audience.

Badges endure. If they're metal, with the volunteer's name, they substantiate the volunteer's worth to the institution. During a tour of duty, they communicate to visitors, including donors, supporters, and board members, that the museum is fulfilling its goal of diversity and inclusion and runs a businesslike volunteer program.

Once the badge is at home on a counter, it reminds the volunteer of their part in a professional organization. More retention, at the home front.

STAIRS, ELEVATORS, AND BENCHES

Accessibility applies to volunteers, too. Just as tour guides indicate the location of elevators, bathrooms, and water fountains, someone needs to warn volunteers:

- How long they'll be standing
- What to expect when working outside
- Weight of tools they'll have to lift

- Need to wear glasses rather than lean too close to an object
- Need, if any, for good hearing

SO MANY CHOICES FOR THE VOLUNTEER-MINDED

Where are volunteers needed these days? Everywhere. As links in the non-profit supply chain, they're widely deployed. They multitask and their 360-degree knowledge of the museum gives them connections. New volunteer positions reward the museum, as well, because it forces them to confront the plusses and minuses in their operation.

Locust Grove, a historic house and grounds near Louisville, Kentucky, drew an organization chart for prospects to find their volunteering fit. Such a chart also suggests gaps where a museum might expand its volunteer wish list. A visitor to the Volunteer page of the website can read:

Why do you want to give to Locust Grove?

- The history
- The people
- The grounds
- The events

You would be great as

- A school tour interpreter
- A gardener
- A baker for the monthly lecture series buffet

Different skills vary by museum and these are some of the requests:

- Photographer and videographer
- Digitization
- Foreign language translation (QR codes come in handy for access to translation sites)
- ASL—signing for the hearing impaired
- Origami—required by Japanese American National Museum for their Origami Docents

Writers: when assembling the museum's needs and wants list, the challenge is to find new wishlist jobs in addition to the usual ones. Go down the list of museum departments and see if they need volunteers. Keep asking the staff and snooping around to unearth opportunities missed before. Volunteers can provide many new ideas if you have an open mind, so write down everything that comes to mind and ask staffers later if this volunteer job description would help them with their job.

"We are not accepting new volunteers at this time. Check back later!" This is a bad idea on a web page headline for viewers looking to give time to their museum. Museums never discourage volunteering. However, openings occur at different times depending on seasonality, budgets (volunteers don't realize how much a training program costs), school breaks, demographics, and the dynamics of hybrid work. What the museum sees as balancing budget and visitation expectations, the viewer might see as phasing out.

This is a good idea for a website page for prospective volunteers: "The Volunteer Office works diligently to place applicants in roles that are meaningful and engaging to them. Applications remain on file for one year."

The best way to demonstrate the strength of a museum is to proceed, business as usual. List the volunteer opportunities. Detail the time, effort, and skill required. And keep the thought, which bears repeating, about working "diligently to place applicants in roles that are meaningful and engaging to them."

VOLUNTEERING AND INTERNSHIPS

"Development" has been dangling at the end of "Fundraising and" for too long. Development means building for the future and identifying long-term prospects.

Investment in community involvement bodes well for the future of volunteerism. It exposes new audiences to social involvement. Cultural institutions that offer teen internships help nurture a new generation of volunteers. What starts as a helping hand for young people becomes a helping hand for staff-short institutions.

Another internship program is that of North Carolina Museum of Science for Historically Black Colleges and Universities. It's called a volunteer-partnership, but acts as a high-quality investment. The museum offers paid internships. Interns get leadership training that in many colleges is a costly credit-hour course. Call it paying forward. It's going to return tangible dividends in the not-so-distant future.

Board of Trustees Volunteers—Another Kind of Volunteer that Works All the Time

On the subject of professionalism and businesslike operation, remember that some of museums' hardest-working professionalisms are the board directors. They come from many business and arts organizations, many of them still full-time jobs.

If you could assemble museums' boards of trustees, look at the expertise in that board room:

Graphic designer
Architect
Lawyer
Digital designer
Technical expert
Entrepreneur
Professor Emeritus

Their professions and titles give donors and supporters confidence in the mission-centeredness of the institution. If your board members have honorifics or letters after their names, use them. They're an honor.

St. Augustine Lighthouse & Maritime Museum has trustees with USN, USA, USAF, after their name. It's impressive and many viewers will be honored to support such a museum.

Whether or not your board has term limits, its members still need to be retained emotionally—with appreciation, recognition, and help.

As the Mississippi Museum of Art says about its slate of new trustees on its website: "They enthusiastically embrace our mission to continuously foster meaningful engagements with art among the communities we serve and ensure that a diversity of voices tell Mississippi's stories."

Writers: remember to check about giving credit where it's due. There's always space enough at the end of a list of names, whether volunteers or board members, for a line of praise. It could be as simple as, "Thank you, Trustees."

Virtual Volunteering

Working in the virtual world will always be an option. Distance is a reality, not a problem. Citizen scientists, for example, have long worked independently, far from the museum to collect and observe the natural world.

Virtual volunteers need to be addressed as valued and essential. Not everyone, for example, can travel to Cooperstown, New York, to volunteer at the National Baseball Hall of Fame Museum. However, the museum's archive and collection of written publications is so vast, online help is essential.

Become a National Baseball Hall of Fame and Museum Virtual Volunteer and help us make historical documents more accessible and searchable. . . .

We are currently transcribing . . . profiles on Major League players, Minor League players, and prospects. . . . Review our instructions for Virtual Volunteers and start transcribing!

And from University of Alabama Department of Museums:

Regular monitoring and centralized reporting among participants across three nations will help us answer some of the many questions currently surrounding dragonfly migration and provide information needed to create cross-border conservation programs to protect and sustain the phenomenon. This site will allow you to submit dragonfly migration observations.

CLOSING THOUGHTS ON JOB OPENINGS

Volunteerism opens new opportunities throughout the museum universe because it opens doors to new kinds of people with fresh energy and talents, different availabilities, new contacts, global vision, and forward attitudes. It is a hard-working concept and it's sustainable.

REFERENCES

"Become a Stowe House Volunteer," Program Committee, Friends of Harriett Beecher Stowe House, https://app.betterimpact.com/PublicOrganization/4cd723be-fa10-4ef8-98f3-7322353d5bd1/1 [accessed 12-19-21]

"Become a Virtual Volunteer," Safe at Home, National Baseball of Fame, https://baseballhall.org/discover/safe-at-home [accessed 1-3-22]

California African American Museum, https://caamuseum.org/support [accessed 12-19-21]

"Choose Your Own Volunteer Adventure! The Croghans and Clarks Loved Adventure—Find Yours at Locust Grove!" Volunteer and Internship Opportunities, Locust Grove, https://locustgrove.org/wp-content/uploads/2017/03/Find-Your-Volunteer-Adventure.pdf [accessed 12-27-21]

"Citizen Science Initiatives," Research & Collections, Department of Museum Research & Collections, University of Alabama Museums, The University of Alabama, https://collections.museums.ua.edu/support-research-collections/citizen-science-initiatives/ [accessed 9-1-21]

"Employment Opportunities at RAM and RAM's Wustum Museum," Employment, Get Involved, Racine Art Museum, https://www.ramart.org/get-involved/employment/ [accessed 9-21-21]

High Museum of Art in Atlanta, "Volunteer," Careers, High Museum of Art, https://high.org/careers/ [accessed 12-19-21]

"In the Community," Queens Museum, http://queensmuseum.org/in-the-community [accessed 12-19-21]

"Intern with Us," Volunteers & Internships, Support, North Carolina Museum of Natural Science, https://sites.google.com/view/ncmns-vip-portal/partner-internships [accessed 9-12-21]

"Internship Openings," Join our team, Museum of Musical Instruments, https://mim.org/join-our-team/ [accessed 12-29-21]

"Looking into the Future of the Looking Glass," Restoration, What to See, Strategic Air Command & Aerospace Museum, https://www.sacmuseum.org/what-to-see/restoration/ [accessed 9-29-21]

McFadden-Ward House, Beaumont, Texas, https://mcfaddin-ward.org/about/get-involved/ [accessed 12-19-21]

"Membership & Donation/Volunteer," Metropolitan Museum of Art, https://www.metmuseum.org/join-and-give/volunteer [accessed 12-19-21]

"Mississippi Museum of Art Announces Slate of New Trustees," September 16, 2021, Mississippi Museum of Art, https://www.msmuseumart.org/mississippi-museum-of-art-announces-slate-of-new-trustees [accessed 1-2-22]

"Restoration project: BT-13," Projects, Fargo Air Museum, https://fargoairmuseum.org/projects [accessed 12-20-21]

"2020–2022 Board of Trustees," Get Involved, St. Augustine Lighthouse & Maritime Museum, https://salh.wpengine.com/get-involved/about-mission-uvp/board/ [accessed 9-19-21]

"Visitors Service Associated," Louisiana Children's Museum, January 1, 2020, https://worknola.com/job/322342/visitor-services-associate [accessed 11-27-21]

"Volunteer," The Fralin Museum of Art at the University of Virginia," https://uvafralinartmuseum.virginia.edu/volunteer [accessed 12-20-21]

"Volunteer Application," Volunteering, Longwood Gardens, https://longwoodgardens.org/volunteering/apply-now [accessed 1-3-22]

"Volunteering at the Burke," Support, Burke Museum, https://www.burkemuseum.org/support/volunteer [accessed 11-8-21]

"Volunteering," Longwood Gardens, https://longwoodgardens.org/volunteering/opportunities/ [accessed 12-29-21]

"Volunteering," Strategic Air Command & Aerospace Museum, https://www.sacmuseum.org/join-give/volunteering/ [accessed 9-19-21]

"Volunteer Roles," Volunteering, Longwood Gardens, https://longwoodgardens.org/volunteering/opportunities [accessed 9-29-21]

"Volunteer Trail Crew," Events, October 16, 2021, Shaker Village, https://shakervillageky.org/events/volunteer-trail-crew-18/ [accessed 12-29-21]

Western Museum of Mining & Industry in Colorado Springs, Colorado, https://wmmi.org/get-involved/volunteer.html [accessed 12-19-21]

"What Can I Do?" Jobs & Internships, Japanese American National Museum, https://www.janm.org/volunteer#volunteer-opportunities [accessed 9-13-21]

CHAPTER 20

Tips for Writers

Writing for a museum involves dozens of variables:

Subject
Audience
Media
Length
Connection to museum's core values

Many more, unknown now, will thwart you later. Fortunately, there's no shortage of tips to guide writers through most assignments. So, without further ado, here they are:

- Never say "without further ado." It's a cliché.

Learn to recognize a cliché when it types itself on your screen. Some examples:

- Crazy, as in it's been a crazy week
- Random
- Bizarre
- Surreal—unless it's Dali
- Curated—except when it's orchestrated by real museum curators
- Magisterial

No platitudes. They're harder to recognize; basically they're what your parents said.

Don't celebrate a museum anniversary. Nobody cares if it's your tenth or hundredth unless you convert your fact into an interesting fact. "100 years ago today Tutankhamen's tomb was discovered" is serviceable for a newsletter announcement from a natural history museum announcing its centennial.

Use quotes. The Mark Twain House has plenty from its namesake; the National Quilt Museum gets quotes from e-mail-writing quilters. Ask your docents what visitors say.

Watch out for nice words. They say nothing. They're delicate.

- Power words are grabbers compared to nice words.
- Strong verbs crush passive verbs.
- Edgy adjectives are invigorating; pleasant adjectives are invisible.

Use negatives. Negatives help you sound funny. Also truthful. In surveys, ask one question that's negative. "What didn't you like at the museum?" Everyone is a critic and they'll answer truthfully.

Corollary: Use scary words.

Avoid: "This exhibition on historic comic book heroes will heighten your appreciation of the illustrator's skill."

Try: "POW! WHAM!! ZAP!#*. This illustrator really nails drawing."

Study the titles for exhibitions written by museum curators all over the world. Curators understand language and use riveting words.

Don't ignore the many words about art museums. Adapt them for your museum.

Avoid generic names like Third Wednesday Sketching Group. Take a cue from the "Bad Drawing Club" at Pulitzer Arts Foundation in St. Louis.

Claiming to be "America's biggest," "only," "most" is called "puffery."

Use superlatives only when you can follow them with a verifiable fact.

Ask non-curators to write a label. Museum professionals have watched visitors and exhibits for years, and have insights into label-reading. Ask interns, docents, volunteers, board members, and sales assistant in the store. Don't spend more than fifteen minutes on this exercise.

CRITIQUING YOURSELF IS CRITICAL

Find a long paragraph in any of your communications, or that of a competitor. Ask your trainee to cut at least thirty words without changing the meaning. It's called editing and every writer must learn to savagely clip, prune, and excise.

Don't use the same word twice in a paragraph. It's okay to use different forms of the same word: Research, researching, researcher.

Use neologisms to avoid repeating an essential word. On the page for Planet Word Museum's store, the text reads: "Present Perfect, the Planet Word gift shop, has something for the wordsmith in everyone . . . books full of wordplay, find word-themed gifts, games, and puzzles . . . to pique the interest of writers, readers, performers, conversationalists, kids, and word nerds." The word "word" appears five times, but differently.

Pretend a good friend has just read a sentence or two and said: "What does this mean?" Explain what you mean.

Read aloud what you write. It could sound terrible. Then talk to yourself, say what you want to say, and write it down fast.

Use nouns instead of adjectives in describing an object:

- For "fascinating artifacts" say "saddles and spurs."
- Instead of "implements early families used" do your homework and write "drop spindle" and "lamp oil funnel filter."

If a paragraph bogs down, switch from keyboard to pen and handwrite what you want to say. You'll omit excess verbiage immediately.

Slash and burn—take any paragraph you've written and edit out 50 percent of the characters. You're more skilled than a trainee.

Don't be shy about using a thesaurus, "define" on the highlighted word task bar, or synonym search. Scan the options, and then stare into space. A more graceful word will occur to you, and it will be your own.

At the end of the day, say 5 p.m., close your application. Reread the next day. Revisions will come to mind effortlessly.

Use scan codes in printed pieces, wall labels, and signage. That's where to store all the communications that would clutter printed text.

Listen to tips from everybody you talk to. Even if they ask you for advice, just talking out loud about writing generates useful self-help.

- Mentally jot down words and phrases you read in reviews.
- For example, these from a review of Milton Avery, who was an "outlier" and worked "blisteringly" hard for modest fame.
- Describe an exhibit on a tour as if a four-foot tall person were looking at it.

The following are thought starters for describing an object. They come from Gary Tinterow, a curator at the Metropolitan Museum of Art and director of the Museum of Fine Arts, Houston. He suggests looking at an object and asking yourself:

- First, what is this thing?
- Is this a replica or a fragment of a larger composition?
- Is it an oil painting or a watercolor?
- Is it an object for religious purposes, or is it a useful piece?
- How does this object relate to other works by that same artist?

- What distinctive feature of this object can help viewers understand the work?
- Is there a quote from the creator of the object that suggests another way to look at it?

Matthias Wascheck of the Worcester (Massachusetts) Art Museum, liked to place groups of objects in proximity to each other and ask:

- What do these objects have in common?

WHO ARE YOU WRITING TO? KNOW YOUR AUDIENCES

Underpinning all writing is an awareness of expanding diversity in audiences. To surface this awareness, look at the people you pass on the street and wonder what they had for breakfast. It helps to picture their home, family, and waking hours. Don't write about visitors, write about them.

Don't overdo tech terms. They're like slang; they change all the time.

Remember GPS and map apps when writing website page footers. Follow the directions of California African American Museum in Los Angeles: "If you are driving, CAAM is at the corner of Figueroa Street and Exposition Boulevard . . . please put that cross section into your maps search or GPS device."

If your museum doesn't have a tag line, get one. It forces everyone to answer the question: "What do we stand for?"

- Search any museum on Twitter and read the profile description that appears. For example, "Harriett Beecher Stowe House: writing the next chapter together."

Written words differ from spoken words. Easy to read on the page may not be easy to understand from a person's mouth. Voice quality of the speaker and hearing acuity of the listener affect comprehension, as do old microphones on both persons' devices.

Example of a written factoid: "A frog can leap several times its own body size."

On a video, a science museum presenter might say, "If you could leap like a frog, you would be able to dunk the ball from the 3-point line! . . . actually from the 3-point line around your opponent's basket." (Above examples from Chip Heath & Karla Starr, *Making Numbers Count.*)

Exercise mature judgment and erase your elegant phrases that make no sense.

E-MAILS

E-mails are writing, perhaps the most frequent and demanding writing you'll undertake.

- Say only one thing per e-mail. You can say it in two sentences, but no more.
- If you have two things to say, send two e-mails. Each has its own Subject.
- Develop your own style for greetings and sign-offs and stick with them.
- Greetings include: Hi, hello, dear, good morning, *bonjour*. I like hello.
- Anyone who starts an e-mail with Hey will be fired.
- Sign-offs include: Thank you, thanks, cheers, have a good weekend, regards, until next time, sincerely, I/we look forward to . . .
- "Thanks" is fool-proof.
- An e-mail signed with yours truly, or best regards, should be written as a letter.
- Do not Reply All. The Alls hate it.
- Avoid u instead of you, thnx instead of thanks, and juvenile abbrevs.
- Get the recipient's name and title and spell them correctly with correct capitalizations. Ask them for corrections in your first e-mail; they'll appreciate your courtesy and thoroughness.
- Don't send clever quotes. You think the recipient will enjoy them? If so, send a link.
- About FYIs. Hold them for a day before you decide if anyone else needs that information.
- If you send an article For Someone's Information, don't use FYI. Take ten words to spell out why you're sending it.
- Don't copy and paste anything longer than a paragraph. Attach it.
- Don't e-mail after 6:30 p.m.
- If your ego demands evidence of round-the-clock industry, send e-mails at 4:00 a.m.

Monday, Tuesday, Wednesday, Thursday, Friday, Saturday, Sunday. In descriptions of an event, these words should precede every date. Visitors plan by day as well as date.

Ongoing, part of series, weekly, monthly. If there are options for attending an event, say so.

Land acknowledgment is customary on all museum websites. Keep yours concise.

What's your address? Ask contacts for their museum's postal address and the map-finding address.

If you have a great phrase, hang on to it. Deploy it frequently. You own it.

Mariners Museum in Newport News, Virginia, owns a great phrase: "Our world's waters."

- "The Mariners' Museum connects people to the world's waters, because through the water, we are connected to one another."
- "We are all connected, even through maritime art! This inspiring series takes you behind the scenes to explore our vast art collection . . . the power of our world's waters . . ."
- "Join us every Monday morning for engaging activities with your children as they learn how we are all connected to the world's waters with story time."

"'I' is one of the shortest and oldest words in the English language . . . the most commonly used word in spoken English today."

Another short word is "we." That's the one to use.

SOCIAL MEDIA

Thanks goes to Blanton Museum of Art for singling out Comments and showing the importance of their staying relevant and on point.

- Keep the comments relevant to the topic, so that we can have this open space for everyone to share.
- Comments are monitored. They'll stay up if they stick to the topic and contribute to the conversation.
- Keep it on point.

Corollary:

- If you have to explain an idea, and then explain your explanation, you've probably wandered off point.
- Find one word in each paragraph you write that is ordinary or unremarkable and substitute a surprising one.
- Social media posts aren't hospitable to grammatically perfect sentences or multisyllable words. There are more appropriate places for that kind of writing. See Blogs, Talks.
- Edit, edit, edit. What looks breezily extemporaneous to the reader has been carefully slashed by the writer.
- Keep it short.

STICK TO YOUR WRITING ROUTINE

Honor your peculiar writing habits: time, place, duration, sweater, coffee mug.

Find one or two workable venues and switch to keep your back from getting stiff.

Don't plan when to write. The right schedule for you will emerge.

Once you've found your groove, stick to it.

Some writers believe three hours a day is optimum, for the writer and the material.

Sometimes writers work through meals without noticing.

Don't talk about your work. What's a labor of love to you is obsessive to others.

Be obsessive.

Remember your peripherals.

REFERENCES

"Accessibility," Visit, The Mariners' Museum and Park, https://www.marinersmu seum.org/accessibility/ [accessed 12-13-21]

"Commenting Guidelines," Digital Community Guidelines, Blanton Museum of Art, The University of Texas at Austin, http://blantonmuseum.org/about/digital -community-guidelines/ [accessed 10-27-21]

"Digital Workshop: Bad Drawing Club," Programs, January 8, 2022, Pulitzer Arts Foundation, https://pulitzerarts.org/program/digital-workshop-bad-draw ing-club/ [accessed 2-13-22]

Gift Shop," Plan Your Visit, Visit, Planet Word Museum, https://planetwordmu seum.org/plan-your-visit/ [accessed 2-12-22]

"Give the Gift of Membership This Holiday Season!" e-newsletter of The Mariners' Museum and Park, December 12, 2021, membership@marinersmuseum.org [accessed 12-13-21]

Heath, Chip, and Karla Starr, *Making Numbers Count*, 111, New York: Avid Reader Press, 2022

Landi, Ann, "Wall Talk: Do We Even Need Museum Wall Labels?" ARTNews, December 21, 2015, https://www.artnews.com/art-news/news/wall-talk-do-we-even -need-museum-wall-labels-5579/

"Old Antique Farm & Garden Tools," Laurel Leaf Farm, https://laurelleaffarm.com /item-pages/antique-tools/antique-tools.htm [accessed 9/10/21]

Peers, Alexandra, "'Milton Avery' Review: A Luminary Outside the Mainstream," Arts, *Wall Street Journal*, December 10, 2021, https://www.wsj.com/articles/mil ton-avery-modern-art-museum-of-fort-worth-abstract-expressionism-mark-roth ko-barnett-newman-11639000990 [accessed 12-10-21]

"Planet Word Museum," e-mail to list, February 10, 2022, https://planetwordmu seum.us14.list-manage.com/subscribe/confirm [accessed 2-10-22]

"Visit," Hours & Directions, Driving and Parking, https://caamuseum.org/visit /hours-directions [accessed 12-19-21]

Index

About the Author

Margot Wallace is associate professor of marketing communication (retired) who researches museum branding and writing. She has written five books and numerous articles on how museums work. She currently teaches member-driven classes in Northwestern University's School of Professional Studies.

Made in United States
Orlando, FL
28 August 2024